MARK DREDGE

THE BEST BEER IN THE WORLD

ONE MAN'S GLOBAL SEARCH FOR THE PERFECT PINT

DOG 'n' BONE

Published in 2015 by Dog 'n' Bone Books
An imprint of Ryland Peters & Small Ltd
20–21 Jockey's Fields   341 E 116th St
London WC1R 4BW   New York, NY 10029

www.rylandpeters.com

10 9 8 7 6 5 4 3 2 1

A CIP catalog record for this book is available from the Library of Congress and the British Library.

ISBN: 978 1 909313 71 2

Printed in China

Editor: Emma Hill
Designer: Eoghan O'Brien
Map Illustrator: Michael Hill
Spot illustrations on pages 8–10, 62, and 91 by Nicholas Frith
Photography Credits: See below

Commissioning editor: Pete Jorgensen
Art director: Sally Powell
Production controller: David Hearn
Publishing manager: Penny Craig
Publisher: Cindy Richards

Key: T=Top, B=Bottom, L=Left, R=Right, C=Center

p4 René Mansi/Getty Images; p5 Lonely Planet/Getty Images; p6 Mark Dredge; p7 Michael Kiser/goodbeerhunting.com; p8 and 17 Vladimir Zakharov/Getty Images; pp10–15 Gavin Kingcome; p18 Josh Smith/theeveningbrews.co.uk; p19 Robert Stainforth/Alamy; p21 Camden Town Brewery; p22 Mark Harmel/Getty Images; p26 Camden Town Brewery/Getty Images; p28 (T) Mypurgatoryyears/Getty Images, (B) Sabine Lubenow/LOOK-foto/Getty Images; p29 (T) Joe Cornish/Getty Images, (BL) Pilsner Urquell, (BR) Philippe Renault/Getty Images; p30 GÃ©rard Guittot/Getty Images; p32 Emmanuel Tychon; p33 Mark Dredge; p34 Westend61/Getty Images; p35 Mark Dredge; p37 Philip Rowlands; p39 AFP/Staff/Getty Images; p41 Justin Sullivan/Staff/Getty Images; p43 Hemis/Alamy; p46 Wu Wei/xh/Xinhua Press/Corbis; p47 Lukasz Wisniewski/EyeEm/Getty Images; p48 Wu Wei/xh/Xinhua Press/Corbis; p49 Lonely Planet/Getty Images; p51 Richard l'Anson/Getty Images; p52 David Soanes Photography/Getty Images; p53 Chris Jackson/Staff/Getty Images; p55 Klug-Photo/Getty Images; pp57–61 Pilsner Urquell; p63 travelstock44/LOOK-foto/Getty Images; p64 Peter Adams/Getty Images; p66–68 Sabine Lubenow/LOOK-foto/Getty Images; p69 Mark Dunn/Alamy; p71 Allen Parseghian/Getty Images; p72 iStock; p79 Ullstein Bild/Contributor/Getty Images; p83 Jorg Greuel/Getty Images; p84 George Tsafos/Getty Images; p86 Michal Krakowiak/Getty Images; p87 Matti Niemi/Getty Images; p91 Janetteasche/Getty Images; p92 Maremagnum/Getty Images; p94 Bob Pool/Getty Images; p95 Maryo990/Getty Images; p98 Travelstock44 – Juergen Held/Getty Images; p100 iStock; p101 Ingolf Pompe/LOOK-foto/Getty Images; p102 Manfred Gottschalk/Getty Images; p104 all Mark Dredge except (CR) Budweiser/Anheuser Busch; p105 (T) Mark Dredge, (B) Justin Sullivan/Staff/Getty Images; pp107–111 (T) Budweiser/Anheuser Busch; p111 (B) Jim Heimann Collection/Contributor/Getty Images; p112 Doug McKay/HMS Group/Getty Images; p115 (T) Michael Snell/Alamy, (B) DPA Picture Alliance/Alamy; p116 Mark Dredge; p117 Eliza Snow/Getty Images; p118 SiliconValleyStock/Alamy; p119 (T) Dave Stamboulis/Alamy; pp121–131 Bloomberg/Contributor/Getty Images; p133 Pete Jorgensen; p134 Mark Dredge; p135 Terence Leezy/Getty Images; p137 Zuma Press, Inc./Alamy; p139 (T) Hemis/Alamy, (B) Anthony Pidgeon/Getty Images; p142 Mark Dredge; p148 Andrew Rowat/Getty Images; p150 Charles Cook/Getty Images; p155 Danita Delimont/Getty Images; p156 Chicago Tribune/Contributor/Getty Images; p163 Justin Sullivan/Staff/Getty Images; p166 Bruce Yuanyue Bi/Getty Images; p168 (T) Blackman's Brewery, (B) Luis Davilla/Getty Images; p169 Mark Dredge except (TR) Albert Photo/Getty Images; p171 Jasper James/Getty Images; p172 Richard l'Anson/Getty Images; pp174–175 Bloomberg/Contributor/Getty Images; p176 Gavin Hellier/Getty Images; p177 Mark Dredge; p179 Luis Davilla/Getty Images; p180 Mark Dredge; p181 Albert Photo/Getty Images; p182 Mark Dredge; p183 Peter Unger/Getty Images; p184 Dave Stamboulis/Contributor/Getty Images; p187–188 Dircinha Welter/Contributor/Getty Images; p190 Mark Dredge; p191 Ingolf Pompe/LOOK-Foto/Getty Images; p192 Dircinha Welter/Contributor/Getty Images; p193 DeluXe-PIX/Getty Images; pp195–196 Blackman's Brewery; p197 Peter Harrison/Getty Images; pp198–201 Blackman's Brewery; p205 Gerard Walker; p206 Matteo Colombo/Getty Images; p207 Chad Ehlers/Getty Images; p208 Donald Iain Smith/Getty Images; p209 Rachel Lewis/Getty Images; p210 Oliver Strewe/Getty Images; p211 LazingBee/Getty Images; p212 Ed Norton/Getty Images; p212 Birrificio Italiano; p213 Mark Dredge; pp214–218 Birrificio Italiano; p219 Marcus Richardson/Getty Images; p221 Mark Dredge

ENAME
La Trappe

CONTENTS

THAT QUESTION

APRIL 2015. LONDON. THE COCK TAVERN, HACKNEY. DRINKING A PINT OF CAMDEN TOWN BREWERY IHL.

Whether consciously or not, the last 10 years of drinking have been a never-ending search for the best beer I can find. When I had that first pint that made me realize that beer could be delicious—a pint of Old Growler at a beer festival in Chatham, Kent—I had no idea that my life would lead up to this point; I had no idea that as research for my third book about beer I'd end up traveling to five continents within two months, that within a year I'd drink in 20 countries, get on over 50 planes, visit more than 200 breweries, and drink in more bars than I can remember. And that's on top of all the breweries and bars I'd visited in the five years before it. The whole thing seems completely ridiculous to me now that it's all over and I'm sitting in my favorite local pub a few minutes from my house. In fact, it seems completely ridiculous to most people who know what I do. Which is why **that** question is something I've faced so often.

I could prepare all I wanted for the question but an answer never came out right. What answer did they want to hear? Did I say something that they'd never heard of and which meant nothing to them? Did I give them a flippant "this beer" or "my next beer" and sound like a dick (because I hate that as an answer)? Did I talk about a beer brewed by Belgian monks that's really hard to find? Did I tell them about the amazing beers brewed in America or Italy or Australia? Did I argue that the American Budweiser could be the best because it has an amazing story and pioneering past? Is it a beer some bloke made in his garage? Is the best-selling beer the best tasting in the world? Is it a cold lager on a hot day somewhere exotic with someone special? Or did I just say the first beer that came to mind to give them an answer. Any answer?

The trouble was that I really didn't know the answer to the question. And I really wanted to know the answer. It frustrated me that I'd been asked the same question hundreds of times and still didn't have a response to it.

Casks of beer waiting to be delivered.

With such a respected, historic brewing tradition, could Belgium provide me with the answer to that question?

It annoyed me that all I could do was mumble and deflect the question in an awkward way ("Ah man, I don't know, there are so many to choose from... Gosh... I had this great beer in Germany once... How about this weather? What a lovely day!).

So I went to find the answers. I traveled as far around the world as my wallet would allow, drinking all the beers I possibly could while searching for the most interesting beer stories: I lived as a monk, I spent days searching for the best-selling beer in the world, I was left speechless at the Budweiser brewery in St Louis, I sat on Vietnamese streets drinking the cheapest beer in the world, I tried to brew my own perfect beer, I went to Brazil to celebrate Oktoberfest, I chased IPAs around California, I looked at the fiercest local rivalry in the world of beer, I planned my own perfect beer day. And I did all of this so I could answer a few seemingly simple questions: What's my favorite beer? What's the best beer I've ever tasted? What's the most important beer ever brewed? And what is The Best Beer in the World?

All I knew at the beginning of the search was that every beer was worthy of consideration and, in context, every beer had the potential to be the best. And that made this search exciting.

Now let me tell you about the best beer in the world.

I'd end up traveling to five continents within two months... within a year I'd drink in 20 countries, get on over 50 planes, visit more than 200 breweries...

DAD'S BEER: THE WORST & MOST IMPORTANT BEER IN THE WORLD

"Can I try some of your beer?" I ask, reaching a hand up toward my dad.

He passes me the stubby green bottle. I can barely fit my small hand around the wet glass. He is with my uncles and grandad. They all drink the same thing and I want to drink it, too. I might be seven years old but I want to be like the grown-ups.

I take a sip and I can still taste it now, somewhere in the farthest corner of my taste memory: icy cold, harshly fizzy, then a flavor I've never had before, like sucking a new penny, and then it hurts my mouth, as if it's just been hit by a frozen metal rocket. "YUCK!" I give it back to dad and run off and play.

That's the first beer I remember drinking.

If there was an award for worst beer in the world then it might go to "Dad's Beer as Tasted by a Seven Year Old." That beer is one of the most horrible-tasting things any child could ever have, worse than cough syrup, even worse than vegetables. But if there were a lifetime achievement award for the most important beer of all time then Dad's Beer would take that prize.

Even as a little boy, seeing the adults standing around and drinking made me see some importance to the beers in their hands. I see the green bottle, something that I know is called beer, and it's a symbol of grownupness that they all like drinking, so it must be good. So I keep asking for sips and keep giving it back with a scrunched up face saying "EURGH!"

"Why do you drink that?" I ask.

"One day you'll like it, too," says my dad.

He wasn't wrong. And back then I'm pretty sure he wouldn't have foreseen that over 20 years into the future he and I would be sipping sour beers in the cellars of a dusty old Belgian brewery or that we'd be on a roadtrip up the West Coast of America, where I'm still asking the same question: "Can I try some of your beer?"

My dad and I drinking at Toronado in San Francisco during our roadtrip through California and Oregon.

IS THERE A BEST BEER IN THE WORLD?

Hill Farmstead Brewery in remote rural Vermont is considered by beer geeks to be one of the best in the world.

This is my quest to find the best beer in the world, my chance to look through the past and present of beer and see which ones stand out for their importance as well as how they taste. I chose the stories in this book based on the beers, breweries, and places that I objectively think are most interesting and relevant in a general sense, though the experiences are subjective and personal to me. It's impossible to separate the subjectivity because what I've found is that it's the experience that tends to have the biggest impact.

What I hope this book achieves is a sense of a beer's story and history, a sense of the people who make it, and the places where we drink it, and why it all matters. Ultimately, I hope it makes you wonder what you'd say is the best beer. What do you think is the most important beer brewed? Is there one single incredible beer experience that stands out as the best you've ever tasted? And if you had the chance to do a similar journey, where would you go and what would you want to drink?

When people have asked what this book is about during the writing process they all asked the same thing: "have you found it yet?" My answer was always the same: "I'm still looking." While I can now say that I have some answers, the truth is that I'll always be looking because I love beer and I'm forever after new experiences and new flavors and I drink with the never-ending hope that the next glass of beer I drink will be better than anything I've had before; there's always the chance of finding a new favorite beer or best beer.

What I hope this book achieves is a sense of a beer's story and history, a sense of the people who make it, and the places where we drink it, and why it all matters.

THE SEARCH STARTS AT HOME

Every journey of this worldwide search begins and ends back at my flat in London, so it makes sense that before I go anywhere I want to explore the places nearest to me. This means brewing and drinking with friends in the city that I call home.

CAN I BREW THE BEST BEER IN THE WORLD AT HOME?

I want to try and brew the best beer in the world in my house. Or, more exactly, at my mate's house because he already brews in his kitchen and has all the stuff. Plus he really knows what he's doing. My thinking is that I can cook great food at home but can I make great beer there? Can I think up a recipe for my ideal beer, get the ingredients I need, and then actually make the beer I was dreaming of? I know I can do that with a recipe for my dinner. But beer is different. Beer feels more challenging to me.

Homebrewing is important. Since the first time someone deliberately mixed grain and water and let the sugars ferment into alcohol, beer has been brewed by people in their homes. It was once as normal—and essential—as baking bread. Brewing meant boiling water, making it safer to drink than the natural source; the grains gave calories and nourished through the day; the alcohol warmed and relaxed through the evening; plus it tasted good.

If it was once done for necessity then in more recent years it's been done for recreation, and the revolution of craft brewing really has its heart in homebrewing; so many breweries tell the story of a homebrewer going pro—someone who refined their skills in a kitchen or shed and eventually decided to turn it into a career. What's interesting is that amateurs are at the forefront of brewing. They don't have commercial constraints, no financial restrictions beyond what's in their wallet, no creative limits; they can combine ingredients in new ways and learn from it very quickly. It's small-scale, small-cost, small-risk, but it can create superb drinks.

So I'm going to homebrew some beer and try to nail a perfect Pale Ale. It's a style I drink often and know well. In my head I can imagine and taste what my ideal version would be like, so I want to make that. I'm also going to brew a second beer that's best described as "experimental" because I love how homebrewers can innovate in ways that professional breweries often can't.

To do this I need some help, which is why I'm going to the house of my good friend Chunk, who has been homebrewing since September 20, 2009. I know the exact date because he has a book with all his recipes neatly written in it. He's that kind of detail-driven guy, which is what helps him to make some seriously excellent beers.

GETTING STARTED

We're in Chunk's small kitchen and on the hob is a big silver pot of water heating up. Opposite this on one of the worktops is the "mash tun"—a large plastic vessel wrapped in an insulated mat, the kind you more often see used for camping. Because he's fastidiously precise and neat, he's put out all of the grains into separate bowls, which he's spread out on his kitchen counter top.

"These malts are all measured out and ready to go. That water is nearly hot enough so chuck all of that into the mash," he says, passing over the bowls of crushed grain.

On the other side of the kitchen are three fridges. Three. The first is for food and next to this are two fridges on top of each other. One is the beer fridge, filled with bottles. Above this is his fermentation fridge—it's where all of his homebrew goes, and he even has a special thermometer to ensure it's at the exact temperature he needs for whatever beer is in there. Gill, his wife, is very understanding, but then she does get to enjoy a lot of good beer.

The water that's on the hob came from bottles bought from the supermarket. "Bottled water has the exact composition on it, which is important," Chunk says. "It's really hard to get accurate and detailed mineral reports on tap water, plus London water is really hard, making it difficult to adjust it to what you need it to be." By "adjust", Chunk is talking about adding things to the water to balance it and make it ideal for brewing this type of beer. Water composition influences the flavors of beers in different ways, so brewers—whether kitchen or industrial—need that control over this crucial element of their brew, with different beer styles working best with different water types.

THE RECIPE

I've told Chunk the ingredients I want to use and the flavor profile that I would like to achieve, and he's translated that into an actual recipe.

The grain bill for my Pale Ale is mostly Pilsner malt because I love how simple, clean, and bready it is. We're adding Munich and Vienna malts for nutty, biscuity flavors, with the Munich also contributing some extra color. And we're adding flaked wheat and malted oats simply because I like wheat and oats in beers and want to know how it'll influence a Pale Ale. As a homebrewer I can make those calls.

For the hops, I'm using Czech Saaz because they give a clean, sharp bitterness to beers plus a lovely lemony, peppery, floral aroma—it's probably my favorite hop. I'm then adding Australian Galaxy and American Citra hops, both famous for their fruitiness—I want this beer to smell like a bowl of tropical and citrus fruit.

The grain bill is carefully measured out before starting the brew.

"All bottled waters are a bit different. This one is really soft, meaning we can more easily tweak it," he says. "You have to add something to it to play with the balance of sulphate to chloride. For example, water high in sulphate will accentuate the bitterness, whereas if the balance is toward chloride it'll round out the malt profile."

"This beer is skewed to chloride for body and malt," explains Chunk. I nod as if I know what he's talking about but clearly he sees through my vacant look. "Water chemistry is seriously complicated!"

He's been saying all of this while standing over the hob with a thermometer in the water. "74—we're ready." I ask why we're shooting for 165°F (74°C). "That's based on the volume and temperature of the grain." I look blankly back at him.

"Imagine if you're brewing outside on a really cold day—the grain will be a different temperature to if you're inside on a hot day. So when you add the water to it it'll change the overall temperature of the mix and when we pour this into the grain we want it to get to 67°C."

Chunk pours the water over the grain that I put into the mash tun and mixes it together, filling the kitchen with the sweet smell of malt. He checks the temperature: 153°F (67.2°C). Next he does something that I've never before seen in a brewery... He picks up the mash tun and runs into his living room. He places it under his stairs and then wraps it up like a baby in large blankets and pillows while I just stand and watch perplexed. "What the hell are you doing?!"

"Insulating the mash tun," he says as if it's the most obvious thing in the world. "We need to hold the temperature as constant as possible, so I just wrap it up and leave it under the stairs. It's inevitable that the temperature will drop a degree or two but this keeps it pretty constant for an hour."

During the mash, we're aiming to convert all the starches in the grain into sugars. Later we'll add yeast and that will convert those sugars into alcohol, so this conversion is important and it will happen at around 153°F (67.2°C).

We leave the mash under the stairs, and prepare for the sparge. For this, Chunk takes 2 gallons (8 liters) of bottled water and heats it in a large pan. "We need to get to 80°C."

"How do you know all of this stuff?" I ask.

"I guess I just learnt it. And I use brewing software for the figures." On the side he has two laptops open. I thought they were there just to play the podcast that we're listening

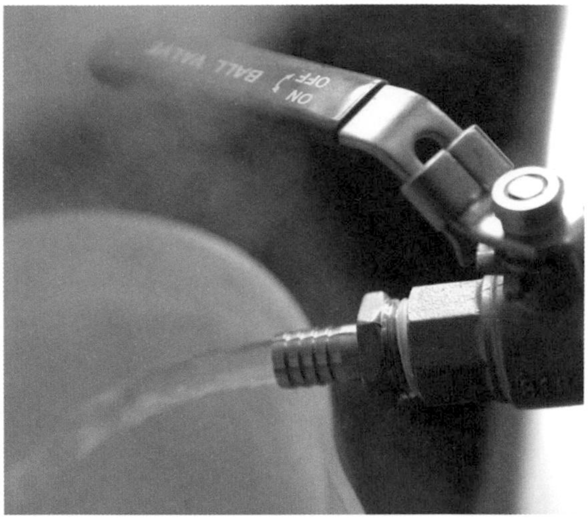

Once the water reaches 153°F (67°C) it's ready to be added to the grain.

to, but no; there's a special beer recipe program open. Called BeerSmith, it's the primary resource for homebrewers, who can punch in any number of variables and get exact details on their beer. For example, put in the temperature and volume of your water plus the amount of each different grain you're using and the program will tell you the exact color of your beer and the expected alcohol level. Change the temperature by half a degree and the whole equation shifts; add some different grains and you get something different again.

"How did you get into this in such a big way, dude?"

"My personality is that I can't do something just a little bit. If I do something then I really get into it properly and have to understand it. I never used to drink beer but when I started I wanted to know everything about it and understand it properly. Homebrewing was kind of an obvious thing for me to do." He's brewed about 80 batches in five years, often changing small details, processes, or ingredients to understand how they affect the flavor.

His day job involves working in IT. "Before that, I was thinking about becoming a chef, but it's long hours and the pay's bad, so

I went with the money. But brewing is like cooking, plus it's great to to drink what you make and then be able to identify the ingredients in commercial beers." To Chunk, it's about learning and being able to nail ingredients and processes.

READY TO SPARGE?

With the hour-long mash period over and the sparge water heated up, Chunk unwraps the blankets and brings the tun back to the kitchen. "Ready to sparge?"

He lifts the lid off the mash tun and a cloud of sweet steam fills the kitchen. He pours in the 176°F (80°C) water and lets it mix in briefly while he lines up a big silver pan on the floor beneath a tap on the mash tun—the sparge water is there to help push all the liquid out. He then opens the tap and golden, sweet "wort" flows out like a fountain into the pan beneath.

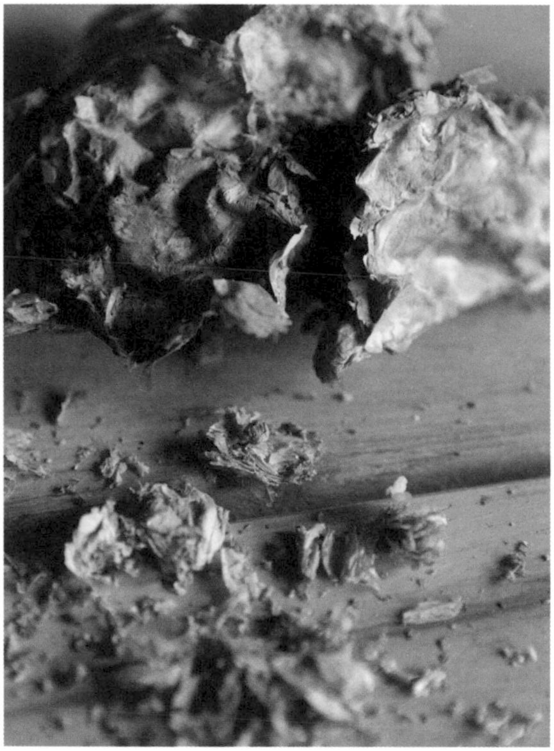

I chose Czech Saaz, Australian Galaxy, and American Citra hops for my dream brew.

We've now got all of the important sugars from the grain and only need the liquid, which will become our beer—the spent grain is no use to us now. Or at least it wouldn't be if we weren't planning on a second brew... But that's happening later.

With all the liquid strained through he lifts the pan onto the kitchen stovetop. He then does something else which makes me stop and stare in disbelief: he takes a wooden spoon and puts it into the pan: "We've got 11.2 liters," he says.

"What the hell?" is all I can say as I look at the spoon, which I now see has black scratches notched into it.

"Didn't I tell you about this spoon!?" he says, passing it to me. "I made it to measure volume. I weighed out a liter of water, put it in that pan then marked the spoon. Then I just kept on doing it all the way up the pan." I can't help but laugh at him. "If Gill uses this spoon when she's cooking then I go mental!"

With the pan of wort on the hob, we turn up the heat and bring it to the boil. While this happens, Chunk gets three vacuum-packs of hops out of the freezer and we weigh out 0.8 oz (25g) of Saaz hops, which doesn't sound like a lot but for this volume of liquid it's a considerable amount. As the wort begins to roll into a boil, we add the hops from which bursts out a fragrant and spicy aroma, turning the brew a soupy green.

When the kitchen timer beeps to tell us that 65 minutes is up, Chunk fills his kitchen sink with cold water and places the whole pan into it: "We need to cool it down to 80°C. It's kind of arbitrary but below 80°C is the best time to add the hops," he says. And of course that's not arbitrary. Neither is the amount of hops we're adding. It's based on Chunk reading all the brewing material he can find, then working out a consistent volume of hops for successful beers, then using BeerSmith for accuracy, and applying all of that to his own beers.

The liquid cools quickly and the rest of the hops go in, throwing out a dank, citrusy aroma to the kitchen. At this point Chunk uses a hydrometer to measure the amount of sugar we've extracted from the grain—the "gravity" of it. Using another equation, he combines the temperature of the liquid with the reading on his hydrometer to give him an accurate number: 1.045. Exactly what we're aiming for to produce a beer of around 4.4% ABV.

From here we just wait for the wort to cool down before it gets transferred into the fermenter—the empty water bottles we used for the brew. When that liquid gets to 64°F (18°C) the yeast will be pitched into it.

HANDLE WITH CARE

Hops will give a beer its bitterness. The thing with hops is that they contain acids and oil. The acids give bitterness once they isomerize (or become soluble in water), which happens after an extended boil, while the oils will give the beer aroma and flavor. However, the oils are volatile, so the longer you heat them the more likely it is that you'll boil them away, meaning the later you add hops the more aroma you get. Typically, a beer will have multiple additions of hops in order to get bitterness plus flavor and aroma. For this recipe we're going to boil the beer for 65 minutes, take it off the heat, and add the Galaxy and Citra hops—this should maximize the aroma from the oils.

GONZO BREWING

Ordinarily Chunk would now be mostly done, apart from some cleaning, and would open a beer. But not today because we're doing something he's never done before. Something very few people have probably ever done before. We're sacking off the science, the known processes, the theory, and we're going gonzo. And it's now that I get three coconuts out of my bag, because I've always wanted to brew a beer with coconut water.

My thinking with brew two is that it'll be a rich, dark beer loaded with coconut. Because we're not following the usual rules, we're not going to get to that dark beer by starting a completely new brew. Instead we're following a centuries-old process. You see, years ago, people brewing in their homes would make a couple of different beers from one batch of grain. After they've mashed it, the first liquid to drain off would be rich with sugars from the grain. As more water was sparged over it, the sweetness would lessen. Separate them into two fermenters and you get one strong beer and one weak beer. We're kind of doing that, just in reverse and with some extra stuff thrown in...

The Pale Ale we've just brewed will form the base of brew two. To bolster it we're creating a small, intense mash of dark, sweet liquid flavored with coconut water and we'll blend that into the Pale Ale. We kept the spent grain from the first brew and into that we put lots of chocolate malt for dark color and a dark chocolate flavor, then we add a grain called Carafa III, which will add color but not give it too much bitter coffee flavor. We also add more wheat and oats and 3.5 oz (100g) of dried coconut chips (because—screw it—we can). We heat water to 176°F (80°C) and Chunk pours that into the mash tun and stirs it around. While this steeps, I carve the coconuts and pour out the sweet water, which gives us 30 fl oz (900ml) of liquid.

After the grain has steeped for 15 minutes, we drain it off into another pan and bring it to the boil on the hob, adding some more hops for bitterness. About 10 minutes into the boil (we're only shooting for about 15 minutes of boiling in total, so much shorter than you'd usually do), we pour in the coconut water, add some fresh vanilla pods (because I love vanilla), then add a lot of

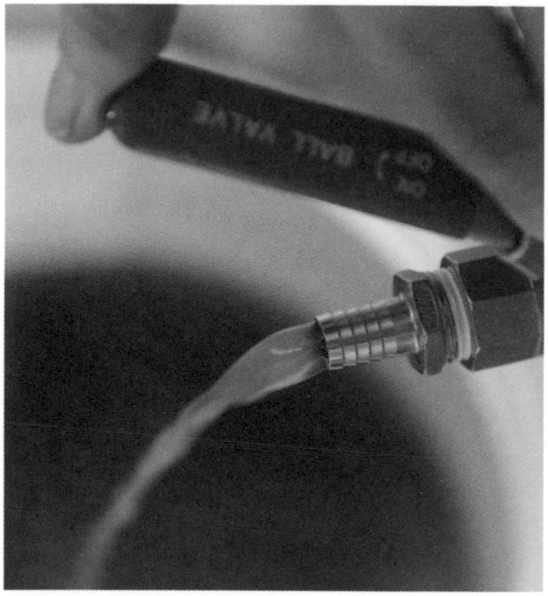

Chunk drains the wort from the mash tun.

dark candy sugar to give it a lot more fermentable sugars to convert into alcohol (I want this to be over 6% ABV), plus this will give some dark, dried fruit flavors to the brew, like a dark Belgian beer.

Far from the calm cleanliness of earlier, it's now carnage in Chunk's kitchen. Neither of us really knows what's going on. There's coconut and grain dust everywhere, hops on the floor, pans and spoons and thermometers in places they definitely shouldn't be, but somehow we manage to get something resembling a second wort, all sweet and bitter and black.

Once both liquids have cooled, it's time to fill the fermenters. After sanitizing them, which is incredibly important to avoid any unwanted flavors, and placing a funnel into the top, we take a large sieve and strain 1.3 gallons (5 liters) of the Pale Ale into one of the bottles. This leaves us a couple of liters of pale liquid to go into the other fermenter, which we top up with the dark coconut liquid to reach 1.3 gallons. Once the liquor has cooled to 64°F (18°C), Chunk adds in the yeast and closes the door on his fermentation fridge. It's taken about six hours but with that the brews are done.

JUDGEMENT DAY

Over the next few weeks I get regular updates on how the beers are doing. We add extra hops into the Pale Ale to give it even more aroma. The dark beer goes a little crazy and ferments further than expected, making it drier than I want, so we add lactose sugar to give body, sweetness, and richness, again just making it up as we go along. We also add more coconut chips, just because.

Three weeks after brewing, I'm back at Chunk's house with our mates Matt, Pez, and Lee. "Is everyone ready to drink the best beer in the world?" I say confidently as Chunk starts to pour out the Pale Ale that he's put into a mini keg.

He hands me the first glass and I'm genuinely excited: in my head this is my idea of my perfect Pale Ale; could Chunk and I translate that idea, that flavor in my mind, into a great glassful of beer?

It's bright gold and clear enough to see through, with just a slight haze. The foam is full and white and it looks great. We all have beers and we all say "cheers" before taking a mouthful. WOW!

I wanted the beer to smell like mango, pineapple, and mandarin and I get all of that and more. It's so fruity, almost like tropical juice. Around me everyone is making excited sounds. I look at Chunk and he's swirling the beer around his glass, chasing those aromas, analyzing them. And he's smiling.

I take a mouthful and that's perfect, too. Full yet still light, there's a hint of biscuity sweetness, a depth of juicy hops, then a dry, balanced and clean bitterness. At 4.4% ABV it's a beer I could drink all day and it's even better than I'd hoped for. Everyone else agrees: "Dude, when are you going to quit your job and become a brewer?!" "This is awesome! I love those hops!" "Chunk, you're a genius." Clearly in their praise they've overlooked and underestimated my own efforts in the brew, but I don't care, because it tastes so good.

"Is everyone ready to drink the best beer in the world?"

Next we move on to brew two. I wanted, via the roundabout route we took, to get something like an Oatmeal Stout with coconut in it. As he passes around glasses of dark beer with a thick tan foam it definitely looks like I want it to...

Where last time there were "wows" of excitement, this time there are "woahs" of confusion. To me it smells like dark chocolate and coconut and it immediately makes me laugh—rarely does a beer create such an unexpected reaction like this. It's exactly what I wanted from this beer—to be surprised by it, for it to make me smile.

"I'm not so sure about that one," says Lee. "Me neither," says Pez. Matt likes it better: "Ha, that's weirdly delicious!"

I think it's amazing, though not exactly amazingly good. It's not like any beer I've had before. It's chocolaty, full-bodied and ever-so-coconutty in the silliest of ways. The others prefer the Pale Ale, and I agree, but there's something fun about this beer that just cracks me up.

The Pale Ale is genuinely brilliant. It's not necessarily the best beer I've ever tasted but it was exactly the beer I hoped we could make. The coconutty brew was weird in the best of ways and I loved that, too, but the unusual processes and tail-chasing that we did to make it happen resulted in something not quite as complete as the Pale Ale. Plus you really need to love coconut to like the beer.

THE FIRST STEPS TOWARD THE BEST BEER

Today an increasing number of people are brewing at home, where with each batch they hope they'll get something delicious to drink with their friends. Some of these brewers do it for fun; others end up making the move to professional breweries. And that's exciting because it's the future of the beers we drink at home and in bars.

Chunk is a great brewer; watching him is inspiring and makes me want to brew more of my own beers. I love the challenge of coming up with recipes and seeing if I can make something great in my house. I also love how I can completely design a beer that's exactly to my taste—I can imagine the best beer in the world and then I can try my best to make it. If I don't get it quite right then I can try again, tweaking it until I'm satisfied. That's the fun of the challenge and I reckon I can nail that coconut stout next time...

Two glasses of the finished pale ale.

PERFECT LONDON BEER DAY

"You're 25 minutes late for your own pub crawl!" shouts Matt when I finally drag myself into the pub. "And I thought you wanted to get lunch here? Why did you text Chunk to say you've already eaten?" Matt and Chunk are the guys I drink with every week. They're also the ones I've been planning today with. The first part of that plan was simple—meet at 12 and eat a pub lunch.

Long story short: I was hungover, went to the gym, felt worse, and ate some eggs. That made me late and not hungry. It has also left me unprepared and today is an important day as I'm hoping to find the best beer in the world in my favorite city by going to my favorite pubs with my favorite people.

"It's my day and I can do what I like! It's important to have some spontaneity, you know. Now who wants a beer?" I ask.

We're in The Mayflower in Rotherhithe, right on the bank of the River Thames. It's a historically significant pub because in 1620 the Mayflower ship set off from here on its nation-establishing pilgrimage across the Atlantic. Fittingly, the dark-wood walls are covered in sea memorabilia, making it feel like an old ship. Being a romantic for starting-line stories like this, The Mayflower feels like a decent place to begin the day. Luckily for me, Matt, Chunk, and his wife Gill got here on time because it meant they got a great seat on the outside decking area that overhangs the Thames. And that's the real reason we're at the Mayflower: I love being by the river in London and can spend hours in its company, enchanted by it, excited by it, endlessly fascinated by the sights.

Looking west I see the sharp point of the Shard, London's tallest building; there are the bottle green curves of the Gherkin; there are factories converted into apartments; pubs and docks and a skyline of cranes keeping the construction going. There's so much activity and I can see both the history of the city and the shape of things to come. There are also so many stories down here, so many things have happened here during the life of the river.

Looking east and that's the direction the Mayflower would've sailed—into the large width of water, starting a great adventure. And like the ship did almost 400 years ago, we've taken on fuel, we've collected passengers, and now, having finished a pale ale and some fries, today's pilgrimage can properly begin... which means getting on a bus to Bermondsey.

THE CRAFT REVOLUTION

London is a city with a rich history of beer making and there are over 80 breweries across the capital. Despite the heritage, this surge in new brews is recent, with less than 10 of those breweries open before 2009. It's also incredible to know that the second oldest still-active brewery in London is Meantime, which started in 1999. London is brewing itself back toward the top of the best beer cities list and by living here I'm getting to see it happen every day.

If there's one thing that any beer lover should do on a Saturday in south London,

A view of the Thames looking west. The day begins at Rotherhithe, in the bottom left corner of the picture.

it's visit the Bermondsey Beer Mile. Beneath, or next to, railway arches going in and out of London Bridge Station, there's a line of excellent breweries and a bottle shop, plus some cool food markets, all just south of the Thames. Conveniently within walking distance of each other, people are coming here on a Saturday and trying to drink in all of them. At the eastern end is FourPure and walking west beside the bridges you pass Partizan, The Kernel, Brew By Numbers, Anspach & Hobday, and Southwark Brewing Co.

The Kernel is where we're going. Coming in from an industrial estate car park, where there are people spilling outside, many carrying bottles wrapped in the distinctive brown labels of the brewery, you can see through the deep arch, over a table of bottles, and down to the brewhouse at the back. It's packed inside and standing room only—it's like this every Saturday even though they only open for a couple of hours. Drinkers crowd the front counter, taking a close look to see what's available: there are Pale Ales and IPAs, each named after the hops used in them; there are strong Stouts based on recipes from over a century ago; there are sour beers aged in wooden barrels. We all order Pale Ales and IPAs, the beers that The Kernel is best known for. They are American-inspired but definitely London delivered, with their appealingly hazy gold color, the smell of fruit bowls, and a full and satisfying texture. I drink a lot of these beers in London.

This kind of beer is important to me because it was these fruity, hoppy pale brews that got me excited enough about beer to want to start writing about it. These American-hopped Pale Ales were so different to the brown Best Bitters I'd been drinking, and one taste made me want to find more and know more. Without beer like this I wouldn't do what I do now.

Bottles for sale at The Kernel Brewery.

MEMORY LANE

As we leave and walk toward London Bridge, via Brew By Numbers for a quick half of their excellent hoppy Saison, we're joined by Pez and Sofia—two more of my favorite people to drink with. The next stop is a return to a pub that featured in my early beer biography. During university a group of us would regularly get the train into London and go on beer crawls. The Rake, near London Bridge, was our go-to pub for trying new beers at a time when there were hardly any beer bars around. After that we'd go to The Market Porter, a handsome corner pub right in the middle of London's Borough Market. It's well dressed in bright flowers and always busy with people crowding the streets outside cradling their beer.

Inside, soldier-like handpulls stand along the large bar top, each with a colorful clip stuck on the front to show what's on. These are the real ales and that's what you drink when you're at the Market Porter. Along with tea, this is Britain's drink, and nowhere else does it like we do it, making it a wonderful idiosyncrasy. A decade ago we'd work through as many beers as possible, learning about different styles, finding beers we loved and beers we hated—it's where we learnt about beer.

"Remember Pete Postlethwaite's Bitter?" "What about the time we came here then went to the German place next door for steins and it took you two hours to get home?" "I was looking at old Facebook photos the other day and saw some from in here—it's just the same today as it was then!" "I still remember that pint of Old Growler in here—it was so good!" "Was it here we came after you pulled an all-nighter to get that essay done and then almost fell asleep over there?" We rarely drink in the Market Porter anymore so it's good to return for a pint. The next stop is somewhere we drink most weeks.

A massive part of my London life is Camden Town Brewery. I started working there in September 2011 and it was a big step for me. I'd gone from being a beer blogger and writer on the outside of the industry to having genuine influence in how a brewery was working. Being at Camden every day, I got to talk to brewers all the time, asking them questions, learning about the processes and the industry, and uncovering all the small details of running a brewery.

Every morning I'd go into work and ask the boss, Jasper Cuppaidge, why there wasn't a bar at the brewery. To me it seemed crazy to have a space and not open it up so people could come inside and be able to drink the beer fresh. Then one day, after about five months of nagging, I arrived at work and some builders were measuring up the space.

And whether at the brewery or elsewhere in London, Camden Town's Hells Lager is the beer I drink most of. I love Hells for how it's been present at many momentous life events in the last few years: working at the brewery; drinking the beer the night my first book came out, which I wrote while working at Camden; it was the beer I drank while doing my best man speech at Matt's wedding; the beer I've taken on numerous weekends away with friends; the beer I was drinking when I realized a 10-year relationship was over; and the first beer I put in my fridge when I moved to London and started a new life. Hells is ever-present in my life and it's more than just a drink to me. Sitting outside the brewery, on long benches in the sun with friends, a Hells is exactly what I want. Here we're joined by Sara, another of my best friends and Matt's wife, plus Chris Hall, a beer-writing friend.

"Tell me again what you're doing today?" asks Sara as she also drinks a pint of Hells.

"Attempting my perfect London beer day for the new book. I've basically planned my ideal drinking day and I want to see if it's actually any good."

"Hmm... I think my perfect drinking day would be very different to yours," she says before others start to throw in their ideas for their perfect drinking day.

"You have to go to some classic old pubs, like Sam Smith pubs where you get cheap pints. And you need to go to a Wetherspoons pub—the ones we used to drink in at uni. And a Fuller's pub for a pint of London Pride—that's proper London drinking."

"The best pub crawls just sort of happen and aren't planned. How many great nights have we had just walking into a random bar after 10pm when we're already drunk?"

"I think it's the people that matter. Wouldn't it be depressing drinking on your own all day? You want to be with friends and just get really drunk with them."

"I'd want to go to some of my favorite pubs because you just feel at home there. I'd want a nightcap of good whiskey or gin or cocktails. I'd want to go somewhere with a good view of the city or just something interesting to look at. And fried chicken at the end, obviously."

The Market Porter, situated in London's best food market, Borough, is a honeypot for foodies and beer lovers.

"The best pub crawls just sort of happen and aren't planned..."

"You know, I really like the idea of a personal pub crawl like we're on today; going to places that have a meaning to you, and that you've been to loads of times already because they are important and you like them. But when I'm drunk and happy I just want to walk into places and see what happens."

We have a few beers in the brewery, including the incredibly delicious IHL, a mega-hopped lager, and talk and laugh for a few hours. As we say bye to Pez we jump on the train and head east to Haggerston and The Fox, a big corner pub on Kingsland Road.

I've spent Sunday afternoons in here playing board games and eating a roast dinner, I've written parts of this book in here, there have been warm evenings sitting on the roof, and too many nights where I've got too drunk on IPA.

I live nearby, so come here often, plus it has the best beer selection in this part of town. Most of us choose Beavertown's Gamma Ray, an American-style Pale Ale from a brewery which originated in Duke's Brew and Cue, a barbecue restaurant just around the corner.

"This is still my favorite beer in London," says Matt.

"Neck Oil is also pretty great. And Smog Rocket," says Chunk.

"Have you had Smog with the ribs at Duke's? It's amazing!" I add, immediately aware of how hungry I am. And also how drunk I am. Somehow we've now been drinking for over eight hours, so with a slight giddiness in my head and sway in my legs, the next stop is for food and that means we're going for The Best Burger in London.

Improbably, I spend more time reading about burgers than I do reading about beer. It's a bit of an obsession. I've been thinking about this particular burger all week, about the soft sweet bun, the juicy beef patty, and the saltiness of the American cheese—I'm just about ready to eat my arm as we finish the 15-minute walk to The Sebright Arms, where Lucky Chip cooks the brilliant burgers. Then my phone buzzes and I see that I've got a voicemail message from Sofia, who cycled ahead to get a table. I play it back: "THEY'RE OUT OF BURGERS! WHAT DO WE DO?!" (I've since had to delete the message because the genuine distress in her voice is something I can't handle hearing ever again.) How can they be out of burgers?! The kitchen doesn't close for another 90 minutes! Oh my god. OH MY GOD!

You know when you leave it too late to eat and you get angry and that's exaggerated by being hammered, and you're empty of food and full of beer and it's a dangerous mix? We're all there right now. "What are we going to do?" "If I don't eat soon I'm going to die!" "I'm starving!"

We walk to Broadway Market, perhaps my favorite street in London (I might as well carry on the favorite theme) and manage to grab some pizza, but this burgerless blip has thrown the day. It's later than we thought and we're all drunker than we should be. I'd been planning another bar after food, just a random pub that I've never been to before, but it's too late now. And as Chris leaves us, there's only one pub to go to at this stage of the evening.

This makes me realize that it's the moments that matter more than the liquid in the glass.

THE LOCAL

The Cock Tavern, by Hackney Central station, is my local. It's a very British thing to have a local. I love this place because when I walk in I feel like I've stepped into a second living room, especially when I'm greeted by Tim the manager. The pub is busy and there's a smoke-like haze in the air that always seems to be here, adding to the old, worn atmosphere of the place. There's a feeling of comfort here and that's important in a pub; that's what a local is. The Cock is where I come to read and write, it's where I come for quiet pints on weekends, it's a solace after a shitty day at work, and it's where I usually end up late at night on Fridays and Saturdays for one more beer.

There's a small brewery in the cellar, there's a long line-up of hand-pulled ales and ciders, plus some great kegs of cold beer.

We get six pints and all sit around a tiny table, with Mark, Matt, and I squashed on one small bench and Gill, Sara, and Sofia opposite. We're talking shit and laughing. I'm not entirely sure what's happening and I don't know what I'm drinking, but I don't care because all that matters to me right now is being here with these guys.

Today's crawl has taken in some classic pubs, some new pubs, a few breweries, and some places with personal significance; it has been the kind of day with friends that I love. Now it's late and as we talk about the last 12 hours I can't remember much of what I had to drink or how anything actually tasted. But I can remember the places, the people, and the way I felt in those moments. What this makes me realize is that it's the moments that matter more than the liquid in the glass. And thinking back to some of the best beers I've ever tasted, I can tell you where I had them and who was there before I can tell you what the beer was like. Beer is great because it's social and the best beer experiences I can have will be ones I can share with other people.

I don't think I drank the best beer in the world today but I did drink some of my favorites and I shared them with my best friends. And now, sitting with them in the pub late at night, is a moment that I won't forget.

Drinkers outside the Camden Town Brewery bar.

BRITISH CASK BEER

With a firm pull on the curved wooden handpump, the pale liquid pours into the glass, white foam bubbling then bursting as another pull almost fills the vessel. One final tug and the beer is placed on the bar, a gentle haze gradually easing upward and forming the beer's foam, leaving a bright, golden pint.

A selection of cask ales from Fullers, one of London's largest breweries, on display at the bar.

The aroma is gentle and lightly fruity, yet it's vibrantly fresh. It's cool against the lips, the body is soft and clean, a gentle carbonation giving it life on your tongue, pushing forward a subtle hop flavor before the malt comes through with the taste of biscuits, bread, and toast—rich yet light. Then the hops return; they are dry and bitter and leave you thirsty for more. This is what makes cask beer great.

Cask beer is England's thing. Here, beer is born in the brewery and then raised in the pub, where the bar staff have an important role in how the beer tastes in your glass.

Brewers fill casks with fermented, uncarbonated, (often) unfiltered beer. They may also add more yeast (or fermenting beer) and sugar, plus some form of fining agent to help to clear the yeast from the beer. (It's worth noting that isinglass is the most common fining and it comes from the dried swim bladders of fish, so vegetarians or vegans might want to consider this.) Then a bung is knocked in and it leaves the brewery.

When the cask arrives at the pub, it's not ready to drink immediately. Instead, it needs to sit in the cool cellar where the yeast still in the beer will continue to work, undergoing a secondary fermentation that creates a gentle carbonation and enlivens more of the flavors and aromas. The beer is brought to life in the cellars and it transforms within a couple of days. When the beer is ready to be sold it's hooked up to a cask line in the cellar. Back in the bar, the handpump pulls the beer from the cask and straight into the customer's glass.

Catch a cask beer at the perfect moment and it's an unbeatable beer experience, but the delight of it is also its ultimate downfall. These beers are alive in the barrels, gradually maturing and changing, and as the beer improves it will only continue to get better until a certain point, when it begins a decline that can slide down the bad side until it's sour and undrinkable. The fact that it's being pulled from a cask in a cool cellar does not guarantee it'll be good, so if you want the best cask beer then go to a busy pub, one that you can see sells through their cask beers quickly, and one with good staff who know their stuff.

A good British cask beer is one of the best beer experiences in the world.

MIGHTY MARIS OTTER MALT

Maris Otter is the best known and most distinctive of British malts and arguably it is to British beer what C-hops (Cascade, Centennial, Citra, etc.) are to American beer. It gives a biscuity, nutty, toasty depth of flavor, which cask beer's gentle carbonation can highlight in the best of ways, compared to the harsher, livelier bubbles in bottles and kegged beer. To really celebrate the mighty Maris Otter malt, you want that beer on cask.

TOP 10 BEERS IN TOWN

Harvey's Best is russet brown and pin bright; there's autumnal fruit, some toasty malt and a deep, clinging bitterness in this classic cask ale from the south of England.

Timothy Taylor's Landlord has a richness of British malt and then a whole barrage of hops come at you, earthy and spicy and with a depth of marmalade. Another classic, this one from the north.

St Austell Tribute has all that chewy English malt in the back and then in come the lightly citrusy, floral hops that can go into a lemon pithiness. Lovely pint.

Fyne Ales Avalanche shows off Maris Otter malt's bready qualities and then whacks in loads of floral and grapefruity hops in this ever-refreshing Golden Ale. As a bonus, it's named after I Am The Avalanche, one of my favorite bands.

Salopian Brewery Darwin's Origin has created the perfect evolution of British ales, celebrating the biscuity sweetness of malt and then the floral, zesty aroma and dry bitterness of the hops.

Moor Revival is a snapshot of modern British beer. Very pale in color, delicate malt, bursting with aromatic American hops, lightly hazy because it's unfiltered, and boldly bitter yet balanced.

Oakham Citra is rightly celebrated as one of Britain's best cask ales. It's all about the Citra hop's vibrant mango and tangerine juiciness but it also has this remarkable soft body of malt, which cask beer highlights like nothing else can.

Fuller's London Porter on cask is a rare and wonderful treat. It has a body like silk, with cocoa, coffee, and smoke. It's smooth and rich and layered with complexity and flavor.

Siren Soundwave shows how good a West Coast IPA can be on cask, where all the fruity, resinous hops turn deliciously fleshy and fresh and the lush malt gives some toffee-like sweetness to balance.

Thornbridge Saint Petersburg is proof that big beers can be cracking on cask; the deeply roasted flavors combine with chocolate and dark fruit and become elegant and soft in this half-pint-by-the-fireplace kind of brew.

CITY GUIDE:

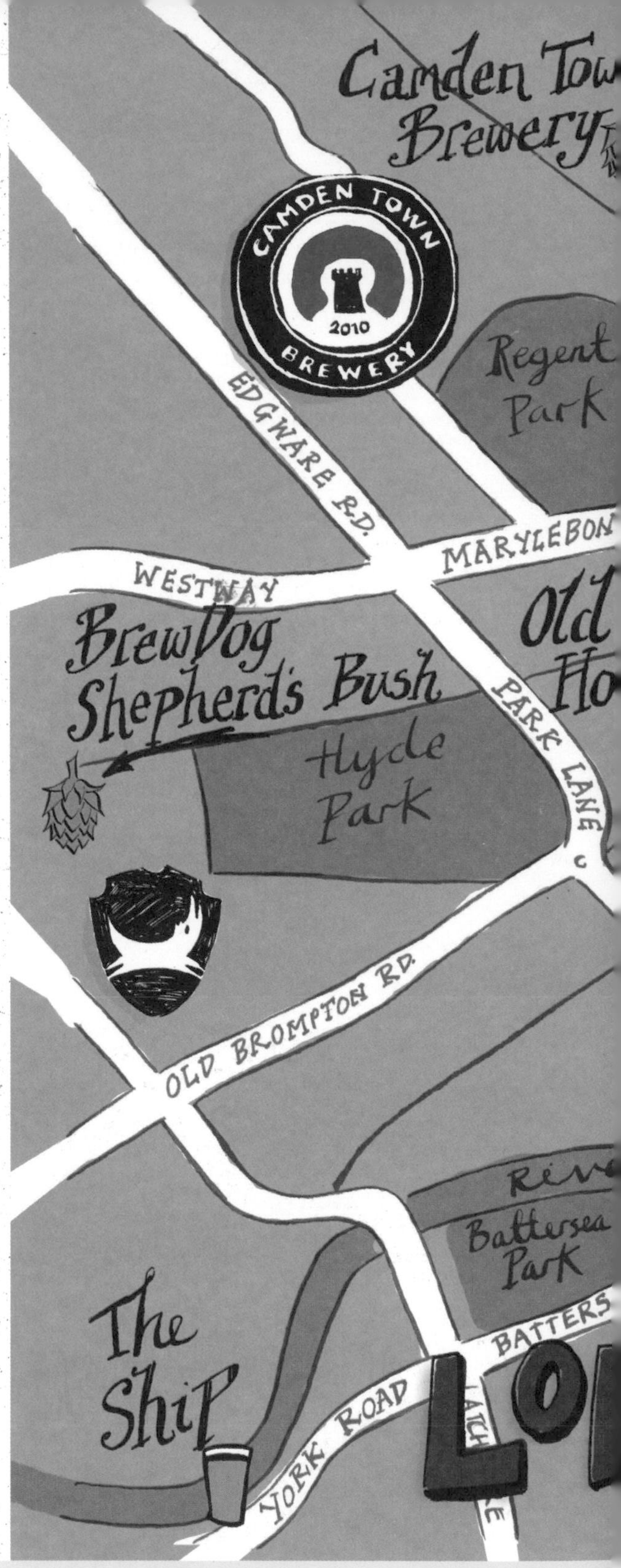

• CITY GUIDE

LONDON

Once the greatest brewing city in the world, it somehow turned into a terrible place for great beer toward the end of the 20th century. Now it's back near the top of the list of beer cities to visit, thanks to the combination of classic old pubs, modern bars, the ever-growing list of breweries, a huge variety of beers, plus a lot of great food.

The Parcel Yard
Duke's Brew & Que
The Fox Craft Beer House
Crate Brewery & Howling Hops
Victoria Park
Earl of Essex
Well & Bucket
Queen's Head
The Craft Beer Co
Ye Olde Cheshire Cheese
The Kernel Brewery
River Thames
Thames
EUSTON RD
PENTONVILLE RD.
CITY RD
UPPER ST.
KINGSLAND ROAD
SHOREDITCH HIGH ST.
WHITECHAPEL
COMMERCIAL RD.
TOWER BR. RD
NEW KENT ROAD
KENNINGTON RD
OLD KENT ROAD
CAMBERWELL NEW RD
PECKHAM HIGH ST
A107
THE KERNEL
PALE ALE
5% VOL
DON

CAMDEN TOWN BREWERY

55-59 WILKIN STREET MEWS;
WWW.CAMDENTOWNBREWERY.COM

It's always better to drink beer fresh and in the brewery. Camden has a cool taproom where they'll have up to 10 of their beers on tap. Outside you'll find a rotating choice of great street food.

THE KERNEL BREWERY

ARCH 11, DOCKLEY ROAD INDUSTRIAL ESTATE; WWW.THEKERNELBREWERY.COM

Only open on Saturdays and only for a short time. Go there and try their incredible IPAs and superb dark beers. When you're done at Kernel, follow the railway arches either east or west and you'll find a few more breweries.

THE QUEEN'S HEAD

66 ACTON STREET;
WWW.QUEENSHEADLONDON.COM

I love this pub not far from King's Cross. Good people, good beers, and always a good atmosphere—it's a real gem which not enough people in the city know about.

Camden Hells Lager, a personal favorite and you'll find it at many of the best beer pubs and bars in London.

CRAFT BEER COMPANY

82 LEATHER LANE;
WWW.THECRAFTBEERCO.COM

This is a growing group of great pubs popping up all over the capital. Leather Lane is their original pub, and still one of the best with a long list of great British and imported beers. Go to their Islington venue for a cozier, classic pub atmosphere.

THE FOX

372 KINGSLAND ROAD;
WWW.THEFOXE8.COM

A big corner pub with a cool roof terrace, The Fox always has a brilliant range of the best beers you can find, so look for some of Britain's best—Moor, Magic Rock, Summer Wine, and Thornbridge.

DUKE'S BREW AND QUE

33 DOWNHAM RD;
WWW.DUKESBREWANDQUE.COM

This is the original home of Beavertown Brewery, before they moved out and into a bigger site in Tottenham. You can drink all the Beavertown beers here, plus great guests. Make sure you eat here too because the ribs are some of the tastiest in the city.

THE WELL AND BUCKET

143 BETHNAL GREEN ROAD;
WWW.WELLANDBUCKET.COM

Skull-faced Victorian portraits line the walls of this cool East London bar that always has a great range of beers. Grab some sliders to go with your brew, and there's also a cocktail bar downstairs if you fancy something different.

YE OLDE CHESHIRE CHEESE

145 FLEET STREET;
WWW.SAMUELSMITHSBREWERY.CO.UK

The Samuel Smith Brewery runs some of the best classic old pubs, offering no brand-name drinks and the full range of their products, including Old Brewery Bitter, which is a great pint and one of the cheapest in town. The Cheese has many levels and centuries of stories for you to get lost in. Also try the Princess Louise and the Cittie of Yorke (Holborn).

MOTHER KELLY'S

251 PARADIS ROW;
WWW.MOTHERKELLYS.CO.UK

Not many weeks pass when I don't visit Mother Kelly's. In a railway arch close to Bethnal Green station, this is a bar with 20 of the best taps in London, always varied and interesting with many rare beers, plus a superb selection of bottles to drink in or take away.

THE PARCEL YARD

KING'S CROSS STATION;
WWW.PARCELYARD.CO.UK

This large pub inside King's Cross Station is run by Fuller's Brewery, giving you a chance to try all of the beers brewed by London's oldest remaining brewer. Harry Potter fans will notice that it's also next to platform 9¾.

THE EARL OF ESSEX

25 DANBURY STREET;
WWW.EARLOFESSEX.NET

Check out the huge beer board on your left as you enter, then walk around the bar to see the small brewery in the back. There are 20 beers on tap and a beer-infused food menu.

THE OLD COFFEE HOUSE

49 BEAK STREET;
WWW.BRODIESBEERS.COM

It's surprisingly difficult to find great beer in Soho, so the Old Coffee House, which is run by the excellent Brodie's Brewery, is the place to go. A proper boozer, the beers are very good and there's a great charm to the place. You can also enjoy Brodie's ales in the William IV in Leyton, East London—that's where the brewery is located.

BREWDOG SHEPHERD'S BUSH

15-19 GOLDHAWK ROAD;
WWW.BREWDOG.COM

With 40 taps of great beer, around half from BrewDog and half as guests, you won't be short of choices. BrewDog have bars all over the city so if you can't get over to SheBu then you're sure to be near another.

THE SHIP

41 JEW'S ROW;
WWW.THESHIP.CO.UK

The Ship is the place to go for a great pub meal and a view of the Thames—it has a huge outdoor space, though it gets busy quickly. They serve Meantime Brewery Fresh Lager from handsome tanks.

CRATE BREWERY AND HOWLING HOPS TANK BAR

THE WHITE BUILDING, UNIT 7, QUEEN'S YARD; WWW.CRATEBREWERY.COM AND WWW.HOWLINGHOPS.CO.UK

One of the hippest locations in London, this brewpub is situated on the canal in Hackney Wick with a view of the Olympic Park. Have a pizza while you're there—they are very good.

Next door is Howling Hops Tank Bar. The brewery started in the basement of the Cock Tavern in Hackney Central and they've since added a new site a little further east. Here they've filled an amazing space with a shiny brewery in the back, long sociable benches in the middle, BBQ food to one side, and, most significantly, a bank of serving tanks from which all draft beer is poured. A game-changing venue for London.

TOP 5 BEERS IN TOWN

Camden Town Brewery IHL
IPA meets lager and one of my favorite beers

Beavertown Smog Rocket
A super smoked London Porter

Kernel IPA
Always excellent and loaded with hops

Fuller's London Pride
A classic brew that you have to have on cask

Fourpure Session IPA
Massive hops, modest ABV

EUROPE

If you want to drink classic beers, then Europe is where you need to go and where you'll find so many famous styles—ranging from the best Czech golden lagers through to the darkest Belgian ales. On my European adventure I want to live as a Trappist monk, see how beer creates rivalries between two German cities, drink the most famous dark beer in the world in Dublin, enjoy cold beers on hot beaches, find the origin of golden lager, and more. Europe is also incredibly exciting for the way modern influences are changing things and new styles are now sitting next to the classics.

GUINNESS
IS GOOD
FOR YOU
GUINNESS'S EXTRA STOUT
JAMES'S GATE DUBLIN

De Troubadour
In De Schaduw Van De Kathedraal
Bieren Pannekoeken Wafels Snacks De Troubadour

TRAPPISSED IN BELGIUM

"Dude, you can do this spiritual stay thing at Orval and actually live with the monks, do prayer and stuff like that. You fancy it?!"

I've just hit send on that email to my friend, Chunk, and I'm chuckling to myself at the prospect of us actually living like monks, something I can never imagine happening. Yet I'm in the middle of planning a road trip around the Belgian Trappist breweries and I've seen that you can stay at the Orval Abbey. I'm only half serious about it until he replies... "Let's do it!"

THE ROAD TO SPIRITUAL ENLIGHTENMENT

Two weeks later, on a cold and foggy February morning, I'm driving Chunk and myself through the flat Belgian countryside. We've passed nothing but forest for miles until we turn down a long, narrow road, flanked by tall trees, running streams, and muddy, misty fields. At the end of the lane the Abbaye Notre-Dame d'Orval appears like a secret castle hidden in the forest. This is where we're going to be living like monks.

The ruins of the old monastery at Orval.

"Woah! Look at this place! That's insane," says Chunk.

It's a magnificent old sandstone farmhouse with gray slats on the roof where the morning's frost is melting around smoking chimneys. There are turrets, a tall clock tower stands at the back, and it's all walled-in. The entrance looks like an old English schoolyard with Tudor-style dark wood.

"Are you ready for this?" I ask because in truth I'm not ready for it. I have no idea what to expect. What does living like a monk mean? What will we be able to do? What won't we be able to do? The only information I have is that silence is observed, notably at meal times, and prayers are in French.

We walk into the visitors' center, something hundreds of people do every day. Where they turn left into the bright, open gift shop, we're told to turn right, through a heavy, closed door. This is presumably a time warp as it leads into an eerily silent courtyard that throws us back a few hundred years. There is no modernity, just old buildings. We walk inside and enter a small office that smells like lavender and soup, where we struggle in our best French to register our arrival. We're given our keys and pointed down a dark hallway that could easily have been used as a location for Hogwarts in the Harry Potter movies. We follow the cold, small hallway and walk out into the middle of the Abbey ground.

WHAT IS A TRAPPIST BEER?

In 1664, the Abbot at the Cistercian monastery of La Trappe in France decided to introduce some new rules and in doing so created the Order of Cistercians of the Strict Observance, or Trappist as it became known. These monks follow the rule of St Benedict and go by the motto of "Ora et labora"—prayer and work—where they live frugally and obediently in a general atmosphere of silence. There are around 170 Trappist monasteries in the world today and one of the fundamental ideals of a Trappist monastery is that they are self-sufficient, so they produce goods and offer services (guest rooms, a café) to provide income for themselves and also to aid the local community.

As of April 2015, 10 Trappist monasteries brew official Trappist beers: Achel, Chimay, Orval, Rochefort, Westmalle, and Westvleteren in Belgium; Stift Engelszell in Austria; La Trappe and Zundert in Netherlands; Spencer in USA; an eleventh, Mont des Cats in France, has Trappist beer but it's brewed at Chimay. To qualify as a Trappist beer, and be allowed to use the official hexagonal logo, it must satisfy certain criteria:

- The beer must be brewed within the walls of a Trappist monastery, either by the monks themselves or under their supervision.
- The brewery must be of secondary importance in the monastery and must be run using business practises proper to a monastic way of life.
- The brewery is not a profit-making venture. The income covers the living expenses of the monks and the maintenance of the monastery. Whatever remains is donated to charity for social work and to help persons in need.

The Trappist appellation is for where the beer is made, not what's made, meaning they can brew any type of beer they want. Despite this, they all make similar styles—Dubbel, Tripel, and Quadrupel are the most common, plus a lower-strength "Patersbier" for the Monks, ostensibly a Singel or Einkel. Orval is the outlier, making an idiosyncratic dry-hopped and wild yeast re-fermented Pale Ale.

There are many similarities in the brewing of these beers. They all tend to start with simple grain bills of Pilsner and Pale malt and use European hops—a lot use hop extract as well as pellets or flowers. Almost all of them use sugar to add to the fermentables. In Dubbels and Quadrupels, a dark or caramelized sugar is used and this is where the ruby-brown color of the beer comes from. The benefit of the sugar is that it's highly fermentable, meaning the beers can be strong without being overly full-bodied or rich, something which helps their digestibility.

"Jesus Christ!" I say without thinking.

"Yep, right there," Chunk laughs, pointing across a lake to the huge church with a tall statue of the Virgin Mary and baby Jesus carved into the front. I've never seen a more handsome church in my life. It's this hulking mass of pale stone, three tall peaks grandly pointing upward. There's the clock tower to one side and there are more buildings reaching back beyond the church. Dark cloistered arches line the inside of a large quadrant and the surrounding gardens are in an immaculate condition. To the left are ruins of the original monastery. It's all astonishing.

Our room looks out onto this awe-inspiring view but those feelings of awe deflate as soon as we step inside. Compared to the incredible grandeur of everything around us, the word "basic" seems too glamorous—there's a table with a bible on it, a small desk chair, an armchair, two single beds, and a sink. And it's freezing cold.

I remind myself where we are and why. This isn't a luxury retreat. We're here to learn about the monks and their way of life, to have time for work and quiet reflection. We need to be mature and respectful of that, I think, just as Chunk rips out a disgusting fart. "That'll warm this place up a bit!"

The grounds of the Abbaye Notre-Dame d'Orval, with its spectacular church to the left of the picture.

Next to the bible is a leaflet with all the details for our stay and welcoming us into a "Space of peace and beauty, silence and song, prayer and fraternity," where "The community that inhabits this place is happy to welcome you home."

Inside is a list of information. The first word is "Silence". We need to be quiet inside our rooms and outside. Meals are taken in silence but with music. On the back page is listed the times of meals and prayer.

"5am prayer!? Holy shit!" says Chunk, then laughs to himself. "Holy shit, indeed."

BEER HEAVEN

We have some time before "Prières de midi," so we head off to explore the grounds. It's so quiet and there's no one here. We're just slowly shuffling around this place, whispering nervously and wondering where we're allowed to go on this stay. We have access to the inside of the monastery, something tourists can only see from outside, but what's off limits?

We walk under the dark arches and don't need to speak to know what we're ultimately looking for, where the smoking chimneys seems like the obvious place. You see, while we're intrigued by the spiritual side, the obvious truth is that we're really here for the beer. So when we pass through a small gap between buildings and see endless orange cases we experience the same awe-filled exclamation as when we first saw the church. "Look at all the Orval! Man, I want to drink that so bad."

Amongst beer lovers, Orval is one of the most revered beers in the world. Its skittle-shaped bottle familiar to so many; the unique-tasting beer loved by so many. I never expected I'd ever come here and see this place and now I'm standing by the brewery in this unbelievable Abbey, next to thousands of bottles, and I can barely believe it. Yet despite all the beer so near to us, we genuinely don't know if and when we'll be able to drink it (is it wrong to drink it while on a spiritual stay?). And we're already thirsty...

As we walk back into the center of the Abbey, the bells chime to call us into the midday prayer. A few people are slowly walking toward the church so we follow, turning back when we're standing beneath the Virgin Mary: it's mesmerizing how spectacular this place is.

It's just as remarkable inside. Dark and silent, it smells like cold wood, old books, and burning incense. The monks are already at the front of the church, arranged in a semicircle at wooden lecterns. They are dressed in white robes, long sleeves hanging from their wrists. There are 12 of them but I can't quite see their faces. A single stained glass gives a distant kaleidoscope of color through it all. And what happens next is one of the most wonderful things I've ever experienced—the monks begin to chant. Calming, hypnotic, their usually silent voices bounce around the cave-like chapel, lulling and lifting. It's hauntingly beautiful and rhythmic as they sing back and forth, seemingly in conversation.

After one of the monks reads a passage the lights are dimmed and they sit in silent prayer. In this calm I have a chance to properly look at the monks. There are definitely fewer than I expected; just a few men in this huge place. Around half of them fit the "monk" stereotype in my mind: old, gray hair or bald, glasses, and one of two extremes around the belly—portly or very thin. A few of the others are middle-aged and look like they might work in I.T. or as history teachers. And there are three guys, all around 30 years old, who look like the kind of people I hang out with at home. Maybe it's my naivety, but I didn't expect that and I wonder why they are here: what makes someone choose to dedicate their life in this way? A quiet (celibate!) existence dedicated to work and prayer.

After 15 minutes the bells above us ring in deep, long booms, groaning as they beat, like a train passing, reverberating through the building. It's another amazing sound and it hangs with me long after we've left the church and returned to our room. We don't talk for a while, less out of the respect we know we should show, more because we're both left silenced by the experience and thoughts of what this way of life is really like.

Lunch is at 1pm so we walk to the gift shop in the spare time before we eat. A man is buying a few cases of Orval."Do you think we can get away with buying a case?" Chunk says. "It says room doors close at 9pm. Then what can we do other than drink?"

"It's going to look pretty bad if someone sees us carrying cases to our room."

"Maybe, but we can't come here and not drink, can we?"

Chunk is already looking at the cases, picking out the bottles and checking their bottled-on date. The thing with Orval is that the flavor evolves and changes over time thanks to it having a wild yeast—called Brettanomyces, or Brett—added into the bottle. Mention Orval to any beer lover and the conversation will come to what age they prefer (9–12 months is a common favorite, some like older, others younger).

"5th of November. Three months old. That'll do." He looks at a few more and then checks a different pallet. "Oh my god, dude, this one's like 30 days old!"

I've never had it this young and it takes me about three seconds to make my decision: "Fuck it, we're getting some. I want to take a case home anyway." We buy two cases of beer—one of each batch—and walk as quickly and quietly as we can back to our room, dipping our heads and speeding up when we see a monk heading toward us.

An Orval truck outside the brewery.

TIME TO EAT

Lunch is in a large dining hall that takes us a long time to find, meaning everyone is already sitting in silence and eating soup when we enter a few minutes late. There are 18 of us lined up facing the same direction and a monk watches over us (the other monks live and eat in a different part of the Abbey). And there are bottles of beer on the table, but this beer is different to what we've just bought. It's the same skittle-shaped bottle but it doesn't have a label. This is Petit Orval, the beer the monks drink. From what I know, it's only brewed a few times a year and is essentially the same brew as Orval, only more water is added before fermentation to lower the alcohol (3.4% ABV according to Stan Hieronymus in **Brew Like a Monk**, though it could vary up to 4.5% ABV).

As we fill our bowls with vegetable soup, the monk opens the bottles, which force out a booming "PFFFT" of carbonation. This beer is only available to the monks and people on a spiritual stay. An actual monk opened this beer for me. And I'm sitting in the Abbey right now. Of all the beer experiences that I've had, this is undoubtedly one of the rarest.

A lunch of sausage, sauerkraut, and potatoes, washed down with a glass of Petit Orval beer.

The beer is the same copper color as the regular Orval and has a big, Brett aroma—peppery, earthy, lemony—so it's clearly a few months old. It's complex yet light in body and the hops hang around at the end. I really want to talk to Chunk about it because I can see him swirling his glass, taking in all the aromas and trying to understand the beer, but I can't speak to him. All I can do is point and nod as enthusiastically as possible without drawing attention to myself.

The soup is replaced with trays of pork and sausages, boiled potatoes, and sauerkraut. Dessert is a baked apple with dried fruit. It's good food—frugal but filling—and when everyone has finished eating, the monk says thank you and then requests that we help to clean up, which means scraping leftovers into a bowl, placing anything dirty into a hatch through to the kitchen, then wiping down the tables and laying them for the evening meals. In this community we all play a part.

IT'S FOR THE BOOK

It's now 1.30pm. The next prayer session is at 5.30pm. If I were a monk I'd now have four hours for work, reading, or private prayer. I can't see where anyone on the spiritual stay has gone so have no idea what they're doing. And now we have no plans.

We decide to take a tour of the ruins. The original buildings were destroyed years ago and the brewery was added to provide income to build a new Abbey. There's also a museum where we learn about the history of the monastery as well as the brewing processes. A video shows the inside of the brewery, which is the closest we'll get. (I'd emailed asking if we might get to see the brewery and got a terse response explaining that a spiritual stay and a tourist visit are different... Not that tourists can see the brewery.) The most interesting sight is the dry-hopping process: brewers fill huge sacks with hop flowers and stuff them into the tanks then pour the beer on top of them. They stay in tank for 2–3 weeks.

Then before the beer is bottled it's centrifuged to clear out the yeast and then new yeast, including the Brett, plus some sugar, is added into the bottle. It then gets stored for 3–5 weeks until it's ready, meaning our 30-day-old beer is as fresh as you can get it.

Learning more about the process has the inevitable effect of making us thirsty.

"Should we go for a beer?" I say in the same tone as if I'd suggested taking a selfie during prayer.

"I think we should... I think we can get away with it," Chunk says quietly in case anyone hears. "The café closes early so we need to go soon. And I think it's important you see it for the book, right." Chunk's right, of course. I do need to go. It's for the book. We'll just have one.

A l'Ange Gardien—the Guardian Angel—is a bright, modern café near the Abbey entrance where visitors can drink the beer and eat the cheeses that are also made here. They have an exclusive beer on draft called Orval Vert, which is 4.5% ABV. You can't drink this anywhere else in the world. We order two and it arrives in the Orval chalice that shows off the rich copper color of the beer and the thick white foam. The aroma is a surprise: bready, strawberries, pepper, hop sack, chamomile, all sorts of fragrant things but none of the Brett we associate with Orval. It's softly carbonated, there's a deep malt flavor, then the bitterness drives through leaving an almost savory depth. Wow. Our glasses are empty within a couple of minutes and the one-beer limit is immediately forgotten as we order two more and some cheese.

"It's so good! I never expected that. I love the hops and how there's none of that Brett." Chunk says. "Should we get some bottles now?"

They have young and old—the latter promises to be at least one year. We're visiting on February 19, 2015; the young was bottled on October 19, 2014 and the old was 19 October 2013. We get one of each. The difference is instantly obvious,

THE ORVAL NAME AND LOGO

The widowed Mathilda of Tuscany was walking here one day and she dropped her wedding ring in a spring of water. She prayed for its return and at that moment a trout rose with the ring in its mouth. She exclaimed that this place was a valley of gold, or Val d'Or, in French. The spring is still there today and it still provides water to the monastery and brewery.

A l'Ange Gardien café is the only place in the world you can drink Orval Vert.

The way sound travels in the chapel is spectacular.

especially compared to Orval Vert. Young Orval still has a hop aroma that mixes with the earthy, lemony Brett before a pronounced bitterness makes it sharp and balanced. Old Orval is more aromatic; there's a tannic berry quality, it seems more oxidized than Bretty, bitterness is lower, the body is thinner but overall it seems more complex. I favor the younger version.

We've still got time before 5.30pm prayers so we order another Orval Vert and more cheese. This beer really is special and so easy to drink, and as we'll probably never get it again we decide we can't leave here without having just one more. It's too good.

TIME FOR REFLECTION

We have to sprint to make it to the 5.30pm prayer and we shuffle breathless into the chapel just as the chanting begins. From the bright café to the dark chapel is a huge change of scene. The sound of the chanting is hypnotizing, beautiful, sobering. There are some readings followed by a kind of communion which neither Chunk nor I take part in; we want to be respectful (as much as we can be turning up slightly pissed for prayer) but we have our personal religious beliefs and communion goes beyond those. It's dark when we leave and head across for the evening meal, which is bread, cheese, and a tasty potato salad, plus a beer.

Before the final prayer of the day we have some more beer in our room. The 30-day old is like the one we've just had on draft. There's no Brett aroma, instead it has yeast esters like pear, banana, and apple. The hops are really bitter and dry, the malt is toasty, bubbles are soft, and it's really drinkable. We open a three-month old to compare: the Brett gives that distinctive lemony, farm-like aroma plus a much sharper carbonation. The Goût d'Orval, the way that it always tastes a bit different, yet always interesting, is why so many people love this beer.

The 8pm prayer is the calmest of them all, almost like a lullaby. The way the sound travels in the chapel is spectacular. It's rare to see and hear something so beautiful and it's a sound made by this small group of men who otherwise spend their days in silence.

Chunk and I return to our room and open more beers. And then more. And more. Until we finish a case between us. Of all the drinking nights I've had, drinking Orval while in the Abbey is unquestionably one of the most memorable.

What's less good is the way we feel when our alarms go off for the 5am prayer. The grounds are so dark and we can't see a thing as we stumble, thick-headed, in the icy February morning. There are just two other people in the church, plus the monks (and not even all of them are there)—I guess the others on the spiritual stay didn't fancy the early alarm call. At least Chunk and I are taking this seriously.

The monks would now have their breakfast but we both fall back into our beds, woken by the bells ringing for 7.30am prayer. After this our breakfast is bread, cheese, jam, and fruit. Yesterday I found the mealtime silence awkward but by breakfast I'm calmed by it and I enjoy it. The enforced silence makes me think, but I expect that my thoughts are different to the ones the monks are having. I'm thinking about how I can tell this story; about the travel plans I need to arrange for next week; I have moments of un-monastic lust when I think about my girlfriend. Later, Chunk tells me that during one prayer he was trying to think up a homebrew recipe for Orval Vert.

The rest of the morning I spend doing some work, following the flow of a monk's day more closely than we did yesterday. It's a relaxing, inspiring place for me to write, free from modern distractions. What's most remarkable is how peaceful it is.

The 12pm prayer gives us one full rotation through a monk's day. The 15-minute quiet prayer gives me another chance to reflect on the experience. Here I am, at a monastery, and in front of me are monks in silent thought—what is in their minds right now?

THE BELGIAN TRAPPIST BREWERIES

Trappist beers from (l–r) Achel, Chimay, Stift Engelszell, La Trappe, Orval, Rochefort, Westmalle, and Westvleteren.

Achel

In the northeast of Belgium, straddling the Dutch border, is De Achelse Kluis, producers of Achel and the smallest Belgian Trappist brewery. Monks from Westmalle established a monastery here in 1844 and by 1852 they were brewing beer. The brewery was destroyed in World War I and the most recent resurrection of brewing came in 1998. On brewing days, someone drives to Westmalle to collect yeast. A secular brewer leads operations and monks monitor production. They brew Blond and Bruin versions of a 5% ABV beer, available only at the monastery café, Blond and Bruin 8% ABV, and Blond and Bruin 10% ABV Extra.

Chimay

The largest of the Trappist breweries, Chimay is located in southwest Belgium. The Abbey de Scourmont was founded in 1850 by monks from Westvleteren and beer was first brewed in 1862. The brewery has four beers: Dorée is a blond beer made with coriander seed and curacao (it's effectively their Singel; the beer the monks drink); Red, White, and Blue give the classic triumvirate of Dubbel-Tripel-Quadrupel. They also produce their own cheeses. You can drink the beers a short stroll from the Abbey at Poteaupré Inn, which also has accommodation.

Orval

In the far south of Belgium, by the French border, is the Abbaye d'Orval. A monastery was initially founded here in 1070 with brewing first recorded in 1628. It has been sacked and rebuilt several times since then, with the current incarnation constructed literally by the money earned from the brewery, which re-fired its coppers in 1932. Orval is a dry-hopped amber beer that's re-fermented in the bottle with Brettanomyces wild yeast. The brewery also makes a lower-strength Orval Vert which is available on draft at the brewery, plus Petit Orval which is a bottled version of Vert made for the monks. They produce around 70,000 hectoliters of Orval a year—that's over 21 million bottles. They also make their own cheese. The Abbey is a popular tourist attraction with over 100,000 people visiting a year. There's a shop and café on site.

Rochefort

The Rochefort beers are made at Abbaye Notre-Dame de Saint-Remy which is toward the south of Belgium. The Abbey was founded in 1230, with Cistercians taking over in 1464 and brewing first recorded in 1595, though it likely started long before this. Today, a number of monks help out in the brewery though it's run by a secular brewer. They make three dark beers—6, 8, and 10—each of increasing complexity and potency and each made with sugars plus a little coriander seed. You can't visit the Abbey.

Westmalle

Abdij der Trappisten van Westmalle, in the north of the country, was founded at the end of the 18th century with brewing beginning in 1836. As with others, it had to be rebuilt after World War I, selling beer again in 1920 and a new brewery opening in 1934. It's the second-largest Belgian Trappist brewery, producing 120,000 hectoliters a year. They make two year-round beers, Dubbel and Tripel, with a rarely seen hoppy blonde called Extra. They are generally credited with creating the modern template of a golden Tripel while Dubbel is one of the few Trappist beers available on draft. They make one cheese and there's a large café opposite the Abbey.

Westvleteren

Monasteries have existed at Sint-Sixtusabdij, in Vleteren, since 806, though it was in 1831 that a Trappist monastery was formed and brewing began shortly after in 1839. Today the monks are active in the brewery—the most active of all the Trappists—helping to brew, package, and sell the products. They are three Westvleteren beers: Blond is a hoppy pale beer, while 8 and 12 are dark ales. They make cheese and have a café next to the monastery.

They have somehow felt a calling to come into this life and dedicate themselves to god, their monastery, their work, and this quiet and unchanging routine. There's no way I'll understand it properly but in honesty I'm here out of curiosity and for the beer. And the beer does seem removed from the monastic way of life; it's this thing which happens to the side of the monastery, it makes them money to live, it enables them to be charitable, allows them this amazing Abbey, but I can't see how the brewery impacts upon their life at Orval, especially as it's run only by secular brewers. That part is unexpected.

Considering how far removed this last 24 hours has been from our normal lives, we're actually both reluctant to go; there's something wonderful about this place and the experience, and that's without even considering the beer. As I drive away from the Abbey I'm fairly certain that one day I'll return and do the whole thing again. But not before I've visited the five other beer-brewing Belgian monasteries.

ROCHEFORT AND ACHEL

The Rochefort brewery is an hour north of Orval. Unlike the other five abbeys, this one has no café or shop and you can't visit, but we still want to see it for ourselves. We park at the entrance and the church is right at the front. We walk around as much as we can and get to see the beautiful copper brewhouse through large windows, but that's all we can see, which is disappointing. Also disappointing is the lack of bars nearby so we stop at a local supermarket and buy a case of Rochefort 8—we have to buy the beer in the town it's brewed in.

They make three dark beers at Rochefort—6, 8, and 10—each of increasing strength, depth, and complexity. Later that night we drink them in a bar in Liege. These are classic dark Trappist ales: dried fruit, cocoa, spices, dark sugar, fresh bread, with lively carbonation and dry bitterness making their elevated ABVs refreshing to drink. The ones we drink are all young, but I prefer them to mature for months or years because they lose a hoppy harshness and everything mellows into a doughy, sweet, fruitier brew; they really are world-class beers with astonishing depths of flavor.

The next morning we drive north to De Achelse Kluis, the home of Achel. Seemingly in the middle of nowhere, down another long driveway, we turn into a large walled complex. The area for the monks is blocked off, as you'd expect, but there's a large open courtyard with an excellent beer shop at one end and a café from where you can see into the small brewery at the other. The café has an odd vibe, but it sells beer so we get a glass each of the Blond and Bruin 5% beer that's only available here on tap. The Blond is a hazy gold and looks great. It's all malt, so no sugar is added, giving it a nice cereal quality before spicy, floral hops come through. It's ok, not especially exciting, but better than the Bruin that neither of us enjoy—maybe we just got a bad batch.

Next we open bottles of Blond and Bruin 8. The Blond 8 has honey and spice, a nice depth but not as much complexity as other similar beers. The same is true of the Bruin 8 that has some dried fruit flavors, a spicy depth, but not much more.

WESTMALLE-BOUND

An hour west, not far outside of Antwerp, is Abdij der Trappisten van Westmalle. Set back from a main road and up a long tree-lined drive-way, it's popular with walkers, runners, and cyclists; you can pass around the grounds but you can't go in them. It's a shame you can't go inside and look around, though you can see endless pallets of beer cases and mountains of stinky spent grain.

Opposite the Abbey, looking like a bright service station, you can visit Café Trappisten. It's a busy modern café-restaurant and Chunk and I order the Westmalle Dubbel, which they have on tap. It has a thick, dark foam and rich hazy brown body. It's surprisingly hoppy, there's a deep bitterness, some bitter fruits, plums, almond kernels, then it's very dry with a herbal quality.

Westmalle Tripel is 9.5% ABV, bright gold with a white foam. There's peach skin, apricot, a little sulphur and esters come from the yeast. Somehow the body is light yet muscular, while the bitterness grips hold in the middle and doesn't let go. It's malty yet not, hoppy yet not, spicy yet not. It's an incredibly precise, balanced beer.

They have one cheese, reminiscent of Cheddar, and it brings out more of the fruity flavors in the Tripel, which we drink for the rest of the night because it's so tasty.

CHIMAY, CHIMAY YA

Next stop is Chimay. To get to the Notre-Dame de Scourmont Abbey, like the others, has me driving down quiet, remote roads for many miles, passing through the occasional village, until almost out of nowhere a huge stone structure reveals itself through the trees. You can't go into the Abbey but a short distance away is the Poteaupré Inn, a visitor center, restaurant, and hotel, where we're staying for the night.

We start by paying €6.50 for a short self-guided walk through the story and history of the Abbey that is moderately interesting but worth doing if you've made the effort to go. The tour ends in the large wood-paneled restaurant with a glass of Dorée, the blond beer that used to be reserved for the monks but is now available to regular drinkers. Here it's drawn from cask giving it a lovely soft body. It's spiced with coriander seed and curaçao making it perfumy, floral, and orangey. It really is very good.

Chimay Red, the Dubbel, is surprising light for a dark beer, it has tannic fruit skins and some hop bitterness but is otherwise unremarkable. White, their Tripel, has a lot of really interesting stone fruit aromas, it's rich with malt and yeast and has a nice depth, though doesn't compare with Westmalle Tripel; the Blue, also known as Grande Reserve, is a Quadrupel with dried fruit, bread, yeast, cocoa, and lots of fizz and again it's good but again it doesn't have the same complexity as something like Rochefort 8 and 10.

A monk walks past cases of Trappist beer.

We buy some cheese and some bottles of beer and take it all back to our room upstairs. As it's the winter, this place shuts at 6pm, meaning the rest of our night is spent lying in bed eating cheese and drinking beer, which is just as weird as it sounds.

WESTVLETEREN PILGRIMAGE

There's one last monastery: Sint-Sixtusabdij, home of the Westvleteren beers. If Orval is the beer that geeks cherish, Westvleteren is the one they idolize and put on an impossibly high pedestal. It's a god amongst beers and is the one most frequently talked about as the best. This is because ever since 2002, Westvleteren 12 has been the top-rated beer on RateBeer.com, where it averages 4.44 out of 5 from over 3,300 votes (as of April 2015). Reading the ratings is like reading personal love letters. The praise put upon this beer is crazy, something expected with the hype that you're drinking the best beer in the world.

Part of the reason it's so highly regarded is that it's very difficult to buy Westvleteren beer. They don't brew much of it, tightly controlling their output based on how much they need to brew to sustain themselves, rather than how much they could brew to make loads of money. Plus you can only buy it from the monastery or the café opposite.

If you want to buy cases of this beer then it's complicated: on certain days, and between certain times, that fit around the monks' schedule (the monks are active in the brewing, packaging, and selling of the beer), a phone line opens at the Abbey. Only one beer is available to reserve at a time, meaning you call up, reserve your beer (you can get two cases), and then you collect them on another specified date and at a specified time from the brewery gates. A case of 24 bottles of Westvleteren 12 costs €40—I've seen single bottles costing double that on the black market.

I checked the brewery website and saw that the day I was planning on visiting was a day when Westvleteren 12 could be collected, so a couple of weeks earlier, on a day that the phone lines were open for the 12, I dialed the number as soon as the phone line opened. It didn't connect so I dialed again. Still nothing. After about 20 calls I got the busy tone. The next time I got nothing again. I hung up and called constantly for four hours and I didn't get through. I dialed over 300 times.

There was a two-hour window the following morning, so I did the same thing again. A couple of times I got the busy tone, otherwise I got nothing; it just didn't connect. Frustrated, I decided to just call one more time before the lines closed. And guess what? It actually connected. A monk answered and I panicked. I'd given up all hope of this happening and didn't know what to say. It didn't really matter: "I'm sorry, we just sold out of the 12," he said. I finally got through after 500 phone calls and they'd sold out.

Like I said, it's difficult to get Westvleteren beer. The only way to guarantee you can drink it is by going to In de Vrede, the monastery's café. There you'll find a gift shop in the corner where you can buy cheese, mustard, glasses, and cases of beer, where typically one of their three beers (Blond, 8, and 12) is available—today it's the 8. The actual café is a modern place and pop music plays, which is not what I was expecting, and I can't help but feel like I'm in the wrong place—it'd be like drinking a great American IPA in a museum gift shop. There's a complete incongruity between beer and place.

We order a bottle of each of the beers and they arrive in big bowl glasses lined with gold. The Blond is hazy, pale, and looks fantastic with its thick white foam. It has a lovely aroma; floral, honey, fresh bread. The mouthful is surprisingly creamy and full, it's fruity and dry and there's a long, deep bitterness. The Blond rarely gets talked about in the shadow of the dark beers, but it's absolutely brilliant.

The 8 has a great aroma of licorice, chocolate, cola, rum, dried fruit, and bakery bread, the carbonation is brisk, which makes it dry and it stands out for the incomparable depth of flavor in it—it just keeps on giving you more.

Then there's the 12. Rich and full-bodied, it's deeply bitter, with raisins, toast, booze, cookie dough, and brown sugar. Again it's so complex with an endless depth. I'm always excited to drink this beer, surely conditioned by its "best beer" standing, but also because it's amazing.

While we eat toasties made with Westvleteren cheese, Chunk and I fight over the Blond. This is the beer which surprises us the most. The 8 and 12 are great, but I think they both benefit from aging, where the harsher bitterness and the booze mellow and push out more fruit, tea cake, chocolate, and port-like flavors. The Blond is best as fresh as we're drinking it and it fits its surroundings better than the dark beers.

The beers here are extraordinarily good and stand up to their hype. But being in this bright café with Belgian pop music playing is a jarring experience that detracts from the beer. This is the first time I've felt this way: usually I travel to drink a beer where it's made because you can't beat that. Not here. I actually dislike drinking it in the café and I want to take the glasses and sit in a dark Belgian beer bar somewhere. This is true of all the monasteries (with the exception of our spiritual stay experience at Orval) and there's a disconnect between what I associate with these beers and the way the cafés are.

Westy, as beer geeks fondly call Westvletern 12.

Despite these feelings, I know I'll return to Westvleteren again some day because the beers are impressive enough to draw me back. And as Chunk and I leave to travel home we reflect on an unforgettable trip with unforgettable beers, knowing that we've drunk some of the world's best-tasting and best-known beers.

DIVINE BREWS

Beers brewed at Trappist monasteries have a holy reverence placed upon them. It's as if they are automatically elevated thanks to their spiritual place and their history, most of which seems more unknown than exposed. This means they have this wonderful elusive secrecy to them, a kind of mystical, romantic aura that no one quite understands.

There are only six Trappist monasteries brewing in Belgium and that makes them rare. They also undoubtedly make some of the best (and best-loved) beers you can find. I associate these beers with dark, old bars, fridges filled with bottles, shelves stacked with different glasses. That's where these beers are best, not in bright cafés. But it means that these beers work all over the world in a way which others don't—they can travel, they improve by being aged, they suit different environments. It's only their own home in which they seem to feel a little uncomfortable, perhaps analogous with the dichotomy between the monastic life of prayer and the business side of brewing.

There is rightly a romance to these beers, their appeal being the link to a life so different from our own. To me, Westfalen Tripel is one of the best beers in the world; a powerful, majestic, golden ale. Rochefort 10 is an amazing beer, cloaked in a monastic-level of complexity. As is Orval, a beer genuinely living and breathing in the bottle, resting and rising like the monks who oversee its production, while the Vert in the café is a great world beer experience. And there's Westvleteren. Extraordinary beers actually made by the men in the monastery. They could brew four times as much and still sell them all. But they don't because they aren't brewers; they are monks. That's what makes their beers extra special.

THE BEER IS SOUR... CANTILLON

"It's just around here, I think," I say, looking at my map. I'm pretty sure we're close, but it doesn't feel like we're around the corner from one of the world's most revered breweries as we walk through seedy back streets, a few blocks from Brussels Midi Station. I was expecting fine sculptures and elegant architecture, not a chained-up wasteland, gaudy "fashion outlets," and beat-up old cars.

My dad and I are in Brussels on a weekend of beer drinking and we're looking for Cantillon Brewery. It's one of the most traditional breweries in the world and a must-visit destination among beer geeks. But it's not your usual industrial estate brewhouse and Cantillon doesn't make typical things like IPA and Stout. Cantillon is famous for one particular type of beer called Lambic. And it's shockingly, cheek-puckeringly sour.

A STEP BACK IN TIME

"There it is!" We're on a normal-looking residential street lined with cars, but in the middle is an off-white building with a shut shutter. It looks like a house from the outside but this is definitely the place; it says "Brasserie Cantillon" in big letters on the front. There's a brown wooden door and a couple of windows and that's all. It's completely inconspicuous as a brewery and I have no idea if it's open. This really isn't what I was expecting.

Pulling back the door we're thrown through a time warp to a century ago. I gasp—you will, too—as I suck a different type of air into my lungs; it's musty and thick, old and alive, like a second-hand bookshop filled with fermenting wine barrels. The brewery is dark like an old barn, with bare stone floors and wooden beams covered in a creeping film of fungus. It's as if the walls are breathing gently. And there's a lot of people inside this small space: confused-looking Japanese tourists, Dutch guys on a bachelor party, reverential beer geeks, young parents with their baby, a couple of old guys sharing a large bottle.

"That's the head brewer," I say to dad, pointing to Jean Van Roy, the slender blond-haired guy pouring beer from two jugs; an inconspicuous beer superstar. We pay six euros each to take the self-guided tour which leads through a cramped, cobweb-crusted corridor filled with empty wooden cases, dusty bottle tops, and mountains of full, unlabeled bottles lying on their sides. Most breweries pride themselves on being absolutely spotlessly clean. This is different.

We walk into the brewhouse, a small room dominated by two battered and beautiful cast-iron vessels. Gnarly and mangled, seemingly ancient yet offering a hint of a glowing reflection, this is where they brew the beer. The top of one is yanked open, revealing angry-looking mechanical arms, cogs, rakes, and forks that look like torture instruments, while outside copper pipes snake all around. You sense that the

This ancient mash tun shows why they call this place the "Museum of the Gueuze."

Pulling back the door we're thrown through a time warp to a century ago.

arms in these tanks ache and crunch as they go through the brewing process, grumpily moving around. It's mesmerizing.

Dad dips his head into the tank. "What beers do they make again?" I haven't exactly warned him about Lambic yet; he just knows that the first stop of the day is a brewery and that I'm overly excited about it.

"It's called Lambic. It's, er... a bit unusual. Sour. No, not sour because that is bad. It's acidic. It's this really old type of beer aged in wooden barrels for years and it's famous in this specific area and this is the best known Lambic brewery. They use really old hops here, which is very unusual. Most breweries specifically want as much fresh aroma and flavor as possible, yet here they simply want the anti-bacterial qualities you get from hops and not much else."

For years Cantillon have used the same crates to store their recently bottled beers.

We follow the tour route past Cantillon's squat copper kettle and climb up a creaking flight of old steps into the attic of the brewhouse. I know what to expect up here but it still surprises me as I've never seen one of these before—a wide, flat copper pan beneath open roof rafters. "This is the coolship," I say. "The beer comes up here from the kettle and into this pan where it cools down. And then see there," I point at the open slats in the wooden roof and we can see the tops of neighboring buildings. "They open these overnight and let wild yeast come in. That dives right into the sweet liquid in the coolship and starts the fermentation—it's called spontaneous fermentation."

Thousands of years ago, all beer would've been made a bit like this; a mix of grain and water is like a flashing neon light for natural wild yeast who want to eat the sugar and convert it into alcohol. In Lambic production today, the sweet wort is left exposed to the yeast and bacteria naturally in the air, plus whatever microorganisms are in the old wooden building and in the barrels all around. Around 70-80 different yeast and bacteria will combine to make Lambic taste the way it does, with each brewery having their own unique mix adding to their individual mystique. And each yeast and bacteria works in its own way, with sourness typically developing after a few months, meaning the beers of millennia ago might have fermented this way but as they were drunk relatively fresh they probably weren't as shockingly sour.

The barrel room is covered in cobwebs, almost as if the webs are holding the barrels together.

WHERE THE MAGIC HAPPENS

We turn away from the coolship and toward the start of the barrel storage—Cantillon's Lambic is aged in wooden barrels. This dark, dusty room is like an old Belgian farmhouse; there's mold growing and it's covered in cobwebs, almost as if those webs are holding the barrels together. After a night in the coolship, the liquid transfers into these oak or chestnut barrels, a bung is banged in, and all the microorganisms that jumped into the wort are left to ferment the beer. No additional yeast is pitched.

"Some of these barrels are 100 years old," I say, barely able to believe it myself. "Imagine all the beers which have passed through them, all the drinkers who have tasted beers made in them."

We negotiate more stairs down into the cool depths of the brewery and reach the main barrel room, an astonishing sight of time-blackened wooden vessels, lined up and piled high, stretching farther than you thought possible in this seemingly tiny building. Each barrel is marked in secret code denoting its age and type, while spotlights catch a haunting haze in the living air. It's hard to think that we're still in the center of a major European city.

"How... Where... Why?" Dad is as speechless as I am.

Where most beers ferment within two to eight days and are then left to condition for between one and six weeks, Lambic stays in these barrels for up to three years. The casks are individually important because many microorganisms live within them, adding to the ones found in the surrounding air. Each of these organisms has a role to play, changing the beer's aromas, flavors, and complexity throughout. They start working at different times, making the fermentation process long and incredibly complicated.

THE LAMBIC STORY

One of the world's most unique and complex drinks, Lambic is local to the Senne Valley and Payottenland region of Belgium, which rings around Brussels. It's been made for hundreds of years as a farmhouse style of beer and it's the world's most natural and elemental beer, thanks to it being fermented spontaneously by wild airborne yeast. That wild yeast, which works in tandem with bacteria (similar to the kinds you find in yogurt), turns the beer intentionally acidic. On first taste, it's the sort of beer most people have an immediate negative reaction to, unsure why anyone would want to drink something sour. But once you get the taste for acidity it's one of the world's most-loved beers and Cantillon is *the* place to go.

The Cantillon family made Lambic from the 1700s in a town called Lambeek. At one point in time the town had 43 breweries for its 600 inhabitants and many of breweries also made gin, with the stills known as *alembic* in French, so the beer style's origin is likely from the town.

When the Cantillons moved to the country's capital in 1900, they started a lambic merchants and blenders, before making their own beer from 1937. Today it's run by the Van Roy-Cantillon family.

At its peak in 1860, Brussels alone had 3,000 Lambic breweries. Only around 50 of the 3,000 outlasted the World Wars, then this esoteric style started to lose favor and be replaced by less obscure beer styles, such as Pilsner and Pale Ale. But some breweries, like Cantillon and around a dozen others, have kept the tradition going and it's had a remarkable resurrection and increase in popularity around the world, as drinkers develop a taste for the style's tartness.

The barrels are ready for blending.

The initial fermentation is done by a yeast similar to those which make regular ales—this rips through the sugars and creates alcohol in a couple of weeks. Next the bacteria will give a lactic fermentation, producing sourness over a few months. Then comes the slower-working wild yeast called Brettanomyces, or Brett, which continues for years, consuming the sugars that regular yeast can't, and working alongside the bacteria to gradually develop aromatic complexity, often described as funky, leathery, farm-like, and musty. The longer the liquid stays in the barrel, the more the flavors and aromas will evolve. The brewer has no control over all this activity in the barrels, meaning every single batch in here matures differently and will taste unique. And there are a lot of barrels at Cantillon.

The main finished product of a Lambic brewery is not actually Lambic beer. Breweries do make and sell Lambic but it's rare and you'll likely only get it directly from the brewery or at a nearby bar. It's more typically used as a base or a step in the process of beer making, so Lambic breweries make Gueuze (this is pronounced different everywhere you go—I say "gheerz" with hard 'g' and rhyming with "blurs," while others say "ger-zer").

Lambic is a straight beer, in that it comes straight from a single barrel and is poured flat and uncarbonated; its taste

is dependent on how old it is. This becomes more relevant when talking about Gueuze, which is a blend of one-, two-, and three-year-old barrels of Lambic. Where the three-year-old beer is tart, very dry, complex, and aromatic, the younger beer is softer with a fuller body and residual sweetness still present. The skill of the brewer is in blending the different ages of Lambic to get the perfect balance of old and young. When blended and bottled, the sweetness in the young beer and the insatiable yeast still active in the old beer start a further fermentation, giving out carbon dioxide. With the bottle sealed and stored for between three and 18 months, this gas is released and then absorbed back into the beer, resulting in a lively, sharp carbonation, similar to Champagne. So not only do these beers spend years in barrels, they are also left for more months to mature further. It's a slow, dedicated process to make small amounts of this idiosyncratic, unusual beer; the success of a Lambic is almost entirely down to luck and the greatness of a Gueuze is in the ability of the blender to combine different barrels.

The barrel room—the heart of a Lambic brewery—is an incredible experience. You're surrounded by endless old wooden barrels in an Alice-in-Wonderland-like sprawl of space. The whole place moves at a pace that's completely different to anywhere else.

"I love that smell," says dad taking a deep breath in. The air is thick with wine and wood, there's vanilla and citrus, a mustiness, a richness that's deeply intoxicating, sweetly vinous and fruity; it's the smell of slow, gradual maturation and it's amazing. More amazing is that we're in the middle of Brussels in this old building which magically makes this very old style of beer, completely ambivalent to change or modernity.

Next we pass the old bottling machines, completing our loop through the building when we arrive back at the bar and brewery entrance. After the reverential cathedral-like quietness of the slumbering barrels, it's a shock to see and hear people again, but it's good to be back here because now we finally get to drink the beer.

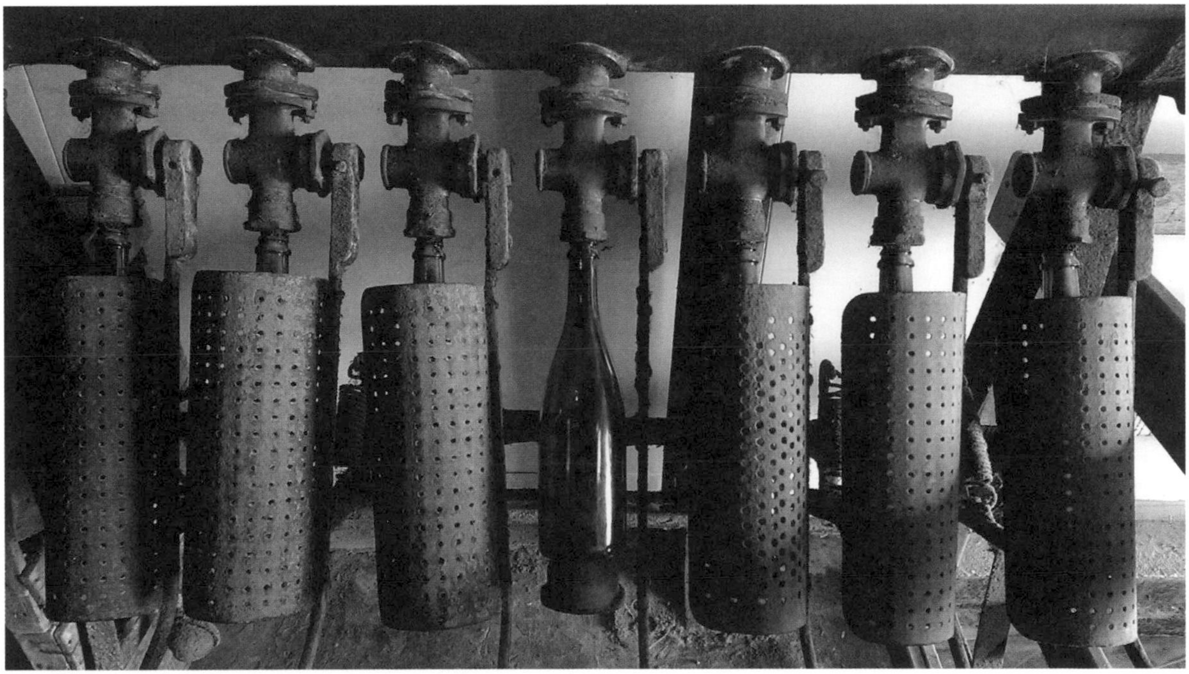

The bottling machines are reminiscent of a medieval torture device.

"IT'S DIFFERENT, ISN'T IT?"

"What are we having?" asks dad.

"There's Lambic, Gueuze, a cherry beer called Kriek, and a raspberry beer called Framboise." I reply. Lambic breweries also make a few other beers, classically containing fruit. The fertile Senne Valley with its vines and orchards (which provide an abundance of the fruit-dwelling wild yeast) grows the ingredients that go into the barrels. Cherries and raspberries are most common, though you'll also find grapes, apricots, and other fruits. These contain sugars, which start another fermentation, plus you'll get the fruit's depth of flavor and a change in color.

At Cantillon they add 10 oz (300 g) of whole fruit into each liter of already-aged lambic (typically 12 to 18 months old) and then it's aged in steel tanks. The fruit contains lots of sugar going in but less than 5% of it remains at the end, so if your cherry beer is like dessert then you've got one made with fruit syrup or extract.

"Is the cherry one sweet?"

"I'll get you one of those and you'll see."

I choose the Lambic, which is about 18 months old. They are poured into small teardrop-shaped glasses. We sit in the corner, a wooden enclave, and I watch as my dad has his first sip of sour beer. "Wow!" he says, his eyes staring over his glasses at the mysterious red liquid. "It's... Umm... Well..." His brow is wrinkled, his nose scrunched. "I wasn't expecting that!" His reaction seems to be the same as most people's: shock followed by wondering why anyone would drink something sour for fun. That was my first reaction years ago.

There's no harsh sourness, just this beautiful dance of wood and acidity. I love it.

For many, the last stop of the tour is the best: the bar where visitors can finally try Cantillon's beers.

My Lambic is an amber color and completely still in the glass; it smells like wood and lemons and orchards and farmyard. A sip and it's so smooth, then sharp in a refreshing kind of way. There's lemon and then it has this rough, brilliant depth of tannic, bitter barrel and a real lip-smacking dryness. There's no harsh sourness, just this beautiful dance of wood and acidity. I love it.

Dad seems to be having a different experience. His face has been frozen in the shocked position—eyebrows raised, lips taut, a perplexed stare. "It's different, isn't it?"

"Can I try?" I slide my beer toward him and grab his glass. It smells like a bag of impossibly ripe cherries, but not sweet, just fresh with a juicy kind of fruitiness. The beer is sharply carbonated and lively, there's a burst of acidity first, then come cherries almost as a whisper, followed by an almond nuttiness and a tannic fruit-skin tartness, somehow powerful yet elegant and refreshing.

Dad's cheeks are now puckered together as he tastes the Lambic. "Bloody hell. It's sour, isn't it? And yours is... more... I'm not sure. It smells different. It's not fizzy. It's different."

Once we have emptied our glasses, I go back to the bar and get a Gueuze for me and for dad I choose a Rosé de Gambrinus, which is made with raspberries. My beer has a bracing carbonation which makes it feel like it's bouncing over my tongue. There's a rounded flavor profile with unfathomable depth, a dry sourness like the pith of a lemon, and a woody, almost cheesy depth from the old hops. Where the Lambic makes you work, this one is more approachable with its fizz, and it's also more refreshing and tantalizing, like a lively, acidic Champagne.

VERY FEW PLACES ARE AS EVOCATIVE AS THIS

Cantillon is a magical and majestic old place. The air is alive, it's filled with history and amazing microorganisms which create these unique beers. And they are unique. No one could recreate a Cantillon beer. This place is too special and it's full of secrets, which no one will ever be able to decode. The intangible wonder of what happens in the cast-iron tanks, in the air, in the roof rafters, in the wooden barrels, in those curvy green bottles, it's all a part of Cantillon and Cantillon alone. It's slow, it's an unknown, it's reliant upon nature for years, and then the important role of human interaction steps in when it's time for blending. I find it irresistibly romantic that every single barrel has its own personality reflecting the way it's matured; a beer which the brewer has virtually no control over. Drinking Cantillon beer in the brewery—sitting amongst old barrels, surrounded by the history, having the special air all around—is remarkable and unexpectedly moving. It's also one of the world's greatest drinking experiences. Very few places are as evocative and unusual as this.

When I finish scribbling love letters to lambic in my notebook, I look up to see that dad has almost finished his glass. "Wow!" he says again. "After the first sips you don't really notice the sourness, do you?" I grab his glass before he drinks it all and it's an explosion of raspberry pips with a fruity tartness at the end.

He drinks from my glass and his brow is furrowed again. He takes another sip. "I could drink that all day," he says. "Shall we have another?"

The marks on these barrels are a code used by the brewers to help keep track of the contents.

IS GUINNESS REALLY BETTER IN IRELAND?

"Guinness tastes better in Ireland." How many times have you heard someone say that? I've always dismissed it, putting it down to the holiday beer effect or happy memories from expats. After all this is a mass-market beer available all over the world, brewed to be completely consistent wherever you drink it. But I'm a curious drinker and if nothing else this worldwide beer adventure has allowed me the opportunities to go on trips just because I want to find these things out for myself. So I'm going to Dublin to see whether "Guinness tastes better in Ireland" is beer's most famous truism.

To prepare myself, I order a pint of Guinness at Stansted airport. I don't care if it's only 7am, I'm having it because it's for research. I also associate Guinness with airports for some reason. It just anecdotally seems to me like Guinness is somehow the beer of choice in British airport bars. And today I'm joining in with the others.

As I sit surrounded by people eating fry-ups and bacon sandwiches, I have a handsome black pint in front of me. I'm not thirsty but this is a serious beer research trip and this, I genuinely believe, is a necessary pint to drink. After one mouthful I'm having exactly the opposite thought. Why am I drinking this? It tastes of cold, fizzy coffee mixed with burnt toast and tannic berries all topped with a thick, bitter foam. It's like all the bad things about breakfast blitzed up and carbonated. At 7am in the airport this is what Guinness tastes like to me. I've had many pints of it before and actually this tastes much like all the rest of them. At least my point of reference is set (albeit very low).

GOOD THINGS COME TO THOSE WHO WAIT

I get in a taxi at the airport. My driver has an accent so thick I can barely understand what he's saying but the reason I'm in a taxi is because I want to ask him an important question. You see, taxi drivers know everything. They are a great resource for travelers. "Where's the best pint of Guinness in Dublin?" I ask.

"I don't know, like. I'm a lager drinker."

Are you kidding me? Of all the cabbies in Dublin I think I found the only one who doesn't drink Guinness. What are the bloody chances?

"But people say it's better here, like," he adds, which at least lifts my spirits.

A few hours later I walk into Mulligan's. It's a pub that a few Dubliners suggested I visit for a pint of Guinness when I asked where I could get the best in town. For over 300 years this has been a pub and walking in I feel the same comfort as when

I slip on a pair of old sneakers, the ones that fit so snugly I wonder why I ever take them off.

Mulligan's is warm with conversation, there's dark wood all around, and the floor is worn with the slow, gradual passing of feet. It's busy already; there are people sitting at the bar, people in groups at tables eating lunch, there's laughter and chatter, some cheery background music, rugby is on TV.

I sit at the bar and order a Guinness. The bartender grabs a glass and flicks open the tap. The dark brown liquid pours out, swirling and surging around the glass, flowing and forming its white foam. He fills two-thirds up the glass and stops. He leaves my Guinness and serves someone else. He steps out from behind the bar, he talks to some customers, all while my beer sits there, as the thick foam settles and the dark brown swirls become solid black. Good things come to those who wait, we've been told.

Watching it entrances me and I now have the most extraordinary sensation of thirst. I want to hold that pint and take a deep drink through the thick foam. I can taste it already in my mind and I want it now. But I have to wait.

The barman returns and takes my glass, opening the beer tap and sending another surge of dark brown through the beer. He's barely looking at my beer as he chats to a guy at the bar, but he knows just when to knock off the tap. He slides the beer across the bar top and places it in front of me silently as I'm mesmerized by the sight of the straight horizon of black and white forming. It's beautiful and it's impossible to deny that. Finally the wait is over. My first pint of Guinness in Ireland.

The first of many pints of Guinness consumed over 48 hours in the Irish capital.

The glass is cold and feels heavy; perhaps because it is, perhaps because I feel like the perceived density of this beer is weighing down my drinking arm, I don't know. The foam is rich as it hits my lips then the beer pushes through it, chilled and somehow lighter than I imagined, refreshing where I expected weight. One gulp becomes two, then three, then four. It's a glorious thing to actually drink. It has this remarkable texture that many assume makes it heavy but it's not, it has a smooth elegance to it. There's a fruity ester quality I've never noticed before, some strawberry or bubblegum. There's a subtlety of dark malt instead of a harshness of bitter barley. There's more fruitiness in the flavor than I've previously tasted. The body is actually refreshingly light while the foam is thick and slips down the glass. It's changed everything I thought I knew about Guinness.

I'm mesmerized by the sight of the straight horizon of black and white forming. It's beautiful.

FROM THE SOURCE

Next I go to the Guinness Storehouse at St James's Gate. This is Ireland's number one tourist attraction and it is just that: a tourist stop. You walk into a gift shop, which has the Guinness logo printed on everything you can possibly print a Guinness logo on, your entrance fee (it's €18 so not cheap) buys you a self-guided tour which is fairly interesting (did you know they brew three million pints of Guinness a day?) as you gradually work your way up to the Gravity Bar on the seventh floor, where a pint and a 360-degree view of Dublin awaits you. In the brightness of this glass-walled bar you can see the beer is actually a deep ruby color. It's also unexpectedly refreshing and fresh. More of that fruitiness I tasted earlier comes through, there's a gentle richness to the body, some caramel sweetness, and there's just something pleasant about actually drinking it—the smooth texture, the foam, the flavor; it's great.

Later that night I'm in a pub across town and, as I wait for my Guinness to pour, the old chap sitting next to me at the bar is just finishing his beer. He nods to the barmaid, says "I'll take another one in there when you're ready," and smiles the smile of a happy Irishman. Then he turns to me. "Good evening there!" When he finds out I'm in Dublin specifically to drink Guinness his eyes light up.

"There's a bar in Donegal and you could fucking live there for a year and still love the beer, I swear!" he says, remembering a trip he took with a mistress (details of which I daren't put in print).

The River Liffey slices through the center of Dublin.

"I can look at a pint and know if it's good, you know," he pauses as my pint is put in front of me ("A pint of Goodness," says the barmaid). "Ah, yes, that's a fine one. A bad one has yellow foam and the foam should cling to the beer and not the glass."

"What makes a really good pint of Guinness?" I ask him.

"The thing with Guinness is you need to drink it fresh. You should go all around town and just drink lots of Guinness and you'll see that it's different. It doesn't taste the same everywhere. But when you find somewhere good you'll stay there."

"I'll take another one in there," he nods, then smiles the smile of a happy Irishman.

THE HOME OF GUINNESS

I end the night in the Temple Bar pub in Temple Bar, the center of Dublin's famously fun nightlife, where there's live music and a great atmosphere. The Guinness tap doesn't seem to stop as glasses are lined up, part-filled then topped up. Somehow

The entrance to the St James's Gate brewery, where the world's bestselling stout is brewed. 10 million glasses of Guinness are drunk each day in 150 different countries.

1 MINUTE AND 58 SECONDS

That's how long it takes to pour the perfect pint of Guinness. It's amazing how the company has managed to completely own a very particular way to pour their beer. How did they do that? How have they managed to make every bartender all around the world go through the two-part pour every time they get asked for a Guinness? It's an incredible worldwide buy-in from drinkers and bars to the point that you'd question it if it wasn't done. And considering Guinness is the go-to dark beer in the world, available virtually everywhere, it's a marvel of a thing.

Guinness just belongs and I can't imagine anything other than a pint of Stout right here, right now. It might be a worldwide brand, available in virtually every city that has a pub (probably an Irish bar...), but Dublin is its home. Some beers just belong in certain places, they are certain places, and Guinness is certainly that in Dublin. And yes, Guinness genuinely does taste better in Dublin.

* As a relevant footnote, while Guinness is better in Dublin than anywhere else I've drunk it, there are better Stouts to drink in the city. I'm a huge fan of O'Hara's and could drink it by the bucket, plus there are many from Ireland's burgeoning craft brewing scene. Check out the Dublin City Guide (pages 76–79) for more of the best places in what is one of the world's best drinking cities.

PILSEN STRIKES GOLD

Over 90% of all beer drunk around the world is golden lager, yet before 1842 golden lager didn't exist. It took 36 barrels of bad dark ale, a Bavarian brewmaster smart to all the latest brewing science, and a city perfectly placed in the middle of natural resources to combine to produce the world's first golden lager. This is the story of Pilsner Urquell.

PILSEN, BOHEMIA. FEBRUARY 1838

"It is unacceptable," said Václav Mirwald, the innkeeper here at U Zlatého Orla, and a prominent citizen of Pilsen. "This is bad beer." The acid smell of smoke and old beer hangs in the dark inn just off the town's main square.

"It is also sour," says Jakub Michel. "It is not the first time he has bad beer," adds Josef Klotz. "And he isn't the only one with beer like this."

"That tavern does not sell it fast enough," says Mirwald as he hammers a wooden tap into a new barrel of beer.

"And then there's the Bavarian beer," says Klotz, causing Mirwald to slam his hammer down on the bar top. "Our town is drinking too much of it."

"It is two crowns cheaper than our beer," points out Václav Stary.

"This is a discussion we have had too often," says Mirwald. "Things must change. We need good beer and it should also be cheap. It is unacceptable to have Bavarian beer take over our town." He pours himself a mug of dark, thick, flat beer, takes a mouthful and spits it out onto the floor. "But Bavarian beer is better than this rubbish."

"We should call a meeting," says Klotz. "We should encourage new laws for brewing and ensure that everyone can make good beer. We cannot have this Bavarian beer invade our town and affect our brewing citizens."

"No," says Mirwald. "That is not enough. We must make an example of this for the town to see."

THE DAY IT ALL CHANGED

A growing crowd is gathering around the Town Hall, rubbing their hands together in the bitter cold. Stacked, battered wooden barrels are lined up, 36 in total. The February sun passes beneath the rooftops as Mirwald and the others stand with their arms folded over their round stomachs, their faces taut and firm. Martin Kestranek, head cooper of the town, stands beside them holding a heavy axe.

When the bell of St Bartholomew's Cathedral strikes, the crowd falls quiet, counting the heavy chimes. After the fifth, Mirwald steps forward.

"Since 1295, citizens of this town have had the right to make beer," his voice is visible in the cold air. "But the beer we have today is not good enough. Some of you are holding onto the best barley. Some of you are charging too much for your beer. Some of this beer is sour. And Bavarian beer is coming; we should not drink this in our town. We should drink beer from Pilsen."

Mirwald turns to the wooden barrels next to him. "These barrels of beer brewed in Pilsen are unfit for use and dangerous for health." He nods to Kestranek, who loosens his wide arms, lifts his axe, and throws it over his shoulder. A barrel smashes open with a ferocious crash, gushing a wave of dark liquid into the gutter.

"This is to show you..." he pauses while Kestranek breaks a second barrel that he once built, "...that we must be better. We need to work together to make Pilsen's beer better."

"We must make an example of this for the town to see."

The townsfolk watch on in silence. There's shame and there's anger, lowered heads and clenched fists, as the bitter brown liquid pours through the streets, filling the icy air with the foul smell of vinegar, sewage, and stables. Mirwald turns to the men beside him: "This will change things and make them better."

"But we must work together," says Stary. "We have over 20 families making beer; we have different maltsters. We have a town that wants to drink good beer but we can't be successful as we are." Another barrel is smashed before them. "Maybe it's time for something new. Maybe just one brewery for us all, like they have in Bavaria. A brewery owned by the people of Pilsen."

Mirwald turns to him: "Let's talk tomorrow."

AN EXTERNAL THREAT

Through spring things improve but by summer the quality of beer declines again in the heat, while the threat of cheaper and better imported brews never leaves. Old habits in the town—primitive breweries in homes, plus a resistance to use the new bottom-fermenting yeast of Bavaria (the more common top-fermenting yeast is preferred)—mean that many of Pilsen's beers are still poorer quality than the imported ones.

Ever since February, Mirwald and the others have been discussing a solution to the town's beer problems: they debate how the citizens with brewing rights can continue to make income from beer, they consider how and where a brewery could be built and the type of beer the town might make. The discussions have lasted months.

As the men talk one Sunday afternoon in November of 1838, Klotz rushes in, breathless: "I have just heard of a storehouse outside of our town. It's used for Bavarian beer, meaning it will be ever-ready to supply the local taverns!"

Mirwald stares back at Klotz then looks at the others: "This danger threatens the burghers. If one such Bavarian brewery business establishes itself, there is no doubt that it will find many followers and flood our city with foreign, cheap beer. We must confront the competition in both quality and price. The citizens with

Pilsen's town hall as it stands today.

brewing rights must build a brewery for themselves, which is then equipped in the Bavarian manner, and by themselves brew beer."

A meeting is arranged with Martin Kopecky, the town's mayor, for the following afternoon. A man of great standing, level-headed, smart, and focused on the best for Pilsen, Kopecky listens carefully as the idea is presented to him.

"We cannot ban imported beers because each innkeeper in the town is free to buy from any brewer he likes, even the foreign ones," says Kopecky. "But only with great beer will it be possible to beat the foreign competition and achieve rich sales outside of Pilsen." After a silent thought, he adds: "I will help you to achieve this goal."

A NEW BEGINNING

On a cold January 2, 1839, almost a year after the barrels were destroyed in the square, the citizens of Pilsen are gathered again by the Town Hall.

Mirwald, standing next to Kopecky, opens a document and makes his announcement, straight and unwavering. "It has been decided that we, the people of Pilsen, will begin work on one new brewery. It will be a brewery for us all; a brewery for the citizens of Pilsen. We will all have ownership of it and we will all work to ensure that it can be a great business for our town. It will create jobs, it will make great beer, and as a permanent property it will be an honorable memorial to our descendants. We will do this by improving the quality of the beer, by proceeding to produce bottom-fermented beers, and in so doing the market for Pilsner beer could be gained even outside the territory of Pilsen."

"We, the people of Pilsen, will begin work on one new brewery."

The crowd calls out: "This is impossible!" "I make my beer!" "This cannot be!" "What about my malthouse?" "This is my job!"

Mirwald looks up at the eyes staring him down, and says firmly: "If some individuals, out of selfishness or unreason, let themselves be seduced into opposition against such a boon, it is to be reminded that such an effort of theirs will be in vain, for a way has been found to accomplish this plan conclusively." The decision is made.

The first job was to hire an architect and Martin Stelzer was their choice. He made plans for an impressive new brewhouse like those he'd seen on his travels around Europe. He decided on a location beside the Radbuza river, a short walk from the town's central square. Beneath the brewery, the soft stone was perfect for carving deep cellars into the ground to create a place that would allow their beer to slowly and gently mature and condition. He also designed a grand malting house so that the people of Pilsen could produce their own malt from the local barley.

Next they needed a brewmaster. It was decided that he should be a Bavarian with experience of brewing lager beers. Josef Groll got the job and he brought with him two other Bavarians: an assistant brewmaster, and a chief cooper to construct all the barrels the brewery required. They worked alongside local citizens who themselves were to build the Burgher's Brewery.

Groll came to Pilsen with new knowledge of brewing that others had yet to put into place, information gained from his time working at pioneering Bavarian breweries. This job was Groll's chance to do something different, and he was very fortunate in because Pilsen has wonderful water that is naturally soft and virtually mineral-free—perfect for brewing clean beers.

The early summer of 1842 saw a good crop of barley, which Groll took into his malthouse; there he made a monumental decision. He had learnt of a new malting technique pioneered by British brewers that used indirect heat to turn the barley into malt. Before now malting was done directly over flames, adding a dark, smoky tinge to the grain and the beer. His beer would not be like that. His malt would be heated without the smoke, without taking on any of the darkness of the fire, slowly turning it sweet and golden in color. It would be the perfect brewing malt for the town's soft water.

Late in August, Groll traveled to the nearby hop fields to check on the harvest and he found big, fragrant, and aromatic flowers hanging heavy on the bine. He rubbed them in his hands and they filled his palms with the smell of spice, citrus, and fresh cut grass. He ordered many bales to be delivered one month from that day.

He just needed one more ingredient: yeast. It was decided that he would use a bottom-fermenting yeast and produce light-colored, Bavarian-style lagers, rather than the dark ales brewers in Bohemia and beyond were still making. Groll knew that his yeast liked to work slowly at cool temperatures, so he insisted that more and more cellars were cut beneath his brewery, and as they were being carved, his team of coopers were busy lining them with large, empty barrels, ready to be filled with Pilsen's new beer.

A portrait of brewmaster Josef Groll.

BREWING BEGINS

On Wednesday October 5, 1842, after nearly four years of work, the first brew day finally came and large copper pans were filled with Pilsen's soft water and golden grains. The liquid churned and simmered slowly. To increase the heat Groll used a decoction process. This took a portion of the mash and moved it into another copper vessel where it was heated hard and fast before it was returned to the brew, raising the the temperature to give a caramelized sweetness to the brew. He did this three times. Later, when the bitter, fragrant Czech hops were added to the boiling liquid the smell of sweet toasty malt, lemon peel, and fresh cut grass filled the town's air, alerting the people of Pilsen that there would soon be beer again.

With the brew complete it was cooled, and transferred down into the cold cellars, where it was poured into a giant wooden vessel before Groll added the yeast.

Every day Groll checked his beer while the town waited. He saw the yeast slowly come to life and create a thick head of foam on the top of the barrel. He tasted it as the sweetness reduced and the alcohol levels increased, pushing forward the hop bitterness. One week became two. The beer was transferred into another wooden tank deeper in the dark cellars to allow it to slowly condition. By the third week Groll was tiring of having Mirwald contact him daily asking about the beer, so told him bluntly to leave and that the beer will be ready when it is ready, not sooner. By the fourth week the beer was maturing well, developing in flavor.

In the fifth week Groll left his usual metal tankard behind and instead took a glass into the cellar, which he held under the tap of the barrel, filling it with beer. He lit a candle and raised his glass to the light. What he saw was a surprise even to him:

a beer so bright and pale he could see the sharp edges of the candle's light flickering through it. He lifted the glass to his nose and took in a spicy, fruity fragrance like he'd never experienced before. He took a deep gulp, tasting a soft sweetness of honey then a long, refreshing bitterness.

That night Groll walked into Mirwald's busy inn. As he entered everyone stopped and turned, for the brewmaster was rarely seen here. Groll sat at the bar, ordered a beer as dark, bitter, and heavy as the faces staring back at him. He drank it quickly enough that no one would come and talk to him. As he finished his beer he passed his tankard to Mirwald, said: "We will drink at St Martin's Fair," and left.

THE ORIGINAL GOLDEN LAGER

Friday November 11, 1842. The crowd surrounds the Town Hall once again, staring at the wooden barrels stacked before them, bringing back bad memories. They are restless; this brewery of theirs has taken years to build, it has taken up their lives, it has changed their lives. And where is the brewmaster? The scowling, coarse Bavarian man of few words who has yet to enamor himself to the people. Could he really make quality beer for their town? Everyone in this town is invested in the brewery—emotionally, physically, financially—so the beer has to be good.

Kopecky, Groll, and Stelzer wait inside the Town Hall. The mayor, wanting to taste the beer before the town's citizens, had invited the brewmaster and architect to see him, but Groll wouldn't allow it. When the crowd is large, Kopecky leads the way into the street, silencing the chatter of the people.

Groll carries with him a large wooden box and a hammer. He places the box down then without pause he pounds a tap into the barrel, spraying white foam as he does. From the box he pulls out an ornate glass jug and, with his back to the crowd, pours the beer while the townsfolk watch on nervously. With the jug full he turns and raises it into the autumn sun. A shocked inhalation sucks the words from the crowd, for Groll is holding a jug of bright beer with a thick white foam on top. They had never seen a beer so golden in color.

"What is this?" shouts one man. "What have you made?" shouts another. "That's not beer!"

Groll takes a taste from the jug and passes it to Stelzer, who takes a long mouthful, nods happily, then passes it to Mirwald, who can barely wait any longer to taste it. He raises the jug to the light and sees the weak golden sun through it. He has one taste and can barely comprehend what he is drinking. He has another taste, and another, and still this beer is new to him, an incredible surprise. Mirwald hands the almost-empty jug to Kopecky who stares at it cautiously, drawn to the glowing brightness, drawn to the sight of the cathedral's spire visible through it. He takes one mouthful of the bright beer, and raises the jug above his head and says: "This is Pilsen's beer!"

Pilsen had struck gold.

Václav Mirwald, one of the men responsible for developing the new brewery in Pilsen.

MODERN PILSEN

Pilsen's main square is a handsome block lined with both new and old buildings in a pick 'n' mix variety of pastel colors, all centered around the large Gothic cathedral of St Bartholomew. But one building really stands out: the Town Hall—an ornate, dark, looming structure. This is the spot where the 36 barrels of beer were smashed in 1838 and that's all I can think about. It's one of the most legendary moments in beer's history. What would it have been like on that day in February?

Walking through the town and over the river, I reach the castle-like gates of the brewery. Behind them is a large, open courtyard; tall chimneys pump steam into the sky, a water tower pokes up like an old lighthouse observing all around it, and a yellow building stands at the back proudly boasting the distinctive red wax seal of the Pilsner Urquell logo. The brewery has been here since 1842, always making beer. The first brew took the name of the town. In 1859, they trademarked "Pilsner Bier" and then in 1898 then added "Urquell", or Original, to mark it out as the first.

The guide who will be showing a group of us around comes to greet us. He takes us to the huge packaging halls then we walk through the maltings where the brewery still produces its own golden malt. We see the cooperage—the last remaining one in a brewery in Central Europe—where eight men work to build and maintain barrels of beer. We see the original copper mash tun used in 1842—one of the beer world's most important museum pieces. We pass the handsome copper tanks of the old brewhouse, then into the stunning new one—a clean and warm room with silver pyramid-like lauter tuns and more gorgeous copper vessels.

The stunning copper tanks of the brewhouse.

We're told how the recipe and process is unchanged since Josef Groll: it still uses Pilsen's soft water, drawn from a nearby well; it uses Moravian barley which is malted at the brewery in Pilsen to give that distinctive bright golden color to the beer; it uses Czech Saaz hops to give a clean bitterness and fragrant aroma; it uses their own "H" yeast strain; it still uses copper tanks, it still undergoes a triple decoction, and it takes around five weeks from start to finish, just like Groll's brew. And this is still the only beer they make here. It's just Pilsner Urquell, known in Czech as Plzeňský Prazdroj. All of this is great to see, but there's one place that I want to go more than anywhere else: the cellars.

MARKED WITH STORIES AND HISTORY

The construction of the cellars began when the brewery was first conceived. They took 80 years to complete and they snake 5.6 miles (9 km) in length, down to 39 ft (12 m) underground, totaling 344,400 ft^2 ($32,000 m^2$). At one time, before artificial refrigeration, this was the heart of the brewery, with almost all workers based underground. The beer was fermented here, conditioned here, and packaged here. Over a century ago, in 1913, the brewery produced over one million hectoliters and all of that was made down here—an astonishing, incomprehensible volume and task. Today, many of the cellars are off-limits as much of the underground area has caved in, but you can still walk around a small section. It's also down here that you get to drink... and by now I'm very, very thirsty.

Just a few steps into these cellars and it's impossible not to be mesmerized by them. Cold and dark, there's a calm stillness like a morning silenced by fresh snowfall. These huge cellars were carved 170 years ago; great tracks cut beneath the brewery, turning left and right, with just darkness and no idea of what lies a few yards beyond. It feels like there's an echo, but it's too cool and damp for our words to bounce back what we're saying. Instead, the "Ohmygods" that I'm whispering to myself are also being repeated under the breaths of everyone else.

We move into a corridor lined on either side with barrels stacked two high: imposing and tight, dark and cold. These barrels are taller than me and wider than my arm span. They hold 3,000–4,000 liters in each and are up to 100 years old. Blackened by time, they are scratched with chalk so the brewers can see what's in them, but more than that they are marked with stories and history: How many men have worked down here? What was their job like? How many beers have passed through them? How many people have drunk those beers?

When the brewery shifted production from all wooden barrels to all stainless steel tanks a few decades ago, they kept making a small amount in the wood to ensure the flavor didn't change during the transition. Called "Parallel Brewing" it still continues today, so when you get to this part of the tour you drink the unfiltered beer fermented in the cellars and matured in these huge barrels, just like it was when Groll brewed it in 1842.

There's a man standing in front of one of the barrels, gripping a copper tap. I put my glass beneath and it fills up. The silent "wow" that I mouth comes out as condensation. Beer in hand, we pass through a narrow gap between the barrels and into another cellar. We stop briefly, looking back to where we were served—it's like the ultimate beer theatre, dark with spotlights showing a haze in the air. The stories that this place could tell are hanging silently around us. We're holding a glass of Pilsner made in Pilsen in the barrels in these cellars.

A pint of Pilsner Urquell poured straight from the barrel, just the way Josef Groll would have tasted it.

The underground network of cellars provides the perfect conditions for the maturation process.

The beer is an unfiltered cloudy gold with a thick white foam. It's unbelievably smooth and rich. There's a slight sweetness to begin and a herbal, dry bitterness to finish. It's so atmospheric down here, haunting almost, and a chill runs through me as I take another sip. This is the beer that Groll would have tasted in November 1842, one which was unlike any other—the world's first golden lager. With over 90% of the world's beer now pale lagers, it's easy to assume that beer has always been this way, but it hasn't. Pilsner Urquell changed things forever, making a beer of singular importance. It's even more extraordinary that we can trace this beer to specific people, to an exact time and place; a rare thing for something so momentous.

What did Groll think when he first tasted this beer? How did he feel? Was he ready to take this beer into the city center and face the people of Pilsen and offer them their new beer? Were the citizens of Pilsen ready for it when they finally got to taste the new beer?

I wasn't ready for it. I didn't expect to get a beer like this. I didn't expect to be wrapped in so much history, to be so romanced by the cold cellars. But it's impossible not to be and it's one of the best beer experiences I've ever had—drinking in the cellars at Pilsner Urquell is an essential world beer experience. This beer might be the best I've ever tasted.

DISCLAIMER: I work for Pilsner Urquell and you may think that I am therefore biased, but you should really go and drink this beer for yourself—it's an astonishing experience and something that all beer lovers must do. I've done it more than 10 times and it never fails to blow my mind.

Credit in this chapter goes to Evan Rail who translated the original documents of the brewery's beginning, which much of this story is based on. It was published in the **Brewery History Journal**, edition 149 (2012), pages 20–29.

MY BEER IS BETTER THAN YOUR BEER!

"You know what's funny?" says my friend Patrick as we sit in a beer garden in Cologne. "When you drive out of the city there's no road sign for Düsseldorf. It just tells you the town after it!"

The competition between Düsseldorf and Cologne is one of the greatest town rivalries in the world. They are 25 miles (40 km) apart on the River Rhine in the west of Germany, not far from the Dutch and Belgian borders. Cologne is the fourth biggest city in Germany and Düsseldorf is the seventh, though Düsseldorf is the capital of the North Rhine-Westphalia region, a fact that the people of Cologne don't like to be reminded of. Cologne has its hugely impressive cathedral; it's a media hub, a center of creative industries, and home to one of Europe's oldest universities. Düsseldorf has technology, business, fine dining, and high fashion. Both have big Christmas markets. Both have a great carnival. Both have a soccer team. And Düsseldorf and Cologne both have their own indigenous beer style, and these beers have become a definitive symbol of the respective city and central to their competitive coexistence.

Düsseldorf has Altbier and Cologne has Kölsch. There's nowhere in the world where one specific, idiosyncratic beer style dominates a city as prominently as in either Düsseldorf or Cologne, yet here we have two cities side by side, each with their own beer, each with numerous breweries within walking distance of each other, and where the citizens of each are certain that their beer is the best.

But which is the best? This is Düsseldorf versus Cologne. It's Altbier versus Kölsch.

A CASE FOR ALT

Düsseldorf's Haubtbahnhof is ugly. Like almost every other major European city, the area around the main station is shitty, but walk to the Altstadt or Old Town and it gets a lot better. It's around here that you'll find many breweries and bars, and at all of them people will be drinking Altbier.

My first stop is to drink the älteste Altbier in the Aldstadt at Brauerei Schumacher. When John Matthias Schumacher started brewing in 1838 he made a beer similar to

WHAT IS ALT?

Go back many years and the majority of beers brewed in Germany, and particularly so in the relatively warm region of the northwest, would've been dark, well-hopped ales. With the encroaching advance of pale lagers, the brewers of Düsseldorf stuck to their bitter brown beers, adopting the name Altbier to differentiate their traditional brews from the golden newcomers. It's still that same dark, hoppy beer today and what marks it out as different from other ales is that it's fermented warm then, as is more common with lager, it's cold-conditioned at a low temperature.

the others, only his was notably hoppier and cold-matured in wooden barrels, from which it was then served. This essentially became the template for other Altbiers and today the majority of beers in Düsseldorf are served directly from the wooden barrel, pulled up straight from the cellar and propped on the bar.

Walking through the expansive restaurant at Schumacher, you can't miss the large dark barrel sitting on the bar, as men dressed in blue waistcoats rush past carrying round trays of small glasses. I find a table and one of those men in blue approaches. He makes eye contact, I say "eins", and he places a beer mat in front of me, scratches a dark pencil tick onto it, then slams a glass down. The deep copper-colored beer has a thick tan foam and a subtle aroma of berries, apples, and spice. It's complexly toasty and roasty from the dark malt and finishes very bitter and quenching, thanks to the earthy, spicy German hops.

The first beer is gone in minutes. This isn't because I'm drinking especially fast but because the glass only holds 7 oz (200 ml)—you can't get Altbier by the pint in Düsseldorf. The glass is called a becher and it's short and squat like a tumbler. The guy in blue passes again, sees my empty glass and without asking he picks it up and replaces it with a fresh one from his tray, adding a second scratch to my beer mat. As I finish number two, I spread a map of the city on the table in front of me; I'm trying to visit all the breweries and beer halls, looking to sample as many different Altbiers as possible in order to find my favorite.

This is Düsseldorf versus Cologne. Altbier versus Kölsch.

Uerige is a busy, big multi-level corner building with loads of drinking space outside and many rooms inside. The Alt

Locals in Düsseldorf gather on a warm summer evening on the banks of the Rhein.

here is especially bitter, registering at 55IBU, making it one of German's most bitter commercial beers. Kürzer is the youngest brewery in town and has a cooler crowd. The Braukon kit stands at the back of the bar while a clear glass "barrel" sits on the bar as a modern take on dispensing the beer. The Alt here is definitely the fruitiest with a big banana aroma and rounder body.

My search of all the Alts takes me to: Im Füchschen (quinine-like bitterness and toastier malts), Frankenheim (earthy, smoky, tobacco-esque quality with a buttery richness), Diebels (the biggest-selling and the least complex), Bolten's (vanilla, toast, aniseed, and floral hops), and Schlösser (strawberry milkshake sweetness and nutty, toasty malt).

Like the ticks the waiters have been marking on beer mats in each bar, I keep my own tick tally in my notebook and I've built quite a few fences across the page when I decide it's time to eat.

Bolkerstrasse is otherwise known as the "largest bar top in the world" thanks to its 1000-ft (300-meter) succession of bars and restaurants. On a Saturday night in August it's packed with revelers, and this is where I'm going for dinner in Zum Schlüssel, one of the largest brauhauses in town.

Despite Zum Schlüssel having almost 1,000 seats, the place is so busy that it takes me 10 minutes of walking around all the various rooms, seeing huge plates of food and hundreds of glasses of beer, before I finally find a table and get a beer. The Alt here is clean and dry, aromatic and bitter, toasty, complex, and refreshingly hoppy with a little apple freshness. Having now had a lot of different Alts, this one strikes me as a perfect composite of the others.

As my first beer disappears, my second one arrives in time to join a big plate of Himmel und Ähd, which is just about the most comforting food you can imagine: soft salty black pudding, creamy mash potato, caramelized onions, and apple sauce (guess which nearby city also has Himmel und Ähd as one of their main meals?).

The restaurant is still packed as three women—grandmother, daughter, and granddaughter—carrying about 20 shopping bags between them, pass and ask to share the table with me. Sitting down, beers are placed in front of them as they carry on their gossiping. That is until they see me taking a photo of my food so I remember what it looks like and so I can put it online and make friends at home jealous. I'm also taking photos of my beer. The three women stare while I line up photos of the beer next to the plate, trying to get the perfect angle. They are still silent and staring at me when I take my pencil and scribble in my notebook.

"Are you a... how do you say... critic?" asks the youngest.

"Oh, no, I just... I just like to take photos of my food."

"What do you write?" she asks.

"I'm writing a book about beer. About this beer." I raise my glass to them.

"You write a book about our Altbier?"

On Bolkerstrasse, one of Germany's most popular drinking streets, you're never more than a few steps away from your next Altbier.

> The Alt here is clean and dry, aromatic and bitter, toasty, complex, and refreshingly hoppy...

"It's about all beer. I'm trying to find the best beer in the world."

They look at each other and the mother says something in German, then to me in English: "But you have already found it," she says completely straight.

"You think this beer is the best?"

"Of course."

"What about Uerige?" I ask.

"Too... bitter."

"Kürzer?"

"For young people."

"Schumacher?"

"We like this beer."

Then I dare to ask the question: "Have you ever had Kölsch?"

They look at each other but don't speak for an uncomfortably long time... "This is best beer," says the grandmother, the first thing she's said so far, as she lifts her glass and drains it, as if to prove her point. "Kölsch is cheap beer. They don't use expensive dark grain and they have less hopfen. Not like our Altbier."

As their food arrives and mine disappears I say goodbye and move on, walking around the Altstadt for a few hours, stopping for more Alts in different bars. With space for one more, I return to Zum Schlüssel.

Generally, if you told me I'd only be able to drink one beer style all day then I wouldn't be so excited about it, preferring to drink more diversely. But drinking only Altbier in Düsseldorf has been fascinating: seeing how some versions are more bitter, others more malty, others fruitier. It's like spending a day eating 10 cheeseburgers and being able to directly compare them and pick out the best. It's rare to be able to have that experience, and I love it.

One final beer in Zum Schlüssel and my personal tick tally hits 21. This is definitely my favorite Altbier; it's complex and interesting, bitter and dry yet with a toasty, nutty malt depth. It's a great beer.

Now it's time to sleep because I've got an early alarm tomorrow morning to catch a train to Cologne.

TALKING KÖLSCH

You should definitely travel to Cologne by train because the station is extraordinary in that it welcomes you with the sight of the huge Cathedral as soon as you exit the Hauptbahnhof.

I walk through the old town to see some sights and build my thirst, ready for another day of drink-based research. Passing the Cathedral and just off the central square, I find Früh am Dom and take a seat in the warm courtyard outside.

In a strange parallel of yesterday, a man in a blue waistcoat, carrying a tray of small glasses approaches. I nod at him and he places a beer mat in front of me, scratches a pencil tick onto it, and slams a beer down.

That first part may have been the same, but the beer is definitely different. The glass is called a stange and it's taller, slimmer, and lighter than yesterday's bechers. The beer in this stange is brilliant gold with a bright white foam on top. Früh's Kölsch is light, clean, and refreshing, there's a subtle fruitiness, some bready malt flavor, and a quenching, dry finish.

Just like yesterday, I'm on a tour of as many breweries and brauhauses as possible. In my second stop, Gäffel, where the Kölsch has a pronounced lemony quality and a maltier depth than Früh's,

WHAT IS KÖLSCH?

Like Düsseldorf's Altbier, Kölsch became a symbol of parochial defiance against the encroach of pale lager. Where Altbier remained dark, the beers of Cologne got lighter, though they never adopted lager yeast, sticking to their top-fermenting ales. Both did take on the cold-conditioning of lagerbiers, leading to the hybrid lagered ales that we drink today.

Cologne has a long history of trying to make the best beer possible. As early as 1396, the city's brewers banded together to form a guild, which worked to protect their beer and their work. In 1603, the guild outlawed bottom-fermenting lager—the warmer weather of the area was far better for brewing top-fermenting ales, and they wanted to ensure the best quality beers for their city.

By the early 20th century, the indigenous pale ales of Cologne adopted the name Kölsch, meaning "of Köln" in local dialect. As other nearby brewers saw the style and tried to make their own versions, the Cologne brewers once again got together to protect their brew and in 1985, 22 of them signed the Kölsch Konvention which stipulated that genuine Kölsch must be brewed in the Cologne area, it must be pale in color, top-fermented, well-hopped, filtered, and around 5% ABV. It now has a Protected Geographical Indication, so only Cologne-based brewers can use the style name in Europe.

One of the many squares in Cologne's Old Town where you can enjoy a beer.

I order Kölsche Kavier for lunch and get a taste of the town's light-hearted, fun-poking sense of humor because this isn't a fine fishy treat, it's blood sausage, a rye bread roll, and some onions.

Päffgen is next: a small brewhouse behind a big restaurant a little walk from the center. They only make draught beer here and it's only sold in the city, where it's all served from wooden barrels. One sip and I immediately love it for its bigger hop aroma, more malt depth, and some subtle citrusy hop flavor. It's a very fine beer.

Walking south, I meet with my friend Patrick in a beer garden, where we drink Hellers beer, brewed just a few hundred meters away. Pat isn't from Cologne but he's lived here for 10 years and is an adopted Kölner, so I want to know about the city rivalry from his perspective.

"We say that we drink Kölsch, we pee in the Rhine, and they make Alt out of it!"

Saying 'bye to Pat, I jump on the Metro because I want to visit Braustelle, Cologne's smallest brewery and one of the most interesting and unusual breweries in the whole of Germany.

"Düsseldorf is the forbidden city—there's no reason to go there," he says. "We love to make jokes on them and we keep up those little gags, like no road sign. We make more jokes on Düsseldorf than they do on us, but the city is in a better position because it is the capital of North Rhine-Westphalia. That is an offence to Köln."

"What do you think of Altbier?" I ask him.

"We say that we drink Kölsch, we pee in the Rhine, and they make Alt out of it!" he laughs before explaining that he does drink it if he's in Düsseldorf but he definitely prefers Kölsch.

I ask about the guys I've seen dressed in blue serving the beer and Pat explains that they are called kobes and the name originates in Cologne, yet Düsseldorfers also use it. As Cologne was once a major pilgrimage point, people would stop in the city for a while and work to earn money before moving on. To save employers having to remember many different and new names, these traveling workers were all called 'Jakob', and kobes is derivative of that. "To be a kobes is an honor in Cologne," Pat says. "It's a difficult job thanks to the small glasses and high drinking frequency."

With our glasses almost empty, I ask what his favorite Kölsch is: "Mühlen," he replies without hesitating. "Let's go to a kiosk and we'll have one."

This kiosk, which is about five minutes away, is like a grocery store with hundreds of beers in the fridges and a couple of tables outside. We grab two bottles of beer with a green label featuring a red windmill on the front—the name means mill. It has toasty malt, some caramel and strawberries, and a lower bitterness than others I've tasted—it's good.

Gaffel is one of the most common beers available in the city.

It feels like a Belgian beer bar as you walk into the cozy corner space. The brew kit is in the back and there are tanks in the cellar. What makes this place different is the beer—here you can find Stouts, Pale Ales, sour ales, strong lagers, plus Kölsch, of course. And they brew an Altbier.

"I am from Düsseldorf and I like Altbier," says Peter Esser, the brewmaster. "When I started people said it's a bad thing and the TV and newspapers came and there was a big taboo." But it didn't stop him. He also eschews the Kölsch Konvention by serving his version of the beer, called Helios, unfiltered, meaning it can't officially be called a Kölsch. Regardless, it's one of the best I've tasted today: creamy and hoppy, bitter and refreshing.

Obviously I also order the Altbier. It has a handsome, hazy dark brown with eggshell foam. It's full-bodied and deeply malty, like dark chocolate, then very bitter—it's more like a modern Brown Ale than the Alts I had yesterday, but I like it a lot.

In the shadow of the famous cathedral and close to the station, the courtyard of the Früh am Dom Brauhaus provides a picturesque and convenient location to drink Kölsch.

Back in town I continue my search and find a few more Kölsches: Brauhaus Sion (nice grapefruity freshness), Brauhaus Peter (clean and hoppy), and Reissdorf (a little sweet, a little toasty).

I'm up to 22 ticks for the day, surpassing my Düsseldorf tally, and I reckon I can manage another beer... and I know the one I want. Around a couple of tight, dark corners and into a large square, I spot the green and white Päffgen sign I've been hunting for.

For me, these are the best beers in this part of the world.

A beer is placed in front of me before I've even sat down and it looks amazing: gleaming, golden, with pure white foam. After two days of these little glasses I love them. There's generally something indefinably wonderful about having a fresh beer in front of you, a perfect-looking glassful with thick foam on the top, regardless of whether it's a stange or a stein. Here, with these small glasses, you get that visual reward more often than in other places. And it doesn't take me long to empty this glass of Päffgen and be ready for another.

AND THE WINNER IS...

So it's decision time: Altbier versus Kölsch, Düsseldorf versus Cologne. Two seemingly quite different cities, but if you look at them closely they are almost ironically similar, as if one deliberately copies the other just to be able to say they can do something better; where the beers are symbols of independence and difference for their respective cities.

I love both beers, I love both cities and I can't imagine a time when I would visit one without the other; they almost demand to be visited as a pair just to be able to get a sense of the similarities and the rivalry. They're the beer world's old married couple who bicker and fight yet co-exist happily. In fact they seem to need each other to be able to thrive and a major part of their culture involves lovingly hating their rival, even if it's now mostly done in provincial jest over beer and sport.

Dressed in blue and carrying a tray of beers, the köbes servers are a familiar sight in both cities.

With another fresh glass placed in front of me by the kobes, my Kölsch tally gets another tick as I continue to scribble down my thoughts and look over my notes. In the last two days I have drunk 10 different beers in each city and feel the Kölsches were within a narrower flavor profile, being relatively similar to each other, whereas Alts had more range of aroma and flavor. Alt is a richer and more complex beer, whereas Kölsch is lighter and more refreshing, itself a nice parallel of the places they're from.

The Päffgen I'm drinking is definitely my favorite Kölsch, being the most bitter and interesting. In Düsseldorf, my favorite Altbier is Schlüssel—balanced, a great toasty depth of malt, then lots of hops. For me, these are the best beers I can drink in this part of the world.

My glass is empty. Three ticks on my beer mat (final score: 21–25 to Cologne) and the kobes is coming with another glass. I shake my head, I pass him some money and he nods a "danke schon" and whips away my foam lace-lined stange. It's decision time. Complex, bitter brown beer versus refreshing, hoppy golden beer. Schlüssel versus Päffgen. Altbier versus Kölsch. Düsseldorf versus Cologne. It's not an easy decision.

I love the complexity and depth of Altbier, and I love drinking it in the Altstadt, but Päffgen is the beer I wish I could enjoy all the time, loving its hoppy freshness.

Kölsch wins!

HOLIDAY BEER & ISLAND HOPPING IN GREECE

I'm in The Local Pub in Athens. It's Greece's top craft beer bar and there are some amazing choices on tap, all made by the handful of microbreweries around the country. As I finish a glass of Greek Pale Ale, a guy walks up to me and I already know exactly what he'll say because I've been asked the same question three times in the last 20 minutes.

AGAINST THE GRAIN

"Why do you like Mythos so much?" he says, bluntly. Like the other three before him, he's perplexed, dumbfounded, and I now have to answer the same question and explain myself again.

"Mythos means sunshine, relaxing, hot girls in bikinis. I just love drinking it on the beach."

"But it's a really bad drink. Why don't you like good beer?"

Mythos is a Greek golden lager. More important than that, Mythos is a Holiday Beer and Holiday Beers have a strong claim to the Best Beer in the World crown.

The people in The Local Pub love good beer and hate holiday lager, meaning they can't understand why I like Mythos. The man behind this pub is Fotis Anastasiou. Covered in cool tattoos, Fotis is Greece's number one beer guy and does all that he can to get the best beers for his bar. He knew I'd be in Athens so he invited some beer lovers along to drink with me. They all found my blog online and seemingly ignored hundreds of other posts and have focused in on the fact that I've written love letters to their least-favorite lager. After we've dealt with the whole Mythos thing, I bounce a question back at them: "What's your favorite Greek beer?" They all reply with the same two names: Septem and Santorini. And all of them are drinking either Septem's vibrantly hoppy Pale Ale or Santorini's rich-bodied Crazy Donkey IPA. Both of these beers are as good as any equivalents in the world.

I speak to Alex Seidanis, who runs www.beer.gr, a website, forum, and homebrew store. He asks exactly why I'm here, so I tell him how I want to learn about Greek microbreweries to write a story about them that tells people they can find more than just Mythos, and Amstel here.

"Ah yes, you like Mythos!" I don't even bother responding and just carry on asking him about the beers.

"So which other Greek beers do you think I should know about?"

He gives me a far bigger list than anyone else so far, names I've never heard of. As I try and keep up, scribbling notes, he stops talking, scratches his chin, grabs his phone, and makes a call.

"Terry!" he calls out to a homebrewer I was chatting to earlier. He says something in Greek, Terry smiles and says, "I'll be back soon!" before rushing out the door.

Fotis brings over another glass of Crazy Donkey IPA and we move to the bar and sit down. When Terry returns, he's got a bag filled with different Greek beers bought from a nearby store.

The island of Santorini provides one of the most stunning backdrops on the planet to enjoy a beer.

We pass around glasses and start trying these Greek beers: there's a clean, tasty lager from Cretan Brewery; a bready Fresh House Ale from Chios that's like a British Pale Ale; Corfu Beer's Ionian Epos, an amber lager brewed with wild flower honey; Zeos's Black Weiss that's unusual and interesting; Piraiki's Pilsner—lemony and bitter; and a really good Rauchbier from Craft Brewery, Greece's first microbrewery, which opened in Athens in 1997. The Greek beer guys are as excited as I am about opening these bottles, eager to share them, to share knowledge of these breweries, and have others learn just how great the Greek microbreweries can be.

Holiday beers have a strong claim to the best beer in the world crown.

With the bottles empty we move back to Septem and Crazy Donkey. It's good to get to know these beers because I'll be visiting these two breweries in the next two days.

A beach on a hot day with a cold beer: what could be better?

THE GRAPES OF BEER

Septem Brewery is on Evia, Greece's second-largest island located a couple of hours northeast of Athens. Lots of small breweries are ugly. They are often found in old industrial units on the edges of towns, there are battered barrels around, broken forklifts, and stinky sacks of spent grain. Septem, in contrast, is like a millionaire's party pad; a modern glass-fronted beer palace, run solely by solar power, backed by beautiful mountains, and surrounded by arable fields. Step inside and it gets better: upstairs there's an open-plan area which leads out to a large veranda where there's a bar and tables, and it all overlooks the sexy stainless steel brewhouse—one of the smartest and cleanest I've ever come across.

Septem was opened in 2009 by brothers Sofoklis and Georgios Panagiotou. Sofoklis is the brewer, a former oenologist and winemaker who went from grape to grain, though his former influences are still important. "The majority of Greek beer is without personality, without bitterness, without flavor. The idea is to produce different beers with personality." Central to this are hops, which Sofoklis calls "the grapes of beer." For him, the key to a good beer is the skillful use of hops to allow their unique character to come through but not overpower. As we tour the tanks, Sofoklis pours samples from each and talks through the beers. "I will never make a lager," he says, passing me his Pilsner. Before I can ask how he differentiates lager from Pilsner, he explains that lager is what everyone makes and drinks, "Pilsner is different, it has more bitterness, more character." And his Pilsner is a golden glassful that sings of sweet tropical fruits, elegant with New Zealand and US hops.

Next we try a floral Golden Ale made with two types of local honey, there's a malty Red Ale, and Greece's first Porter which is toasty and smooth. Then we drink the Pale Ale.

PICTURE THE SCENE

You're on holiday. It's late at night and you've had a few local lagers when you see a beautiful stranger and offer to buy them a drink. They're relaxed, you're relaxed, you fall in love over flaming Sambucas and a sunrise that you'll never forget. The next day you see them on the beach, sun behind them like a stunning silhouette as they flick their hair side-to-side after leaving the crystal blue sea. They smile back at you, remembering last night, and the sun's rays seem like they've woken a hundred butterflies in your stomach. You've met the girl or boy of your dreams, you're sure of it.

You stay in touch over the next few weeks, regularly bringing up those happy holiday memories. Then you decide to meet up on a cold September evening. It's obviously raining. It's cold, of course. Tans have faded. You've been working hard all week so you're tired, plus you had to get the train up here and it was busy and smelt terrible. But you're still excited and can't wait to see your holiday love again.

As you stand at the bar in the city center they tread across the beer-stained carpet, drizzle-dampened hair not swaying from side-to-side, hot body beneath a heavy coat, and no longer is this some beach beauty—they actually work in the local supermarket on the cheese counter. No amount of holiday lager and sunshine could fix the situation you're now in.

Holiday beer is the liquid equivalent of a holiday romance and I'm sure we've all experienced it: been away somewhere exciting, sunny, and relaxing, and we've drunk the local beer, served ice cold in the hot sunshine, and decided it's the most delicious drink in the world. Surrounded by sights and smells, a tingle of sunburn along with the deep-set feeling of holiday calmness, that local beer just completes it all and it's hard to imagine anything ever tasting better.

Deciding it's the best beer you've ever tasted, you put a few bottles in your suitcase to recreate that holiday feeling at home. You wait a few days and then open that delicious, refreshing beer from your travels, expecting halcyon holiday memories to flood back and bathe you in sunshine. But something's not right. The beer that glowed golden in the sun is today looking flat and dull in the glass you stole from the pub a few months ago. The sound of the sea is replaced with the patter of rain against the window. Then you take a mouthful and it's like it's a completely different beer, something not even slightly similar to that perfect pint you had by the beach. It doesn't even taste good. How could this be?

Mythos is my holiday lager romance. I love Greece. I love swimming in the warm sea, reading the books I'd been meaning to read all year, eating local food, all free from the stresses of work and life. Days of pure, simple relaxation and fun. And that lager is there throughout. It comes in frosted glasses and hits the lips like a cool breeze, refreshing and restorative, a little sweetness from the malt balanced by a dry hop finish. I've drunk maybe 100 glasses of Mythos in my life. I love it for its refreshment, for what it means, for the memories it's attached to; it's conditioned in my head to signify good times.

But it's a mass-produced lager made by a company owned by a huge brewing corporation—Carlsberg. In fact, it's the second-largest Greek brewery after Athenian, which produces Heineken and Amstel. Between these two, they control around 90% of the Greek beer market, resulting in Greece being dominated by pale lagers. So dominated that until a few years ago, no alternatives existed. But that's changing. And like the rest of the world, Greeks are suddenly discovering a newfound appreciation and awareness of different craft beers.

As one of the most popular beer styles in the world, there are thousands of examples of this type of beer and this is unequivocally one of the best I've tried, confirming what I was tasting last night in The Local Pub. Sofoklis's wine background and his palate for clean flavors is so clear in his beers, and the judicious use of hops is astounding: this beer is bursting with hop freshness but it remains light and fragrant with a whole bowl of oranges and tropical fruit splashing around in there. It's a wonderful beer; I wish more people knew about it and could drink it.

What I like most about the Septem beers is the clarity of flavor in them. I often think about beers in relation to other things and the best example I have here is of looking at a great photo. If that photo is perfectly in focus then you can see everything in great detail. If the photo is blurry then you don't see it properly. In beer, the analogy is in how a good, clean beer has some very precise, pronounced flavors and not a blurry, muddy quality. So many beers from small breweries have that muddiness of flavor. Septem's are the epitome of clean and fresh, and it's a hugely impressive place with seriously good beers. Put this brewery anywhere in the world and it'd do well, I'm sure of it.

BREWING IN PARADISE

The next day I'm awake early for a flight to Santorini, a rugged black-sand island that attained its unique crescent-moon shape when it was blasted apart by a huge volcanic eruption. The main positive of the explosion is that its new shape became perfect for watching the stunning sunset, for which the island is famous. I'm here to go to Santorini Brewery, known for its "Donkey" beers, which are named after the animal that once did all the hard work of moving things around on this hilly island. The brewery is in an old bakery situated between three vineyards, and with a view of both the sea and the mountains—it's in a good spot. Inside it's the most homely brewery I've been to with sofas, rugs, and personal touches like photo frames and books arranged between the hoses, bottling facilities, line of silver tanks, and the handsome 300-liter brewkit from Austria.

I know Steve Daniel, one of the brewery owners from London. His business partner is Yiannis Paraskevopoulos, a well-known Greek winemaker. The daily running of Santorini Brewery is taken care of by Serbian Boban and American Mayda—Boban brews, Mayda manages everything else. "When we were thinking about starting a brewery, there were only two small brewers in Greece," says Yiannis. "But Greeks consume big amounts of lager, so we started asking Greeks and visitors: 'If you're on Santorini and someone proposes a list of beers with the usual names plus a local beer, what would you choose?' Everyone said they'd go for the local beer, and although Greeks didn't at that time have the local brew culture of somewhere like England or Germany, we knew on the spot that we had a winning idea. It was as if we were inventing something, but we weren't, we were just following the logical idea."

They brew Yellow Donkey, a Pale Ale which is zesty and juicy from the mix of European, American, and New Zealand hops, and like the Septem beers it has a great clarity and freshness of flavor. Red Donkey is ruby-colored, fragrantly hopped with New World varieties, and fermented with Belgian yeast, giving an enticing mix of tropical fruit and bubblegum esters—it's a wonderfully unusual beer. From the tank I drink White Donkey which Boban tells me probably won't be sold anywhere and will be saved for their Christmas party, which is astonishing because it's one of the best wheat beers I've ever tasted, so balanced and full-bodied yet massively easy drinking. And there's Crazy Donkey, their superb American-hopped IPA which I drank too much of in The Local Pub. "IPA didn't exist in Greece so we decided to make it a standard beer in our range," says Yiannis. He also tells me about an idea for Fat Donkey, "a totally local beer, with local barley, probably primed with Assyrtiko grape must, and then aged in oak casks from the winery." As a small island, there's a lot of curiosity about the Donkey beers, especially as they are so different to the green bottled lagers that Greeks are more familiar with. The door is also always open and people continually stop by to have a look, a chat, or to buy some beers, which is exactly what I do before heading to my hotel to see the sunset.

A QUESTION OF CONTEXT

You know that quintessential image of Greece with white buildings, blue domed roofs and amazing view? Well that's Santorini. Given the steep sides of the island, everything is built into the rock and the best rooms have a view out over the caldera's wide horizon-facing arc. And that's where I'm staying tonight. It's stunning, but it's unusual. Unlike my familiar July visits to Greece, it's the middle of December and the island is empty—I'm the only person staying in the hotel. The winter light is bleak, weak, and dark, and while it might be breathtakingly beautiful it's also breathtakingly cold.

I've been here before and last time I saw this sunset it was 86°F (30°C), I had a girl with me, and an ice-cold Mythos in my hand. Today it's 40°F (5°C) and I'm alone with the biting wind chill. I'm wearing two t-shirts, a jumper, a fleece, and a coat and I'm still shivering. I open a Red Donkey and sit outside as the deep red sun falls fast through the gunmetal sky, casting a dull orange glow across the flat sea. Looking around I can see the whole sweep of the island—it's like a black and white photo with the dark rock and light stone buildings. It's mesmerizing. And the beer is an amazing counterpoint of brightness against the bleakness, a burst of fruit freshness and color, somehow a flavor reflection of the sun's orange haze. Another mouthful and the sun is gone, but it leaves behind its blushing glow for another 20 minutes as I battle through the cold with another beer, unable to look away from one of the best views I've seen in real life. The beers are extraordinary and are made even better by the location, even if I do wish it were several degrees warmer.

Any beer can be great in a specific context.

I've traveled to many countries to drink some of the world's greatest beers and yet I still crave a cold pint of mass-made lager on a hot beach—you can't beat the experience of a Holiday Beer. The essential part of this is that we've saved, planned, and traveled to enjoy it, and you can only have that experience in that place. This gives an emotional value beyond just the bottle of beer—it means something specific to the drinker. And every time I see Mythos, wherever I am, I think about a Greek beach in the same way that Estrella makes me want to be back in Barcelona, and a bottle of Saigon has me daydreaming of Vietnam.

Any beer can be great in a specific context. Mythos is a great beer in the context of being on holiday in Greece, but it's not a great beer back home on a cold day. The difference with beers from the likes of Santorini Brewing and Septem is that they are genuinely good wherever you have them. Yet combine those beers with being away and they are extra special—watching the Santorini sunset with a Red Donkey was a truly spectacular experience.

What's exciting is that countries that classically haven't had great beers are now beginning to make some which are as good as any in the world. These brews are like a new higher-level holiday romance, the real kind that you'd bring back to meet the parents. They are beers for life and not just a brief sun-kissed fling.

CITY GUIDES:

CITY GUIDE

DUBLIN

Think Dublin and no doubt you imagine a glass of Stout—black with a creamy white foam on top—but this absolutely isn't a one beer town. In fact I think it's one of Europe's most interesting places to get great beer, and it seems to be growing faster and better than other famous drinking destinations. As well as the great Irish beers, you'll experience the famously friendly and lively atmosphere of Irish pubs.

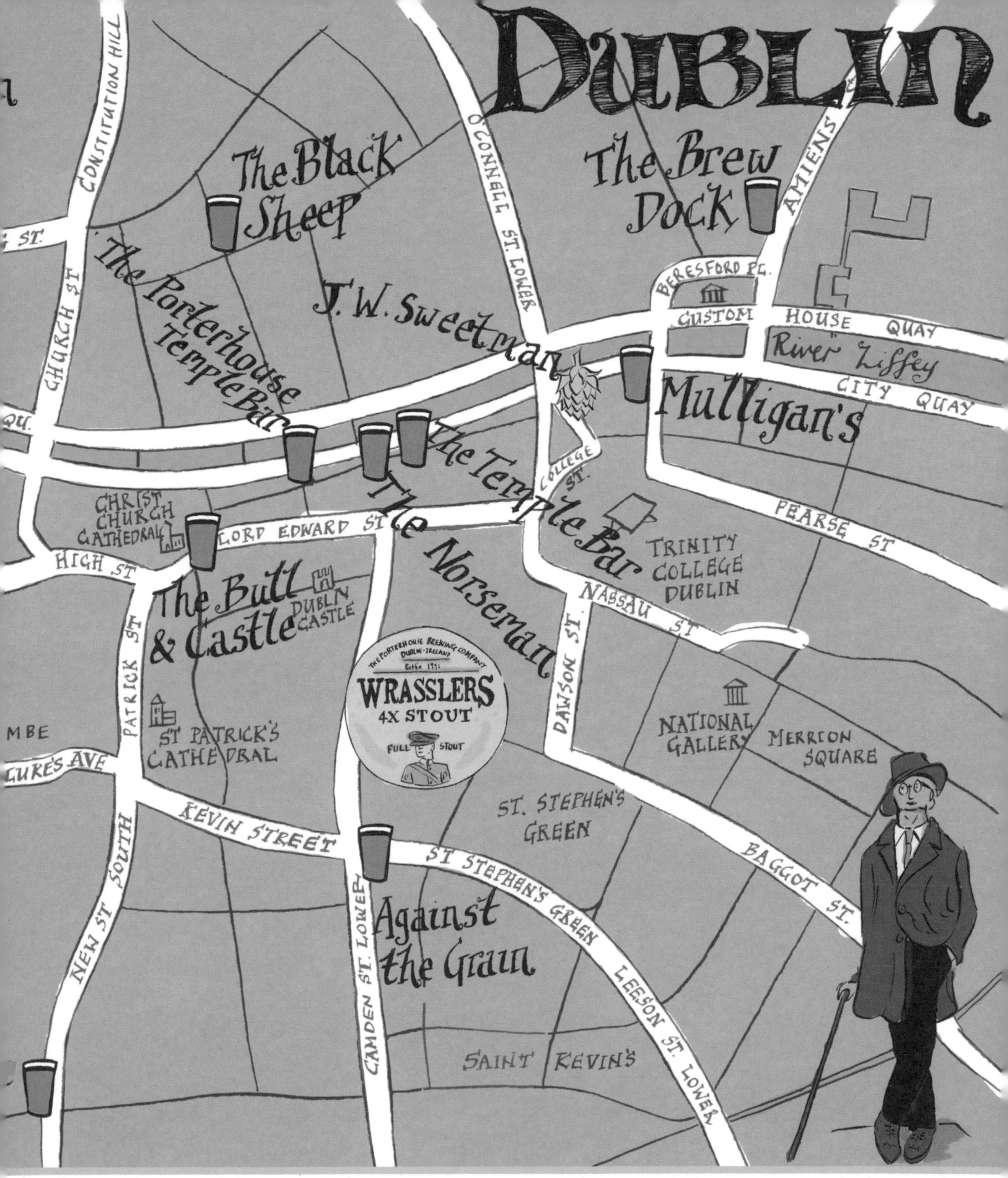

DUBLIN
The Black Sheep
The Brew Dock
The Porterhouse Temple Bar
J.W. Sweetman
Mulligan's
The Temple Bar
The Norseman
The Bull & Castle
Against the Grain
CONSTITUTION HILL
CHURCH ST
O'CONNELL ST. LOWER
AMIENS
BERESFORD PL.
CUSTOM HOUSE QUAY
River Liffey
CITY QUAY
COLLEGE ST.
PEARSE ST
CHRIST CHURCH CATHEDRAL
LORD EDWARD ST
HIGH ST
TRINITY COLLEGE DUBLIN
NASSAU ST
DUBLIN CASTLE
PATRICK ST
DAWSON ST.
THE PORTERHOUSE BREWING COMPANY DUBLIN · IRELAND
WRASSLERS
4X STOUT
FULL STOUT
NATIONAL GALLERY
MERRION SQUARE
ST PATRICK'S CATHEDRAL
KEVIN STREET
ST. STEPHEN'S GREEN
BAGGOT ST.
NEW ST SOUTH
ST STEPHEN'S GREEN
CAMDEN ST. LOWER
LEESON ST. LOWER
SAINT KEVIN'S

THE BREW DOCK

1 AMIENS STREET;
WWW.GALWAYBAYBREWERY.COM

Galway Bay Brewery has a few pubs in Dublin (and beyond) and it's in these pubs where you'll be able to drink some of the very best beers in Ireland. Buried at Sea is their brilliant Chocolate Milk Stout, rich without being sweet; Full Sail is a very good IPA; and Of Foam and Fury is the beer that is rightly celebrated by the beer geeks—it's a monumentally great Double IPA. The Brew Dock is right by the main bus station to and from the airport, so this is the ideal place for your first and last stops in the city.

THE NORSEMAN

28E ESSEX STREET;
WWW.NORSEMAN.IE

If you want the broadest selection of Irish beer then go to The Norseman, right in the center of Temple Bar. Great staff pour every type of beer you can think of from the large list of taps, showcasing the best that Ireland brews. Look for Eight Degrees, Rascals, Trouble Brewing, or O'Hara's ever-lovely Leann Folláin Stout.

L. MULLIGAN GROCER

18 STONEYBATTER;
WWW.LMULLIGANGROCER.COM

Do you like food as well as beer? (Of course you do!) Then L. Mulligan Grocer is the place for you. Well-sourced ingredients are cooked into superb modern Irish dishes, each with a suggested beer match from a well-chosen list. The interior is smart and the staff really know their stuff.

THE BLACK SHEEP

61 CAPEL STREET;
WWW.GALWAYBAYBREWERY.COM

I hope you like the Galway Bay beers as much as I do because this is another of their pubs. The offer is as similarly excellent as the others with great beer choice and classic pub food. You could happily stay for a long time working through the beers.

THE BULL AND CASTLE

5-7 LORD EDWARD STREET;
WWW.BULL-AND-CASTLE.FXBUCKLEY.IE

Once the king of craft beer bars in the city, it's now been overtaken by others as Dublin's beer scene grows and develops, but you won't want to skip the Bull and Castle for their combination of very good beers and superb steaks.

57 THE HEADLINE

57 CLANBRASSIL STREET LOWER;
WWW.57THEHEADLINE.IE

With comfy armchairs and little nooks to hide away in, 57 The Headline is a great, comfortable pub with 20 taps dedicated to small Irish breweries. The food is good and it has a fun, friendly atmosphere—just as you'd expect from a proper Dublin boozer.

PORTERHOUSE TEMPLE BAR

16-18 PARLIAMENT STREET;
WWW.PORTERHOUSEBREWCO.COM

There are three Porterhouse pubs in Dublin and you should make sure you visit at least one of them to drink their excellent range of beers. Dark beer lovers will want to try their three Stouts which are all smooth, rich, and complex. The Oyster Stout (yes, it's actually brewed with the bivalves) has long been a personal favorite from my early drinking days and many visits to the Porterhouse in Covent Garden, London; while the Wrasslers is properly bitter and hoppy while still retaining that roast barley richness.

AGAINST THE GRAIN

11 WEXFORD STREET;
WWW.GALWAYBAYBREWERY.COM

Another great Galway Bay venue and just like the others you'll find good bar food, friendly staff, all of their own beers, plus lots of guest taps and bottles from around the world. If you want to sample a few they will serve you tasting paddles of the Galway Bay beers. You'll still end up on Of Foam and Fury, though.

J.W. SWEETMAN

1-2 BURGH QUAY;
WWW.JWSWEETMAN.IE

This big and busy brewpub, on the bank of the River Liffey, has loads of space for you to sit and enjoy the house beers along with traditional pub food like meat and ale pie, Irish stew, and bangers and mash.

MULLIGAN'S

8 POOLBEG STREET;
WWW.MULLIGANS.IE

I asked a few Dubliners where I should go in the city to get the best pint of Guinness and Mulligan's was the most frequent response. With an ornate wooden front, inside it's dark, cozy, busy, brimming with characters and stories, and it has that intangible feel of a proper old pub. My Guinness was great in there.

THE TEMPLE BAR

47-48 TEMPLE BAR;
WWW.THETEMPLEBARPUB.COM

It's really busy and it's expensive but I think you have to visit The Temple Bar (which is in the busy Temple Bar area of town) when in Dublin—it's surely one of the world's most famous pubs. Go late at night and listen to the live music while you drink from the wide range of different beers—the O'Hara's Stout is a great choice if you want something dark that isn't Guinness—and finish with a whiskey nightcap.

GUINNESS STOREHOUSE

ST JAMES'S GATE;
WWW.GUINNESS-STOREHOUSE.COM

This is Ireland's most-visited tourist attraction. Sure, it's a bit of a beery Disneyland as you walk into a giant gift shop with Guinness emblazoned on everything, but it's fun and at the end of the self-guided tour you get to the Gravity Bar for a pint of the good stuff and a 360° view of the city—it's a must-do Dublin experience.

Temple Bar, the heart of Dublin's nightlife.

TOP 5 BEERS IN TOWN

O'Hara's Stout
One of the best Stouts around

Galway Bay Of Foam and Fury
World class Double IPA

8 Degrees The Full Irish
All Irish-malt, US-hopped IPA

Rascal's Ginger Porter
Zingy, chocolaty, and delicious

Guinness
Of course

CITY GUIDE

BRUSSELS

Brussels doesn't have the beauty or quaint charm of somewhere like Bruges; it has grimy buildings, traffic, and bachelor parties. However, because it's Belgium, it does have some fantastic beer bars and it's a famous beer city that's certainly worth your time, if for no other reason than visiting Cantillon Brewery—every beer lover should see this place (see pages 42–49). Here are my favorite establishments to check out, though there's a whole lot more beyond these. And make sure you eat lots of frites and mayo.

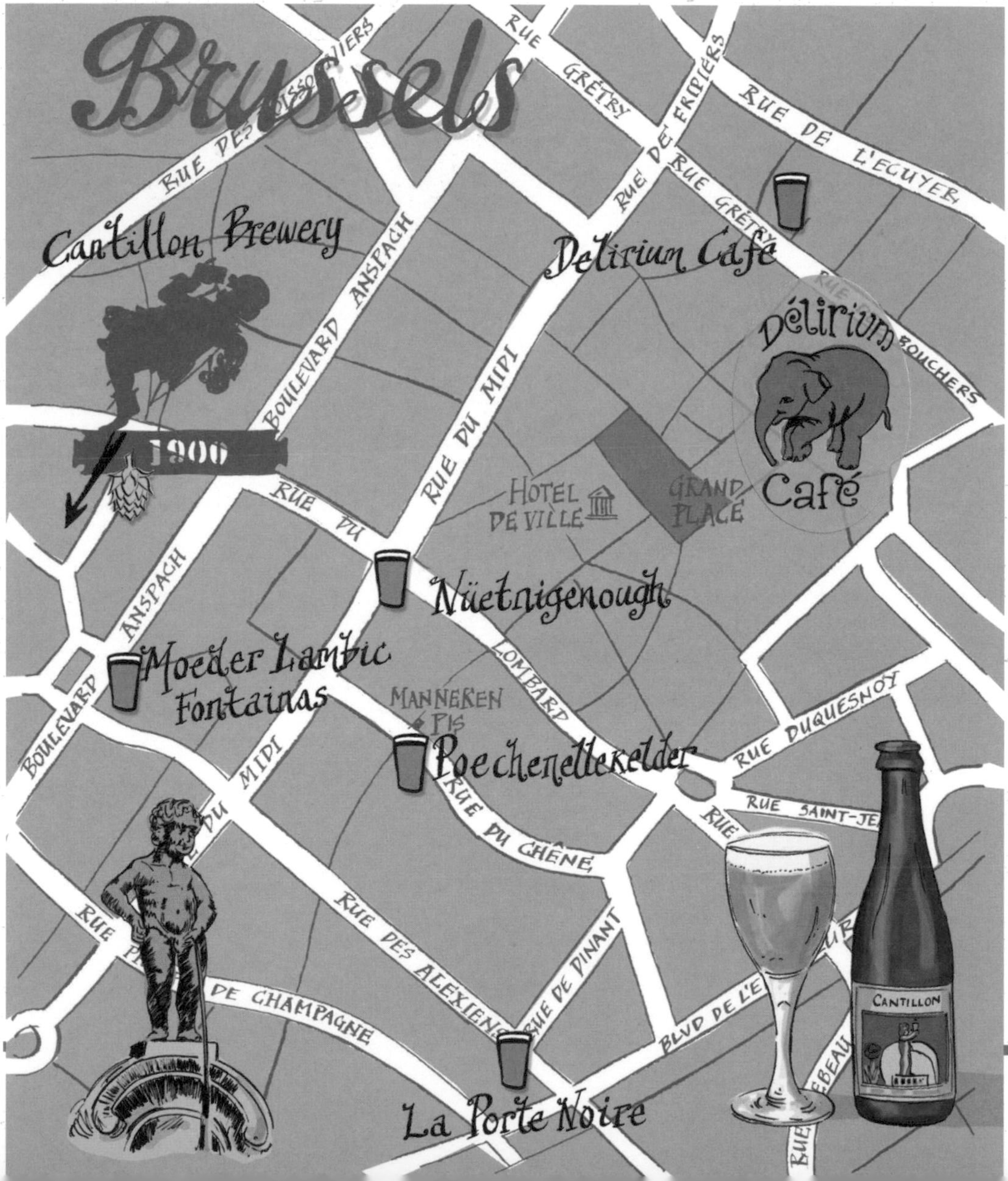

CANTILLON BREWERY

RUE GHEUDE 56; WWW.CANTILLON.BE

I really can't repeat enough how you have to go here: go go go go GO! An astonishing, mesmerizing place that has to be seen to be really understood. It's a short walk from Brussels Midi Station and is the most unexpected location for one of the world's finest, best-loved breweries. Do the self-guided tour and be blown away by the cavernous inner city cellars and then drink through the beers, including the unblended Lambic.

MOEDER LAMBIC FONTAINAS

FONTAINASPLEIN 8; WWW.MOEDERLAMBIC.COM

No question one of my favorite beer bars in the world. It's smart and modern, there are 40 taps of beer with rare Belgians, classic brews, modern favorites, plus interesting imports. I always start with the same three beers—Cantillon Lambic, Taras Boulba, and IV Saison—and then work from there. Order the meat or cheese platter to keep you going. Moeder Lambic Original (68 rue de Savoie 1060) is in the south of the city and also worth your time (though really there's no need to leave Fontainas).

DÉLIRIUM CAFÉ

IMPASSE DE LA FIDÉLITÉ 4A; WWW.DELIRIUMCAFE.BE

Plan to stay here a while because what seems small from the outside opens into a multi-storey beer palace which claims to have 2,500 beers. Check out each of the different floors and see how they're all different—just bear in mind that it can get incredibly busy and loud. The Hoppy Loft is my favorite (and usually where I end up late at night)—it serves mostly craft beers from Belgium and beyond.

LA PORTE NOIRE

CELLEBROERSSTRAAT 67; WWW.LAPORTENOIRE.BE

This is a dark cellar bar with a very good beer list including some hoppier craft beers on tap. Go here late at night if you want to kick the evening on in a busy, lively bar with music.

NÜETNIGENOUGH

RUE DU LOMBARD 25; WWW.NUETNIGENOUGH.BE

Go to this cozy café to eat. The food is excellent and much of it includes beer in the cooking. There are a few beers on tap, including Saison Dupont, and a broad and well-picked bottle list, with lots of classics plus a great choice of Gueuze, making it perfect for you to take your pick to match whatever you're eating. An alternative food stop is the excellent Restobières (Rue Emile Wauters 20; www.restobieres.eu).

POECHENELLEKELDER

RUE DU CHÊNE 5; WWW.POECHENELLEKELDER.BE

I've never worked out how to pronounce this place. I just tell people to go to the Manneken Pis, Brussels' famous statue of a peeing boy, and go to the bar opposite. Sit outside and watch tourists take pictures, or head inside the eccentrically decorated bar and sit surrounded by puppets. A really good beer list includes some newer and rare beers alongside the classics.

TOP 5 BEERS IN TOWN

Cantillon Lambic
A taste of tradition

Brasserie de la Senne Taras Boulba
The perfect Belgian Pale Ale

Jandrain-Jandrenouille IV Saison
Hoppy modern Belgian Saison

Tilquin Gueuze
The new Gueuze blender

Any Trappist Beer
Because you're in Belgium and you should

• CITY GUIDE

BRUGES

Where Brussels is industrial and gray, Bruges is fairytale lovely. With churches, cobbled streets, canals, and market squares, this is the place to go on a romantic weekend away where there's the obvious bonus of brilliant beer (and lots of chocolate, of course). There's not actually that much to see or do in Bruges other than drink and eat, which is fine by me. Here are some places you definitely shouldn't miss.

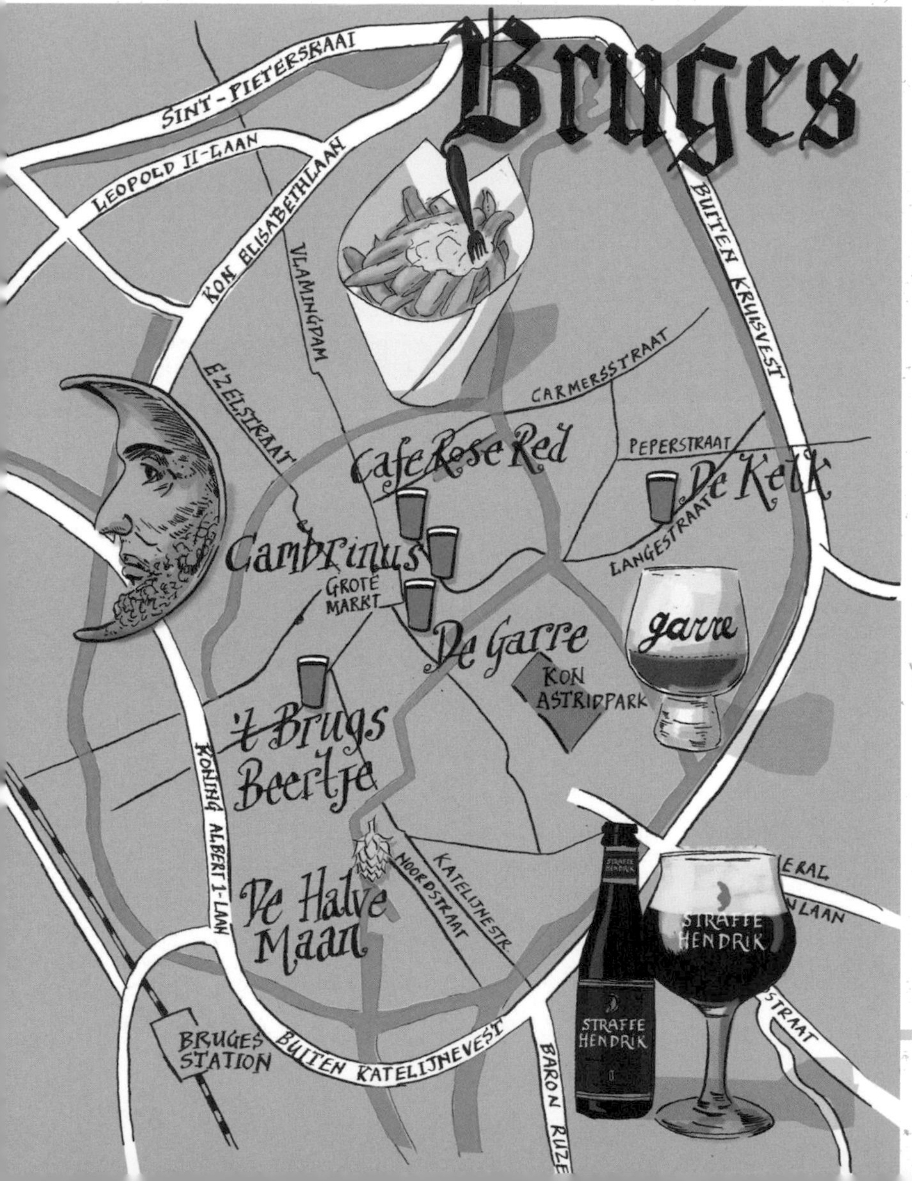

'T BRUGS BEERTJE

KEMELSTRAAT 5;
WWW.BRUGSBEERTJE.BE

A classic world beer bar—you have to visit The Little Bruges Bear. There are a few taps and over 300 bottles in this wonderful, small, dark café packed with beer memorabilia. Cozy up around small tables and have a chat with the friendly locals—it has a great atmosphere. They also have cheese and pate. What more could you want?

CAMBRINUS

PHILIPSTOCKSTRAAT 19;
WWW.CAMBRINUS.EU

This bierbrasserie is where you'll want to stop for food as most dishes are either designed to go with a glass of beer or include a brew in the recipe. It's right in the middle of town, it's old and ornate outside, while inside it stretches back as one large room. The beer menu is thick and detailed so take your time and choose wisely.

Just off the pretty Grote Markt (above) are three of the recommended bars: Cambrinus, Café Rose Red, and De Garre.

CAFÉ ROSE RED

CORDOEANIERSSTRAAT 16; WWW.CAFEROSERED.COM

This is a café in Hotel Cordoeanier, a stroll from the central square. It has a great atmosphere and certainly one of the best-selected beer lists in town, with a mix of traditional and new, loads of Gueuze, plus a vintage choice of aged bottles.

DE GARRE

DE GARRE 1; WWW.DEGARRE.BE

A charming little café which is tucked away down a narrow street—a garre is a small alley—go here for a glass of their house Tripel, a beer that has a glorious thick foam; there's honey and spice, bitterness is bold but then balances out as the booze comes through. It's perfect with the cubes of cheese they give you. It fills up fast but that adds to the atmosphere.

DE HALVE MAAN

WALPLEIN 26; WWW.HALVEMAAN.BE

Head to the Halve Maan—Half Moon—and get on a brewery tour, enjoy a glass of Bruges Zot at the end, and then move onto something bigger and bolder from Straffe Hendrik, like their Tripel or Quadrupel. It's a nice old place to sip a few brews and while away an afternoon. The food is classically Belgian, so obviously works well with whatever you are drinking.

DE KELK

LANGESTRAAT 69; WWW.DEKELK.COM

This small, slightly worn out, dark bar has a superb beer list with a number of rarities (like old Gueuze) if you know what you're looking for, plus beers from craft superstars De Struise and De Molen. There's something quintessentially Belgian about this place.

TOP 5 BEERS IN TOWN

Straffe Hendrick Quadrupel
A wonderfully hoppy Quad

Tripel de Garre
Big, boozy, and best in its own bar, De Garre

De Dolle Oerbier
Super-strong dark ale

Chouffe Houblon
Not local but a world-class hoppy Tripel

Any Struise Beer
One of Belgium's most interesting craft breweries

CITY GUIDE

AMSTERDAM

A fun, relaxed, handsome, and great city, Amsterdam is perhaps most famous for red lights and green leaves but don't overlook it as a place to visit for seriously good beer and food. In the beer bars you'll see how Dutch brewing is largely a mix of Belgian and American influences, creating an interesting mid-point between the two.

There are a lot of good craft beer bars and plenty of cool bars for sharing bottles of Belgian beer, but also seek out some classic old bars known as "brown cafés." These have dark wood interiors, low natural light, and are often small and cozy, with a local feel, almost like an extension of your living room only with better beer. In some of these brown cafés you'll find the freshest glasses of Grolsch and Heineken that you've ever had. They're capable of changing your mind on these beers forever—drinking good local beer doesn't just mean beer from small breweries.

PROEFLOKAAL ARENDSNEST

HERENGRACHT 90; WWW.ARENDSNEST.NL

This should be top of your list as, in my opinion, it's one of the great world beer bars. At Arendsnest you'll only find Dutch craft beers. There's a long and varied list to choose from, perfectly showing off the breadth of the beers being brewed in the country. Essential.

The bar at the excellent Proeflokaal Arendsnest.

PROEFLOKAAL DE PRAEL

OUDEZIJDS ARMSTEEG 26; WWW.DEPRAEL.NL

A brewpub a few blocks from the red light district, De Prael is another must-visit venue. There's lots of seating and really good food, plus a wide range of beers on tap. Nick & Simon is a very good IPA and Mary is a superb hoppy Barley Wine-come-Belgian Ale. Just around the corner they have a gift store with the brewery connecting them in the middle.

BROUWERIJ 'T IJ

FUNENKADE 7; WWW.BROUWERIJHETIJ.NL

Hire a bike and head over to the windmill for some beers. Brouwerij 't IJ is definitely worth a visit to work through their range of brews which includes: IJwit, a Witbier brewed with cilantro (coriander) and lemon; a very good IPA; an even better Black IPA; and superb Belgian-influenced Dubbel and Tripel.

BEERTEMPLE

NIEUWEZIJDS VOORBURGWAL 250; WWW.BEERTEMPLE.NL

This place is like walking into an American beer bar, unsurprising when many of the 35 draft lines are American, and the others are big-name craft brewers. The selection is one of the best in Europe, if that's what you're looking for, and the bottle menu will have you gawping and gasping (sometimes at the beers, sometimes at the prices).

CAFÉ GOLLEM

RAAMSTEEG 4; WWW.CAFEGOLLEM.NL

This is a great example of a brown café and it's the sort of place where you can sit and sip bottles of good beer all night, where the selection is mainly Belgian and Dutch, and all very good.

IN DE WILDEMAN

KOLKSTEEG 3; WWW.INDEWILDEMAN.NL

There are 18 draft beers to choose from in this cozy café close to the center of the city. A mix of Dutch and Belgian beers, you'll also find some interesting American and British imports, plus a hefty bottle list. There's something very welcoming about this great brown café.

TOP 5 BEERS IN TOWN

De Molen
Anything, especially barrel-aged or their Amarillo Double IPA

La Trappe Quadrupel
Drink this from the Netherlands' Trappist brewery

Emelisse Black IPA
A big, black, bitter brew from this great brewery

Brouwerij 't IJ Columbus
It's like a super-hoppy Tripel

De Prael Mary
A great hoppy Belgian Strong Ale

CAFÉ DE SPUYT

KORTE LEIDSEDWARSSTRAAT 86; WWW.CAFEDESPUYT.NL

With a few decent brews on tap and a long list of bottles, mostly Belgian (including the much-coveted Westvleteren beers), this brown café is another which pulls you in like a big hug and makes you want to stay in its cozy embrace for another beer or two.

CAFÉ DE DOKTER

ROZENBOOMSTEEG 4; WWW.CAFE-DE-DOKTER.NL

Café De Dokter is one of the smallest pubs in Amsterdam. It opened in 1798 and has remained in the Beems family for six generations since that time. It's a tiny brown café with an intangible charm, and the place where I drank the best glass of Grolsch I've ever had.

DE BIERKONING

PALEISSTRAAT 125; WWW.BIERKONING.NL

If you want to buy bottles to take home then you have to visit this superlative store. Beers from all over the globe, including a huge Dutch selection, make this a world-class bottle shop.

CITY GUIDE

COPENHAGEN

Scandinavia has one of the best beer scenes in the world with some of the most informed drinkers. It's also undoubtedly one of the geekiest beer places, with the seemingly never-ending search for new, rare beers at the forefront of drinking. As a city, Copenhagen is a wonderful place: it's so clean, chilled out, and friendly. The beer range is also hard to better, while food is generally exceptional, whether you want new Nordic Michelin meals or just a really good hot dog after a few strong brews.

There are worse places to be than enjoying a beer by the sea at picturesque Nyhavn.

Copenhagen really is Mikkeller's city so if you go for beer then you'd better like what the gypsy brewer does. All their venues have a similar smart, minimalist aesthetic. And when you look at the beer list your eyes will bulge out wherever you are so brace yourself now for the forthcoming geek-out. **Mikkeller** (Viktoriagade 8 B-C; www.mikkeller.dk) is their original bar in the city and somewhere that you won't want to miss. It's small, simple, and has a world-beating beer list and great staff. At **Mikkeller and Friends** (Stefansgade 35; www.mikkeller.dk) the "Friends" part specifically refers to To Øl and Three Floyds but extends way beyond, which isn't surprising as Mikkeller is probably the most-connected brewer there is. There's also a shop here with over 200 different bottles. **Øl & Brød** (Viktoriagade 6; www.ologbrod.dk) is for great beer and smørrebrød, the famous Danish open-faced sandwich—it's right by the original Mikkeller bar. **Mikropolis** (Vendersgade 22; www.mikkeller.dk) is a cozy cocktail bar with 10 taps of beer and a very good cocktail list if you fancy a different drink. Then there's **Warpigs** (Flæsketorvet 25; www.warpigs.dk). Don't miss the wonderful combination of Three Floyds, Mikkeller, and BBQ food in this great brewpub that opened in 2015. Mikkeller doesn't have a hand in all the bars in the city. **Fermentoren** (Halmtorvet 29C; www.fb.com/fermentoren.cph) is dark and cozy with lots of candles and 20 great taps. If you want a choice of around 60 taps of beer from all over Europe and the US then the appropriately named **Taphouse** (Lavendelstræde 15; www.taphouse.dk) is the place to go. Head to **Nørrebro Bryghus** (Ryesgade 3; www.noerrebrobryghus.dk), a smart brewpub in the city, to work through their nice range of beers. For bottles, go to **Ølbutikken** (Istedgade 44; www.olbutikken.dk) where you'll find a wide and very well picked selection of beers that you can take home or drink in. There are also many other places to visit but how many can you realistically get to? And if you want Danish beers then here are a few names to look out for: **Amager, To Øl, Beer Here, Hornbeer, Ølsnedkeren** (their busy bar in town is also worth visiting: Griffenfeldsgade 52; www.olsnedkeren.dk), **Stronzo**, and, obviously, **Mikkeller**.

CITY GUIDE

STOCKHOLM

Sweden's capital is a beautiful place to visit. There are many brilliant beers and places to enjoy them in Stockholm, plus it has a smart drinking scene with a knowledgeable crowd interested in the best-tasting brews. You'll be able to find plenty of Swedish brews, with many taking all the same influences as other craft brewers around the world, plus there are a lot of very good imported beers. Swedish breweries to look out for include: Nynäshamns, Dugges, Omnipollo, Närke, Nils Oscar, Slottskällan, Oppigärds, Mohawk, and S:t Eriks. Just bear in mind that while the beers may be good enough to bring a tear to your eye, the prices are also eye-wateringly expensive.

Stortorget Square in the center of Stockholm's old town, or Gamla Stan.

Oliver Twist (Repslagargatan 6; www.olivertwist.se) is rightly regarded as one of the world's best beer bars. It's an interesting mix of English pub and American dive bar, the beer list is exemplary, the staff are friendly, and the atmosphere is brilliant. Have a Nynäshamns Bedäro Bitter to start while you figure out what to have next. You might as well order the meatballs because you'll be staying for a few rounds. **Akkurat** (Hornsgatan 18; www.akkurat.se) is another bar that's widely and highly regarded as one of the best there is. Great ever-changing taps, lots of interesting new Swedish brews, a super geeky (though expensive) vintage bottle list, lots of lambic, good staff, and beer-soaking snacks. **Man in the Moon** (Tegnérgatan 2; www.maninthemoon.se) is a very good gastropub with excellent food and a tap list to match it. **Monks Porter House** (Munkbron 11; www.monkscafe.se) is the place to stop after wandering around the cobbled streets of the Gamla Stan. A dark, atmospheric cellar bar, they have a range of their own beers and they can be very good—there are a few Monks venues in the city. **Nya Carnegiebryggeriet** (Ljusslingan 15; www.nyacarnegiebryggeriet.se) is a joint venture between Brooklyn Brewery and Carlsberg Sweden. This brewpub is bright and open, the beers are varied, clean, and very interesting (J.A.C.K is a really good Pale Ale), plus the food is excellent—don't miss it. There are a number of **Bishops Arms** (www.bishopsarms.com) around Sweden and any are worth visiting as the beer choices are broad meaning you'll always find something you'll want to drink, whether it's a rare import or a local favorite. **Mikkeller Bar** (Döbelnsgatan 25, www.mikkeller.dk) is the Swedish outpost of the Danish gypsy brewer and here you can expect the best and most interesting imported beers plus a large choice of the Mikkeller brews in a smart, clean, classically Scandinavian bar. Another brewery also infiltrating the scene with their own bar is **BrewDog Stockholm** (Sankt Eriksgatan 112; www.brewdogbar.se) who have their beers plus others from around Europe. If you want bottles then find any **Systembolaget** (www.systembolaget.se) as they have world-class beer ranges at comparably good prices.

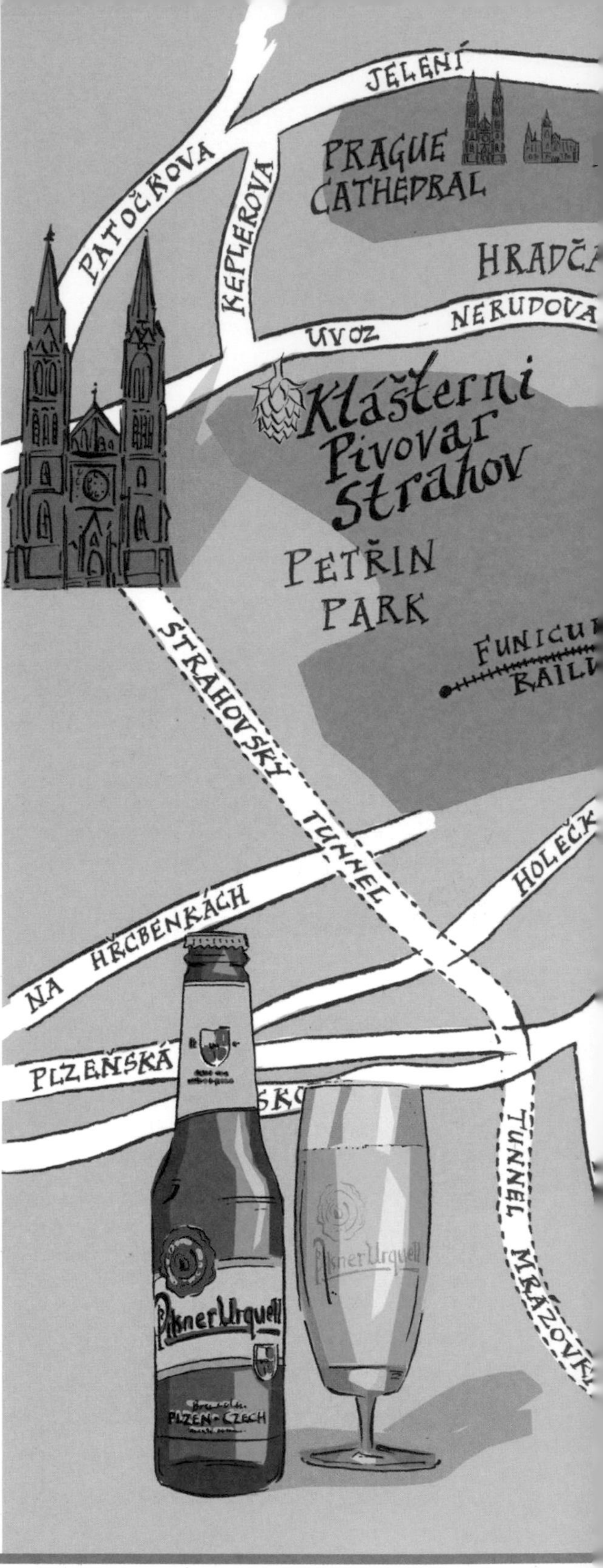

CITY GUIDE
PRAGUE

With old winding streets, a handsome castle perched high on the hill overlooking the city, a river running right through it, and so much good beer, Prague is one of my favorite places for beer. There are classic old bars and some new modern bars serving up craft beers from the Czech Republic, where Pale Ale and IPA are popular styles. Don't be surprised if you go somewhere that only serves one beer—this is typical, and you'll know which one by the sign hanging outside.

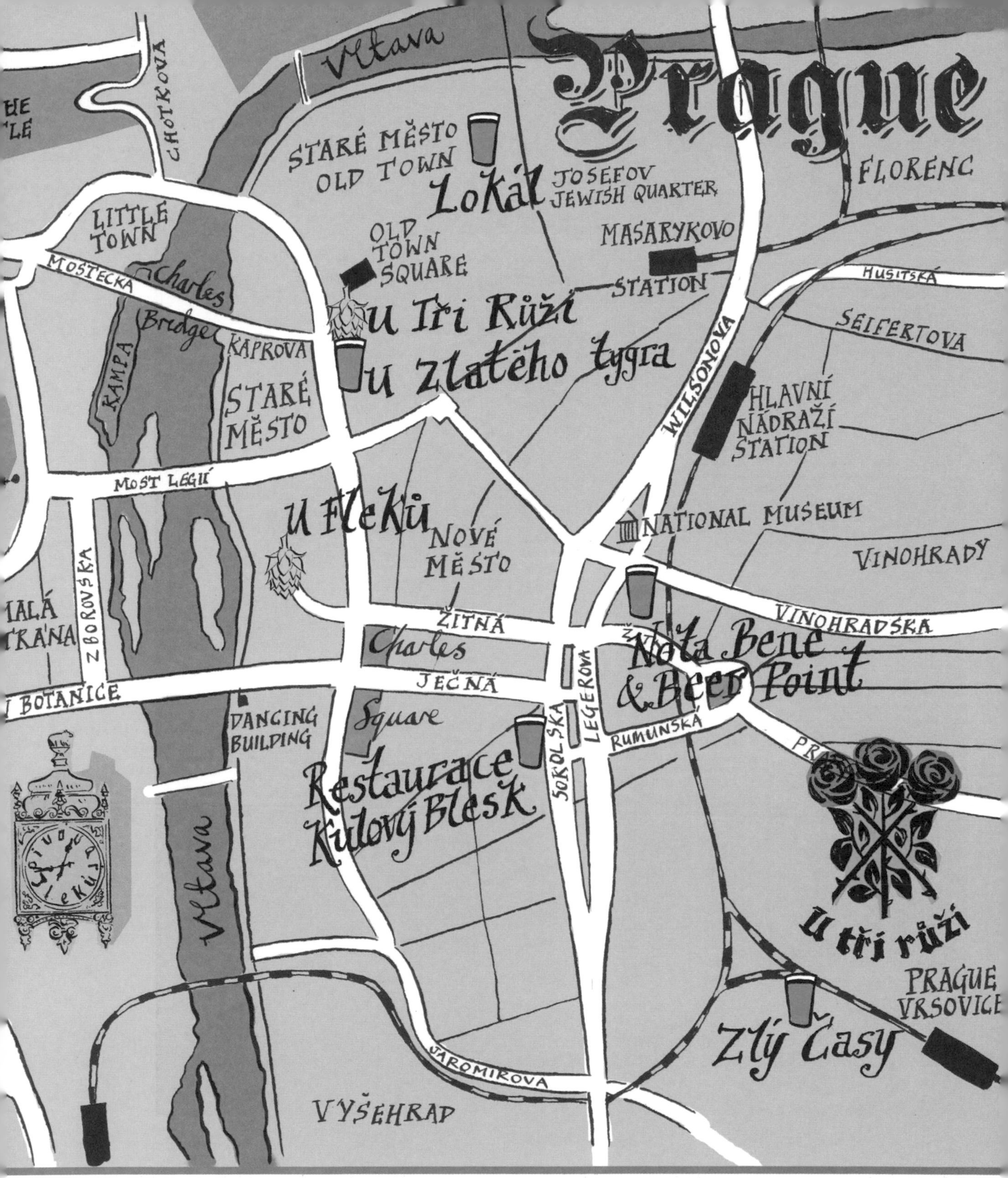
Prague
Vltava
STARÉ MĚSTO
OLD TOWN
Lokál
JOSEFOV
JEWISH QUARTER
FLORENC
CHOTKOVA
LITTLE TOWN
OLD TOWN SQUARE
MASARYKOVO STATION
MOSTECKA
Charles Bridge
U Tři Růží
HUSITSKÁ
SEIFERTOVA
KAPROVA
U Zlatého Tygra
KAMPA
STARÉ MĚSTO
WILSONOVA
HLAVNÍ NÁDRAŽÍ STATION
MOST LEGIÍ
U Fleků
NOVÉ MĚSTO
NATIONAL MUSEUM
VINOHRADY
ZBOROVSKA
ŽITNÁ
VINOHRADSKÁ
Charles Square
Nota Bene & Beer Point
JEČNÁ
BOTANICE
DANCING BUILDING
SOKOLSKÁ
LEGEROVA
RUMUNSKÁ
Restaurace Kulový Blesk
Vltava
U tří růží
PRAGUE VRSOVICE
Zlý Časy
JAROMÍROVA
VYŠEHRAD

U ZLATÉHO TYGRA

HUSOVA 228/17; WWW.UZLATEHOTYGRA.CZ

The Golden Tiger is a classic pub and a quintessential Czech beer experience. It's cramped and busy, one guy pours all the beers while others deliver them to your table. Cozy-up to the locals and just enjoy the atmosphere while you drink perfect pints of Pilsner Urquell.

PIVOVAR U TŘI RŮŽI

HUSOVA 232/10; WWW.U3R.CZ/EN

Right opposite The Golden Tiger is The Three Roses brewpub making classic styles plus some unexpected ones that might include American-hopped Světly, Belgian-inspired Speciál, or smoky Rauchbier. The food is a modern take on Czech bar snacks.

ZLÝ ČASY

CESTMÍROVA 390/5; WWW.ZLYCASY.EU

The name means "Bad Times" but this is the number one craft beer bar in the Czech Republic, and the place to go for the biggest range of good beer. Pick between Pale Ales and IPAs, or just go for an amazing lager. There are three bars inside and each has different beers on, while the food is a mix of Czech (meat-focused) plus some American-influenced burgers and ribs. Next door is a good bottle shop if you want to take something home. Essential.

RESTAURACE KULOVÝ BLESK

SOKOLSKÁ 13;
WWW.RESTAURACEKULOVYBLESK.CZ

This is a brother bar of Zlý Časy with a similarly great beer selection. There's an inside-outside seating area as you enter, or a cozier bar space downstairs. Order a few beer snacks and work your way through the tap list where names to look out for include Kout na Šumavě, Únětický, Matuška, Zhůřák, and Kocour.

NOTA BENE AND BEER POINT

MIKOVCOVA 4;
WWW.NOTABENE-RESTAURANT.CZ

Nota Bene is upstairs and Beer Point is downstairs. Both have a well-chosen selection of excellent beers and the modern food is great.

U FLEKŮ

KŘEMENCOVA 11; WWW.UFLEKU.CZ

Do you want to drink the best dark lager in the world? Then you need to come here. It's been a brewery since 1499 and continues today, making just the one beer—a dark 13° lager. Take a seat and a waiter will bring you beer. The food involves huge portions of classic Czech cuisine.

LOKÁL

DLOUHÁ 33; WWW.LOKAL-DLOUHA.AMBI.CZ

A large, long and modern beerhall, Lokál pours some of the best Tankovná Pilsner Urquell in town alongside Czech home-cooked dishes. If you want to try something different then ask for your beer to beer poured "Mliko"—it comes as a glass of foam which you have to drink really fast to get the full experience of the creamy, soft liquid.

KLÁŠTERNÍ PIVOVAR STRAHOV

STRAHOVSKÉ NÁDVO Í 301/10;
WWW.KLASTERNI-PIVOVAR.CZ

Trek up the hill toward Prague Castle and you'll find a small brewpub in Strahov Monastery making beers under the name Svatý Norbert. The Polotmavý is excellent, as is the bananary Weissbier, but it's the juicy IPA you go to get.

TOP 5 BEERS IN TOWN

Tankovná Pilsner Urquell
The classic Pilsner, unpasteurized

U Fleků's Black Lager
The best dark lager in the world

Kout na Šumave 12
A brilliant pale lager

Pivovar Strahov IPA
US-hopped IPA made in a monastery

Nomád Karel Česká IPA
Superb all-Czech hopped IPA

The view of the city from the famous Charles Bridge.

Saying "cheers!": "Na zdraví!"

Tankovná **means the beer is poured from a large beer-serving tank and is unpasteurized, meaning a fresher and more interesting beer.**

Kvasnicové **is "yeast beer" but that doesn't mean unfiltered, instead it's finished beer which has some fermenting wort or yeast added to it.**

Nefiltrované **means the beer is unfiltered, so will likely be cloudy and richer in flavor–this is definitely the one to look for.**

ORDER LIKE A LOCAL

SVĚTLY is pale lager
TMAVÉ is dark lager
POLOTMAVÝ is an amber lager
ČERNÉ is black lager

Czech brewers use the degree Plato scale:

10° will be around 4% ABV, also known as Výčepní pivo

11-12° is 4.5-5% ABV, also known as Ležák (for example, Tmavé Ležák will be a 5% dark lager)

13-14° (and above) is 5.5-6%, also known as Speciál. It's not uncommon to see 17-18°, while craft brewers may take it even higher

CITY GUIDE

BUDAPEST

Budapest is a brilliant place for great beers and bars—it's one of the lesser-known beery destinations but one that surpasses all expectations. There are a few particularly hip parts of Pest which are reminiscent or Berlin, Brooklyn, or East London, where you can find old ruin bars, hoppy craft beer, and street food coming together in the best of ways. Many of the Hungarian beers I drank were American-inspired and the quality was very high.

Élesztő (Tűzoltó utca 22; www.elesztohaz.hu) is brilliantly Budapest in that there's so much good stuff in one place: it has a big open courtyard outside, there's a grill kitchen, a ham and cheese bar, a coffee shop, a hostel, a restaurant, a brewing school, and you can drink from 20 taps of Hungarian beer. I think it's one of the world's great bars. **Szimpla Kert** (Kazinczy utca 14; www.szimpla.hu) is the most famous ruin bar in Budapest and another of the best bars I've ever drunk in. Sure, it might get overrun with stag and hen parties, but that's just a part of this unreal bar which has so many different rooms, each interesting in their own way. There's great beer, too—drink Keserű Méz, a hoppy honey lager. Go to **Léhűtő Kézműves Söröző** (Holló utca 12-14; www.facebook.com/lehuto.kezmuvessorozo) for that winning combo of craft beer and sausages. This smart, modern bar in Gozsdu Udvar has a good range of local brews on tap and around this area you'll find great street food trucks—and some of these serve good beer, too. **Csak a jó sör!** (Kertész utca 42; www.csakajosor.hu) is that ideal mix of a great bottle shop which has a few good taps of beer and some tables so you can sit and drink—it's tiny and busy and lots of fun. **Szimpla Kávézó** (Kertész utca 48; www.facebook.com/szimplakavezo) is a chilled out ruin bar with a few nice beers on tap and a great atmosphere. **Hopfanatic** (Hunyadi tér 11; www.hopfanatic.hu) is a dark basement brewpub. The paintings of hop-faced superheroes on the walls tell you what to expect from the beers, which are very good, especially the White IPA. **Jónás Kézműves Sörház** (Fővám tér 11-12; www.facebook.com/jonaskezmuvessorhaz) is a smart, modern bar with great views of the Danube, pouring lots of local beers.

And after all that drinking you might want to head to one of Budapest's baths and soak in the natural hot springs—it's a great way to recover after a big night on the beer.

Széchenyi Thermal Baths, one of many outdoor pools that offer an excellent way to beat your hangover.

CITY GUIDE

BERLIN

Unquestionably one of the coolest cities in the world, it took me a few trips to figure out that you don't go to Berlin for the beer—at least not as the primary reason for your visit. You go for the very modern history, you go for the food, for the sights, for the culture, for Berlin. When you are there, however, you can find a lot of very good beer to drink, primarily in brewpubs around the city, plus at some craft beer bars, which are quite rare in Germany.

Brauerei Eschenbrau (Triftstraße 67; www.eschenbraeu.de) is my favorite brewpub in Berlin—there's a house character to all the beers that I love, plus it has a young crowd and a good atmosphere. Finding it can be difficult as it seems to be in the middle of a block of apartments but it's worth the hunt.

Not far from Eschenbrau is **Vagabund Brauerei** (Antwerpener Straße 3; www.vagabundbrauerei.com), a smart and small space brewing on a tiny kit and selling beer on the bar alongside some of Germany's best craft brews. There's a hub of brewpubs right in the center of the city but in my experience **Marcus Bräu** (Münzstraße 1-3; www.brau-dein-bier.de) is the only one worth visiting, with a dark beer and a light beer on tap. **Pfefferbräu** (Schönhauser Allee 176; www.pfefferbraeu.de) is in an impressive location overlooking Schönhauser Allee, though the beers are variable—still, it's likely you'll pass as it's near other interesting things. In the summer head to **Prater Garten** (Kastanienallee 7-9; www.pratergarten.de) beer garden for a more quintessential German drinking experience involving mugs of Prater lager. In Friedrichshain you'll find **Hops & Barley** (Wühlischstr. 22/23; www.hopsandbarley-berlin.de), a warm, welcoming little brewpub with the feel of a café and a selection of very good house beers—I've always liked the clinging grapefruity bitterness in the Pils. Nearby is **Schalander Hausbrauerie** (Bänschstr. 91; www.schalander-berlin.de) with a few brews of their own and tasty flammkuchen. **Bierkombinat Kreuzberg** (Manteuffelstraße 53; www.bier-kombinat.de) is a dark dive bar serving the excellent Shoppe beers—XPA is a great Pale Ale and Black Flag is a super Imperial Stout. For the best craft beer selection in town you have to head to **Hopfenreich** (Sorauer Straße 31; www.hopfenreich.de) which has all of the best of Germany and beyond in a great bar. For food lovers, head to **Heidenpeters** (Eisenbahnstraße 42-43; www.heidenpeters.de) for great street food alongside their selection of craft ales—it's not open all the time so check the hours before you go. **Brauhaus Südstern** (Hasenheide 69; www.brauhaus-suedstern.de) makes the classic German threesome of Helles, Dunkel, and Hefeweizen and they are all good. Sausage-lovers need to go to **Das Meisterstück** (Hausvogteiplatz 3; www.dasmeisterstueck.de) where you'll get all the meat you can eat plus a great beer range. For the best burger in town go to **The Bird** (two locations, both are good; www.thebirdinberlin.com), which also serves some American craft beers. You obviously want a currywurst—**Konnopke's Imbiss** (Schönhauser Allee 42; www.konnopke-imbiss.de) is the most famous and it's great (and close to Prater). After all of that you might want a coffee and there's a lot of good beans in Berlin—**The Barn, Bonanza, Silo,** and **Five Elephant**, to name just a few. Good bars, good beer, modern styles mixed with classic brews, lots of decent food, and a very different experience to the thigh-slapping Oompah and stein-swinging Munich stereotype.

• CITY GUIDE

BAMBERG

Bamberg is one of my favorite beer places and while it might not be as famous as Munich or have the cultural appeal of Berlin, I think it's too good to miss. It's a beautiful city with amazing baroque architecture, plus the added bonus of nine breweries within walking distance of each other.

Schlenkerla (Dominikanerstraße 6; www.schlenkerla.de) is the top tavern in town where you'll go to drink the superlative smoked lagers, the style for which Bamberg is best known. Their Märzen is the deepest purple-brown in color and deeply smoky and rich. The other place to go for smoke is **Spezial** (Obere Königstraße 10; www.brauerei-spezial.de). Less malty, more woody, it's superb, though don't overlook the unsmoked Kellerbier which is delicious. Opposite Spezial is **Fässla** (Obere Königstraße 19-21; www.faessla.de). If you want good, cheap accommodation then stay here where you'll also find classic Franconian brews, including the wonderful Zwergla Dark Lager. Go across town to find two classic old brauhauses: **Keesmann** (Wunderburg 5; www.braugasthoefe.de/en/brauerei-keesmann) and **Mahr's** (Wunderburg 10; www.mahrs.de). Keesmann's Herren Pils is one of the best of its type being fragrant, bitter and so-bloody-good, while Mahr's is most famous for Ungespundet (or just "U"), their bready and rich unfiltered beer, though I prefer the textbook-defining Hell. Back in town, and next to Schlenkerla, is **Ambräusianum** (Dominikanerstraße 10; www.ambraeusianum.de) that truthfully you can skip if you're short on time, though they do flights if you want a sample. Stretch your legs and walk up one of Bamberg's hills (it's built by seven of them) to **Greifenklau** (Laurenziplatz 20; www.greifenklau.de)—it has a great garden with good views over town, ideal for summer glasses of their wheat beer. Head down the hill and go to

Bamberg's historic old town hall, situated right in the middle of the Regnitz River.

Klosterbräu (Obere Mühlbrücke 1-3; www.klosterbraeu.de), the oldest brewery in town, for the best black beer around. If you want to complete the brewery crawl then take a stroll along the river to Kaiserdom's **Brauerie Gasthaus** (Gaustadter Hauptstraße 26; www.kaiserdom.de) for a decent range of brews and good food. Then for something completely different head to **Café Abseits** (Pödeldorfer Straße 39, 96052; www.abseits-bamberg.de) for German craft beers in a cozy bar. In Bamberg, you might go for the smoky beers, but you'll stay because of everything else.

CITY GUIDE

VIENNA

Once a European center of brewing, it's now more interesting to jump in and out of the brewpubs in between seeing the sights and wandering around the pretty streets. What you'll find here is a mix of good classic lager styles, including the reddish Vienna-born Märzen, plus some really good modern styles.

For your hop hit, go to **1516 Brewing Company** (Schwarzenbergstraße 18; www.1516brewingcompany.com), a busy American-style brewpub that makes some seriously good beer. The Pilsner is wonderfully dry and bitter, they make the devilishly hoppy Hop Devil IPA, plus a Cascade dry-hopped Weissbier which is superb. Around the corner from 1516 is **Stadtbrauerei Schwarzenberg** (Schellinggasse 14; www.stadtbrauerei.at) where you can get a house-brewed Helles and Dunkel in a traditional old space.

The Weiner Riesenrad, or Vienna Big Wheel, is one of the city's most popular tourist attractions.

Wieden Bräu (Waaggasse 5; www.wieden-braeu.at) is a good old-style pub with bright branding and classic, tasty beers—try their Vienna. **7 Stern Bräu** (Siebensterngasse 19; www.7stern.at) has the brewkit right in the center of the bar and this makes traditional styles plus a great Rauchbier and some brews with unusual adjuncts like chili and hemp (probably better to stick to the classic styles). Don't miss **Salm Bräu** (Rennweg 8; www.salmbraeu.com) because the food is good, it's in a huge old building, and I think all of their beers are really superb—try the Märzen for a traditional taste of the classic Viennese style which is bready and complex. A little out of the city, but worth the trip, is **Lichtenhaler Bräu** (Liechtensteinstraße 108; www.lichtenthalerbraeu.at), an old timber building with small copper kit in the middle from which comes a good Helles plus some hop-forward styles. Go through the Shamrock Irish Bar and into **Dogstar Craft Beer Bar** (Kirchengasse 3; www.facebook.com/thedogstarvienna) for 10 taps of terrific beer. And do you want to eat the biggest schnitzel you'll ever see (with the world's tastiest potato salad)? Then go to **Figlmüller** (Bäckerstraße 6; www.figlmueller.at).

CITY GUIDE

MUNICH

Go to drink in big Bavarian beer gardens. Go to sit in huge beer halls. Go to savor steins of great lager or tall glasses of hazy Hefeweizen. Go for the massive platefuls of meat. Go for the friendly people. Have the best Helles and Dunkel you can find, drink them fresh and see why these styles are so damn good. Go with the challenge of drinking a beer from each of the Big Six breweries (that's Augustiner, Hacker-Pschorr, Hofbräu, Löwenbräu, Paulaner, and Spaten). Go because it's Munich, one of the world's greatest beer cities.

MAXVORSTADT
THERESIENSTRAßE
LUDWIGSTRAßE
ENGLISCHER GARTEN
Airbräu
Spatenhaus an der Oper
PRINZREGENTENSTR.
PRINZREGENTEN STR.
Wirtshaus Ayingers
Hofbräuhaus München
HB
EINSTEINSTRAßE
Weisses Bräuhaus
FRAUNHOFERSTRAßE
MUSEUMSINSEL
DEUTSCHES MUSEUM
ROSENHEIMER STR
ORLEANSSTRAßE
OSTBAHNHOF
WITTELSBACHERSTR.
Paulaner am Nockherberg
PAULANER MÜNCHEN
AM NOCKHERBERG
WELFENSTRAßE
Tap-House Munich
HUMBOLDTSTRAßE
ANZINGER STR.
ST-MARTIN-STRAßE
Giesinger Bräu
SCHLIERSEE STR.
Forschungsbrauerei
ROSENHEIMER-STR.

HOFBRÄUHAUS

PLATZL 9; WWW.HOFBRAEUHAUS.DE

This is one of the biggest pubs I've been to and you could get lost in the Hofbräuhaus for days. At least you'd be happy with the liter steins of beer—because it only comes by the liter—and mighty meaty meals. It's very busy, very lively and a must-visit pub, where it feels like Oktoberfest every day.

AUGUSTINER-KELLER

ARNULFSTRASSE 52;
WWW.AUGUSTINERKELLER.DE

Under a thick canopy of tall trees, which once provided shade to keep the beer cellars beneath as cool as possible, is a beer garden big enough to seat 5,000 people. Inside you'll find a number of different and interesting rooms plus you can sit in the cellars where they used to store the beer. Drink the Edelstoff that's gravity-poured form large wooden barrels—it's one of the world's best beers. Also check out the Augustiner Großgaststätte in the middle of town (Neuhauser Straße 27, 80331). Stunning outside, it gets even better when you go inside with many amazing rooms of different, handsome designs, while the courtyard feels like a scene from Romeo and Juliet.

ALTES HACKERHAUS

SENDLINGER STRASSE 14;
WWW.HACKERHAUS.DE

The great thing about Munich is how so many of the places you want to visit are very central in the city, all within walking distance of one another, mostly around the Marienplatz. Go to Hackerhaus for the Hacker-Pschorr beers and stay to check out the various ornate, wood-paneled drinking spaces.

LÖWENBRAÜKELLER

NYMPHENBURGER STRASSE 2;
WWW.LOEWENBRAEUKELLER.COM

Walk in and you'll surely say "wow" at Löwenbraü. A huge place; high ceilings, so many tables, and a great beer garden outside. Try the Löwenbraü Pilsner for a dry, snappy pale lager that's wonderfully bitter and a good change-up from the mugs of Helles you'll have been drinking—it's great with the rich, meaty food that you'll no doubt be ordering.

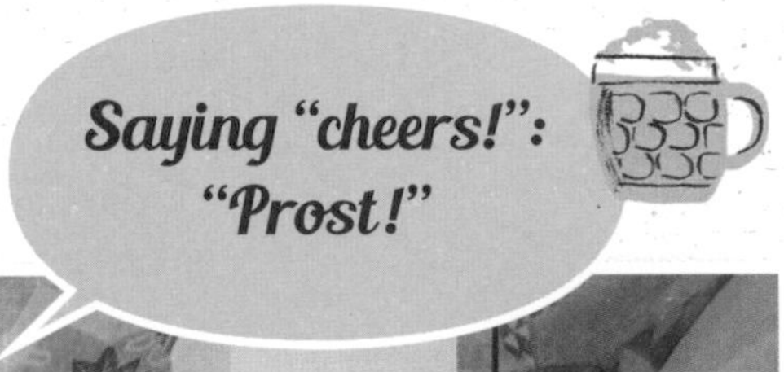

Inside the cavernous Hofbräuhaus.

PAULANER AM NOCKHERBERG

HOCHSTRASSE 77; WWW.NOCKHERBERG.COM

This is another ridiculously big beer venue, capable of seating thousands of people inside and out—luckily it's right next to the brewery so they shouldn't run out of beer. Go for the garden in the summer and sit in the shade of the tree-lined plaza, or inside there are three floors to pick from, including the bierkeller.

SPATENHAUS AN DER OPER

RESIDENZSTRASSE 12; WWW.SPATENHAUS.DE

It's hard to decide whether you should sit inside or out when you visit Spatenhaus. Outside and you're in a busy courtyard opposite the lovely-looking Opera House. Inside and you'll rarely find more attractive rooms to eat and drink in; some modern and bright, some beautifully elegant and traditional. The food is great and so is the beer (obviously, you're in Munich). Drink the Dunkel.

WEISSES BRÄUHAUS

TAL 7; WWW.WEISSES-BRAUHAUS.DE

Do you like wheat beer? Then you have to visit Weisses Bräuhaus owned by Schneider Weisse. They have at least 10 of their own beers and each is very, very good. Tap 5 Meine Hopfenweisse is one of my favorite beers—it's 8.2% ABV and heavily dry-hopped. Don't start with that, though. Instead arrive for a breakfast of the classic Tap 7 with weisswurst and then work through the beers from there.

ANDECHSER AM DOM

WEINSTRASSE 7A; WWW.ANDECHSER-AM-DOM.DE

Drink beers brewed by the Andechs Monastery right by the Frauenkirche. Inside it's exactly what you expect and want from a Bavarian beer hall: it's busy so there's a great atmosphere, the food is hearty and big, looking around at the dark wood interiors you somehow just know you're in Germany, plus the beers are typically excellent—try the Dunkel Naturtrüb; a delicious dark, unfiltered lager.

WIRTSHAUS AYINGERS

AM PLATZL 1A; WWW.AYINGERS.DE

Opposite the Hofbräuhaus, this is where to go to drink Ayinger beer. Have a Kellerbier, their unfiltered lager, which is superb with the schnitzel. For dessert have a Celebrator, the brewery's famous Doppelbock which is a rich, malty treat. The space is modern, open, and warm, making it stand out from the more traditional older locations in this list.

GIESINGER BRÄU

MARTIN-LUTHER-STR. 2; WWW.GIESINGER-BRAEU.DE

This smart brewpub had some serious investment and growth in 2014 and that's allowed them to pump out much more beer and have a brilliant Bräustüberl by the brauhaus. Modern, warm, and relaxed—go to Geisinger and work through the range of Bavarian beer styles and regular specials.

FORSCHUNGSBRAUEREI

UNTERHACHINGER STRASSE 78; WWW.FORSCHUNGSBRAUEREI.DE

The experience of drinking from chunky ceramic mugs should be enough to pull you out of the center of Munich for a few hours. Add in the fact that the beer is excellent, the food delicious, and the beer hall classically Bavarian, and you should jump on the S7 train to München-Perlach and visit Forschungsbrauerei.

TAP-HOUSE MUNICH

ROSENHEIMER STRASSE 108; WWW.TAP-HOUSE-MUNICH.DE

If you want craft beer then this is the place to go. Owned by the guys behind Camba Bavaria, a seriously good brewery based out toward the Austrian border, you'll find every style you can think of. Start with the Camba beers, particularly their IPAs and Pale Ales, then sample some of the exceptional and rare guest beers.

AIRBRÄU

MUNICH INTERNATIONAL AIRPORT; WWW.MUNICH-AIRPORT.DE

Obviously Munich also has a brewery at the airport. With the copper kettles on display and the choice to sit inside or out, it's one of the only airport breweries in the world—you also don't need to be flying to visit (if you are flying then there's also a pub inside terminal 2).

CITY GUIDE

ROME

Rome is a remarkable city to visit. The history is astonishing, the sights are breathtaking and the whole place will leave you in awe. For beer it's also brilliant with a few key bars standing out as being among the top in Europe. One thing to know if you're with a non-beer drinker is that these are beer bars and therefore many of them just sell beer, sometimes with whiskey and water—and that's all.

Ma Che Siete Venuti a Fà (Via di Benedetta 25; www.football-pub.com) is the place to start. The name roughly means "what the hell are you doing here?" and the answer is, quite simply, drinking some of the best beers from Italy and around the world. Opposite is **Bir + Fud** (Via di Benedetta 23; www.birandfud.it). Go for the superb pizzas and the best of Italian craft beer. Cross the Tiber and wind through the small backstreets looking for **Open Baladin** (Via degli Specchi 6; www.openbaladinroma.it). Over 40 taps with lots of Baladin brews. And head to **Brasserie 4:20** (Via Portuense 82; www.brasserie420.com). A cool underground space plus a fun rooftop, the beer list is excellent and the food matches it marvellously. And for one of the best pizzas I've ever had, go to **Pizzarium** (Via della Meloria 43) just outside the Vatican. They often have a few craft beers in the fridge, too.

A bar in the Trastevere district offering locally produced craft beers.

CITY GUIDE

MILAN

Milan doesn't have the stunning sights and history of Rome, instead it's a city of culture, fashion, food, and drink. "Aperitivo" is a big thing, with people stopping at bars to enjoy a drink with a spread of snacks and while a spritz might be the common choice, there are many local craft beers to drink instead.

Head to **Birrificio Lambrate** (Via Adelchi 5; www.birrificiolambrate.com) a busy (especially late at night on weekends), loud brewpub that opened in 1997, making it one of Italy's first micro breweries. Beers include hoppy lagers, great Pale Ales, and a superb smoky Porter—don't miss it. **Lambiczoon** (Via Fruili 46; www.lambiczoon.com) is where you go for a great beer range, including rarities, plus great staff and big burgers. **La Belle Alliance** (Via Evangelista Torricelli 1; www.labellealliance.it) is a fun bar with a really decent beer selection, including cask ales and interesting imports. **Baladin Milano** (Via Solferino 56; www.baladin.it) has all the Baladin beers and you can drink in the café-like upstairs or the edgier, more fun downstairs bar. Nearby is **Eataly** (Piazza 25 Aprile 10; www.eataly.net), the impressive food emporium with a good bottled beer range and some sensational food. There are **BQ** (www.b-q.it) bars all around the city, often small and in interesting places, they have a bunch of their own beers on tap plus guests.

Restaurants and bars line the canal in Milan's Navigli quarter.

CITY GUIDE

BARCELONA

Not so long ago the beer choice in Barcelona was limited to small glasses of cold lager, but that's changing quickly. Spain is still an emerging country for craft brewing, meaning you can expect to find a few duds in your drinking, but the best beers are world-beaters. Barcelona is also just a great place to go with the draw of beach, city, architecture, sunshine, and good food.

The first place to go for beer is **BierCaB** (Muntaner, 55; www.biercab.com), a world-class bar with the best of Spanish and world beer plus seriously good modern Spanish food. Another must-visit place is **CatBar** (Carrer Boria 17; www.facebook.com/catbarcat). It's small, filled with mis-matched furniture, jazz plays, and there are drawings of cats all over the walls. The nine taps feature local and good imports, plus there's a fridge filled with bottles. The food is tasty vegan burgers. A short walk from CatBar is **La Cerveteca** (Carrer d'En Gignàs, 25; www.lacerveteca.com), this is a bottle shop and cool corner bar that feels like an old English pub, especially as they have cask beer on tap. **Ale & Hop** (Carrer de les Basses de Sant Pere, 10; www.aleandhop.com) is another favorite place—go any time for the excellent food, great range of draft beer, and cool space. **BlackLab Brewhouse** (Palau de Mar, Plaça Pau Vila; www.blacklab.es) is a brewpub in a great location near Barceloneta, making IPA, Stout, and more, and serving big burgers and sandwiches plus Asian-inspired dishes. **Edge Brewing** (Carrer Llull 62; www.edgebrewing.com—only open on Fridays at the time of writing, so check opening hours) is an American-inspired place making some of the better beers in Spain. **La Bona Pinta** (Carrer de la Diputació, 433; www.labonapinta.com) is a few streets away from the La Sagrada Familia, and while this little bottle shop doesn't look much from the street corner it opens into a bar with seating inside. **La Cervesera Artesana** (Sant Agustí, 14; www.lacervesera.net) is a cave-like brewpub in town and while they may have lots of their own beers on tap they are not the most consistent or interesting. **Homosibaris** (Plaça d'Osca, 4; www.homosibaris.com) is a smart bar and bottle shop with eight taps mixing local and imports with cosy seating in the back, some snacks, and a good atmosphere. Moritz is a beer you'll see all over Barcelona and **Fabrica Moritz** (Ronda de Sant Antoni, 39—41; www.moritz.com) is worth a visit to have some tapas and drink their unfiltered lager, which you can't find elsewhere. If you want to buy bottles to take home then go to **Rosses i Torrades** (Carrer del Consell de Cent, 192; www.rossesitorrades.com).

A view of the city from Parc Güell.

HOW DO YOU RATE IT?

At times in this book I discuss the two main beer rating websites—RateBeer.com and BeerAdvocate.com—and I want to add background and context to these mentions. Between them they reach millions of beer lovers around the world each month and are active, vocal communities, where all content is user-generated, which all makes these relevant and influential.

The rating part is simple: drink a beer and give scores across a few criteria such as appearance, aroma, flavor, and an overall impression. These scores are collated and averaged to give a mark out of 100. This figure can then be compared to other beers of the same style, from the same brewery, or against every beer that's currently brewed in the world. Users can also rate places like taprooms, restaurants, bars, and beer stores (I find these especially useful before planning beer trips).

When it comes to looking for "the best," the sites become interesting as a reference point. Go to RateBeer and select a beer style and you'll immediately be given the top-rated examples. BeerAdvocate shows the beers with the highest number of rates first, but click one button and you can arrange the list by score. Both sites have sort and search functions so if you want to find the highest-rated Saison or Stout then you can. You can also search for breweries, look over all their brews, compare the beer scores. You can look for the best bar in town or the best beer in a country, plus you can read notes that users write alongside their score. And both sites have an overall list of the highest-rated beers in the world.

Looking at these lists you'll see a trend toward rare beers and high strength—on RateBeer only seven of the Top 50 are under 10% ABV. You'll also see a couple of styles dominating: Imperial Stout makes up 32 of RateBeer's Top 50; Imperial or Double IPA account for 17 of BeerAdvocate's Top 50, and Sour Beers, Wild Ales, and a couple of Belgian beers make up the rest—there are no classic English Bitters, no German Helles. These "best" beers have huge flavor profiles and are often esoteric.

My feeling is that scores are elevated with the increase in flavor as if someone feels they can't assign a perfect score to a Helles because it doesn't have as much flavor as an Imperial IPA. To me this is not true. Sure, I love an Imperial IPA but I also adore the balance and depth in other beers and think they have a place on a "best of" beer list. The other influence here is hype: knowing you're drinking a top-50 beer gives some expectation of excellence and can itself raise the review, as if some taste autonomy is lost.

The sites aren't perfect but they are very relevant and interesting resources. As they are user-generated they're kept going by people who love beer, tracking things in real time, where the averaging of rates should give a decent general guide, though is definitely not always accurate.

THE TOP 5*

RateBeer

1. Toppling Kentucky Brunch Stout
2. Westvleteren XII
3. Cigar City Hunahpu's Imperial Stout
4. Toppling Goliath Mornin' Delight
5. Three Floyds Dark Lord Russian Imperial Stout

BeerAdvocate

1. The Alchemist Heady Topper
2. Toppling Kentucky Brunch Stout
3. Goose Island Bourbon County Coffee Stout
4. Perennial Artisan Ales Barrel-Aged Abraxas
5. Three Floyds Bourbon Barrel Aged Vanilla Bean Dark Lord

*Data taken in July 2015, sites update constantly

KNEE HIGHS
BROTHERS, KENNISON
7.2%
YOUNG GUNS
5.9%
CLEAN AND SIMPLE MALT BILL, MOTUEKA HOPS FROM NZ - A KNOSCHABLE STONEFRUIT PARTY!
ROTATING IPA SERIES
MORPH
IPA w/ tons of pine, grapefruit and soft, tropical notes up front, w/ a bold, clean bitterness + resin finish
CANS
SOMER WEISSE
BERLINER WEISSE WITH LEMON AND GINGER
GLIMMER
GOLDEN STRONG ALE W/ SPICY RYE NOTES, A CRISP HOP BITE AND WARM, EARTHY UNDERTONES
VIVA HABANERA
Rye Ale Brewed With Agave Nectar Aged On Habanero Peppers
THUNDER MOON 5.9%
SUMMER PORTER W/ RICH, DARK MALTS, CITRUSY HOPS, AND GRAINS OF PARADISE
NON-BEERS
SPINDRIFT SODA
TAZA CHOCOLATE
Welcome to Night Shift
Imperial Stout
2014 BARREL SOCIETY MEMBERS ONLY
smooth notes of dark chocolate, berries + caramel

SIERRA NEVADA

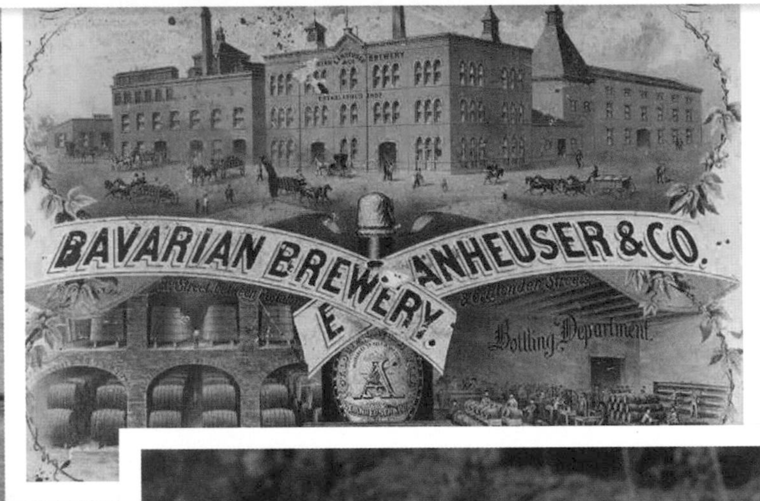
BAVARIAN BREWERY
ANHEUSER & CO.
Bottling Department.

NORTH AMERICA

There's no doubting that North America is at the forefront of craft brewing. For over 30 years it's been constantly evolving and influencing others, with the incredible flavors and aromas from the hops, which have given us IPAs, with cities like Portland which seem to have a craft brewery on every block, with small states like Vermont, where beer is a big thing, and with a brewery like Sierra Nevada leading the way from decades ago. North America is a land of beer.

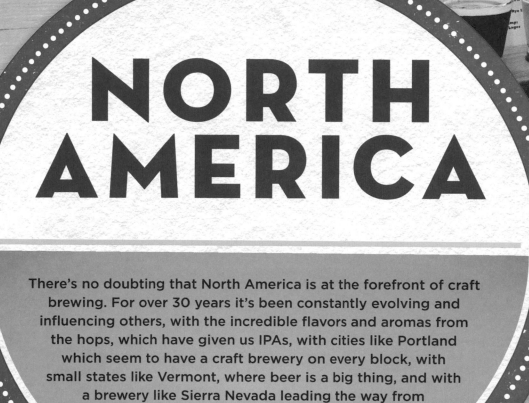

BUDWEISER THE KING OF BEERS?

Budweiser has become a synonym for 'flavorless, mass-made lager,' a word spat out as the best-known example of that type of beer. *Budweiser*. It even sounds like you're forcing it out as a curse. But I think this is unfair and undeserved. Budweiser might not have an impactful, exciting flavor profile and it might be one of the biggest-selling beers in the world, but it's one of the most important beers ever brewed. It's a beer made by a pioneering brewery that started out small, focused on quality ingredients, made the best beers they could, and grew from there. It's also a beer that I like to drink regularly. But is Budweiser really the King of Beers, as it claims?

THE GERMAN CONNECTION

In 1857, 18-year-old Adolphus Busch left his home in Kastel, western Germany, headed for St Louis, Missouri, a city with 160,000 residents, of which a quarter were of German descent. It was here that émigré brewers were making the lagers of their homeland. The migrants would drink these bright and lively beers in bright and lively beer halls, a marked contrast to the dark, rough beers and spirits that Americans were drinking in dark, rough taverns.

In St Louis, Busch met, and would later marry, Lilly Anheuser, daughter of Eberhard Anheuser, the owner of E. Anheuser brewery—one of about 40 breweries in the city at that time. German-born Anheuser, who had made money from soap, was an investor in the Bavarian Brewery, which was founded by George Schneider in 1852. Schneider was struggling and in 1859 Anheuser decided that rather than see the brewing business wash down the sink he'd take it on himself, renaming it the E. Anheuser Brewery.

By this point, Busch had become a partner in a wholesale beer company and his father-in-law's brewery was one of his customers. Within a decade, Busch had bought into the family business with the name changing to E. Anheuser & Co. Brewery to reflect this—that name remained until 1879 when it changed to Anheuser-Busch Brewing Association. Anheuser died in 1880 and Busch became the boss.

Busch was an ambitious, trail-blazing businessman and as soon as he stepped into the brewery he was making advances. He saw that St Louis was a small, crowded market in a large, open country, and that if he were to increase sales, he would need to develop distribution beyond his city. This plan had two obstacles: firstly, transporting beer by horse and cart was slow and the cargo would quickly go stale or sour. Secondly, there was no point looking north or east because there were already many breweries selling beer—Germans had also settled in Chicago and Milwaukee, several hundred miles to the north. To overcome these issues Busch instead looked south and west, following the railroad that was being built between Missouri and Texas.

Back then, beer was primarily distributed in wooden kegs and served directly from them. Bottles existed, and had done for many years, though no brewery was using them on a large scale. Busch worked out that if he could fill enough bottles then this method of distribution could be profitable for him, but it would be a brave gamble.

The infrastructure didn't exist to have a large bottling facility and so Busch had to find a manufacturer who could build him a bespoke, automated bottle filler. He also had to find a glassmaker capable of producing enough bottles. Busch made it happen and in the early years 40,000 bottles could be filled daily by the 80 employees needed to run the line. The Anheuser-Busch Brewing Association was the first brewery to bottle their beer on an industrial scale like this.

A highly intelligent man, Busch also boldly embraced new scientific research, carefully following developments such as Louis Pasteur's experiments with fermentation in beer. He put Pasteur's work into practise in his brewery and began pasteurizing his beer. This process heats filled bottles to kill any bacteria inside, thus making them stable for longer and less likely to spoil. In doing this, Busch was again a pioneer well ahead of his competition.

The combination of the railroad, bottles, and pasteurization, meant that by 1872—the year the train tracks reached Texas—Busch's beers were available for the first time in the Southwest.

Busch's next challenge was keeping his beer cold. In the brewery the beer was stored in naturally formed caves beneath the city that were additionally chilled with chunks of ice harvested from nearby lakes. What if he could replicate these caves above ground to artificially keep his beer cold?

Anheuser-Busch became the first brewery to introduce artificial refrigeration across all their beer production—years ahead of any other brewer. This cooled beer could now be much more consistent. He then applied this same science to his moving rail cars and by 1875 he had built a coordinated system of ice houses along the rail routes to stock blocks of ice. This allowed trains to stop and refill the refrigerated cars, keeping the bottles of pasteurized beer cool throughout the journey.

AMERICA'S FIRST NATIONAL BEER

After a peak of 4,131 breweries operating in United States in 1873, the numbers declined rapidly, with more than half closing in the 15 years that followed. Yet during this time beer production increased,

The Budweiser sign on top of the brewery in St Louis, Missouri.

as those remaining breweries were growing in size. The beer industry was changing and lagers—not the heavy, dark ales that were a hangover from the Colonial era—were becoming America's drink. By 1900, the average American was drinking sixteen gallons of beer a year, four times as much as he did 30 years before.

While the German-Americans were enjoying malty, amber lagers, such as Anheuser-Busch's St Louis Lager, other consumers were developing a preference for lighter lagers. Busch—well traveled, smart, and perceptive of change—figured this out sooner than most. Along with local distributer Carl Conrad, who would be responsible for selling the beer, he set about brewing a new style for this new drinker, one inspired by the bright beers of Bohemia.

However, Busch was brewing with different ingredients to those European brewers and his six-row American barley was richer in protein than the two-row Bohemian barley. That protein led to a hazy beer and that wasn't acceptable because glass was now the container of choice for most beer drinkers. To reduce the six-row in his beer, Busch needed an alternative source of fermentable sugars. He found that rice would lighten the color and body as well as give crispness and a subtle nuttiness to the beer, plus the grain contains good starches and is low in haze-forming protein. (Randy Mosher, in **The Oxford Companion to Beer**, writes that rice was 23.5% of the grain bill.) But rice is more complicated to brew with than barley, so Busch made this decision based on improving the qualities of his beer and not, as some might scoff today, to make it cheaper. The addition of rice also made it a uniquely American beer style—the American Lager.

In 1876, Anheuser-Busch brewed this new beer using barley and rice, imported Saazer hops, and a clean lager yeast. It was called Budweiser and they sold 250,000 bottles in its first year. This light, refreshing lager, which was capable of being cold-shipped around the country in pasteurized bottles, became America's first national beer brand.

A NEW ERA

The end of the 20th century was a time of great growth for Anheuser-Busch and in 1901 they produced over one million barrels of beer, with Budweiser replacing St Louis Lager as the flagship brand. In 1903 they sold over 100 million bottles of Budweiser.

Adolphus Busch died in 1913. An advert from that same year tells of the scale of the brewery he built, "The largest plant of its kind in the world: three million bottles of Budweiser filled a week; 7,500 employees working in 110 separate buildings over the 142-acre St Louis site, the equivalent of 70 city blocks." Busch's son August (Sr.) took over the family business and continued to grow the Budweiser brand to an astonishingly large scale. Then, early in 1920, Anheuser-Busch went from having one of the best-selling beers in the world to having no beer in the world.

THE FORGOTTEN MAN

Carl Conrad was the co-creator of Budweiser, the trademark owner, and the sole proprietor of the brand, and had all rights to sell the bottles through his alcohol merchants. Budweiser was his beer, and there was no mention of Anheuser-Busch on the label.

The brand grew rapidly and Conrad's business grew with it, though it likely expanded too fast for its own good because in January 1883 he was declared bankrupt. Anheuser-Busch, to whom Conrad owed a lot of money, took over the name and rights of the Budweiser brand. Busch was a good friend of Conrad and kept his C. Conrad & Co. branding on the label for many years, until Prohibition in 1920.

MYTHBUSTERS

As we know, Bohemian beer was the inspiration for Budweiser, and the often-told story is of Busch (or more likely Carl Conrad) traveling to Central Europe and stealing or copying a recipe from another brewery. However, there's no written evidence of either of them going to Budweis and coming back with a recipe. It's more likely that they adapted an existing recipe in the portfolio to meet the demands of the beer-drinking public.

Prohibition stopped alcohol production in the United Stated for 13 years. Anheuser-Busch managed to survive the dry period thanks to its diversification into other areas: alcohol-free beer, ice cream, refrigerated rail cars, baking yeast, sodas. August Busch was close to the situation politically and was clearly a vocal advocate of bringing booze back, so when, in 1933, repeal finally happened he was ahead of others and had a brewery filled with Budweiser ready to go, selling 75,000 cases and 7,000 half barrels in two days.

August Busch Sr. committed suicide in 1934 and his son Adolphus Busch III took over and helped the post-Prohibition recovery. When he died in 1946 his brother August Busch Jr. became president of the company and from there the brewery really launched forward, opening a network of additional breweries and becoming the largest brewer in the United States in 1957, a position they've held ever since.

At the same time, Budweiser became the best-selling beer in America, rising to hit a peak of close to 50 million barrels in 1988. It remained America's bestseller until 2002 when it was overtaken by little brother Bud Light, which was initially introduced in 1982. Both are in the top 10 best-selling beers in the world.

ST LOUIS TODAY

I didn't expect the brewery complex in St Louis to be so beautiful. I'm being shown around by Dave Maxwell, Budweiser's Director of Brewing for North America. It's Dave's job to ensure every single bottle of Budweiser brewed in North America is excellent.

The first stop is the Control Room where four people sit at a long desk with over 30 computer screens between them. Each monitor is bemusingly busy; there are figures and processes everywhere, tanks, flows, numbers, acronyms.

"We have defined the perfect process and recipe for Budweiser and we track that right here," says Dave.

Kelly has 10 screens in front of her. She manages the wort production and then passes that liquid on to Gregory, sitting to her right, who deals with the hops and looks after the yeast, including the original Anheuser-Busch Budweiser strain, which has been used since 1876.

Adolphus Busch, the man responsible for changing the face of the beer industry.

Next to Gregory is Lisa, whose job it is to oversee the packaging streams, working out what gets packaged, when, and into which container (bottle, can, keg, etc., and what size of each). She moves liquid between tanks in what seems to me an impossible brain-teasing puzzle. Next to Lisa is Jeff, who ensures that filtered beer gets to Lisa in perfect condition; he's looking at every beer in every tank and checking it against a strict set of parameters. Jeff is getting the readings right through to his screen, where he's able to check things like the alcohol content, oxygen content, even the calories in the beer. If something is outside of the correct range then he needs to know how to fix it.

I'm scribbling notes while I listen and look around. I'm trying to understand what's going on, but I'm a bit confused about what's actually happening here.

"Dave," I say. "What are the job titles of these guys?"

"These are the brewers." It takes a moment for this to register. They aren't dressed in boots and dirty hoodies on the brewhouse floor, rather they are in smart clothes in a dark, quiet office. Four people, who work on a rotating 8-hour shift, are making all of the beers coming out of St Louis, which means simultaneously managing a large variety of brands, all at different stages of production, all needing different attention.

"It's a lot of pressure because some of these tanks hold 12,000 kegs of beer," says Gregory. That's over 700,000 liters of beer in one tank (something like $2m worth of beer). "When you take care of something and you take pride in it, it's got to be perfect every time."

An illustration of the brewery as it looked around the beginning of the twentieth century.

CHANGING PERCEPTIONS

As we leave the Control Room it strikes me that I've just seen Budweiser being brewed but I haven't seen a single tank or sack of grain. I haven't been to a brewery like this before and it adjusts my perception of what brewing can be. It's remarkable yet also a bit sad: it's like navigating by numbers and not looking outside at the view.

This feeling is reinforced when we enter the red-brick brewhouse, because it's the single most magnificent brewing space I've ever seen. Elegant and opulent, there are bronze handrails and columns gilded with gold, there's majestic artwork on the walls, a glass roof shines light through all the floors, and a huge chandelier hangs in the middle.

The brewing vessels are large, silver tanks with elaborate mosaics at their base. And they spread up and down over all the six floors, a vast number of them coming together as three separate brewing streams, each with six mash cookers, two lauter tuns, and two kettles, all combining to brew the beer. I'm speechless standing here. It's so big, so beautiful, so clean, so quiet, and so not what I was expecting

The grand gated entrance to the brewery.

Dave opens a small door by the brew kettles and a cold gust of citrusy, floral, spicy air fills my lungs. "Welcome to the world-famous hop room!" says Gary, as he weighs out and moves around boxes of green hop pellets. Gary is the only person in the brewhouse.

MARKETING PIONEERS

Looking through archives of Anheuser-Busch adverts is a wonderful thing. From an early push in telling customers just how much beer they sell, reinforcing how they must be good if they sell so much, they then turned to focus on quality ingredients. In the 1950s and 1960s there are great paintings and homely images of beer in family environments and snappy slogans like "Where there's life there's Bud"—the customer was now responsible for making the quality choice. Then in the 1970s things shifted from wholesome to macho with the explicit goal of making Budweiser synonymous with American sport. The 2000s onwards seem to focus on forming a kind of sentimentality around the beer by using their famous Clydesdale horses, cute puppies, or guys that look like your best mates.

A stone sculpture of the famous feature of the Anheuser-Busch logo.

"Here you can see the hop bill," says Dave, pointing at a computer screen. I didn't expect them to allow me to see this and I'm trying to scan all the names—there are German and American hops and the list of varieties is so long I can't read them all.

Pete Kraemer, the brewery's Chief Brewmaster in North America, later tells me: "There are 10 types of hops in Budweiser right now but this might change during the season." You read that right: there are 10 different varieties of hops in each brew of Budweiser. "It's a complex process to keep the balance of the hop in Budweiser the same," says Pete, particularly as they transition from each year's crop. There's a pilot plant at the brewery that's used for research. "Every year we brew batches of Budweiser on the pilot plant with just one hop variety. And we do this for each variety that we might use."

These single-hopped versions of the beer are tasted side-by-side to see how the year's hop might influence the overall flavor profile in the brew, and any necessary amends are made, meaning even a beer like Budweiser shifts its recipe through the year. It's a process that has to

be managed incredibly closely to ensure that the end flavor profile never changes, even if the recipe does. This is a monumental task, made even more complicated because Budweiser isn't just brewed in St Louis; it's made in 50 different breweries around the world. And no matter where it's made, every single glass of the beer has to taste the same.

To ensure they are always consistent, the beers are blind-tasted side-by-side every week. "A certified taster is trained to a point where they can recognize the exact flavor profile in the beer and recognize how close it is to the perfect version of that beer," says Dave.

Next, Dave leads us down into the depths of the cold cellars and again I'm left speechless. The conical fermenters look like huge rocket ships suspended a few meters from the ground. There are banks of horizontal conditioning tanks, lined and stacked like submarines. I stand underneath one that holds 6,000 barrels of beer. It's as big as a three-story town house and contains enough Budweiser to fill over two million 12oz bottles.

Dave tells me that Budweiser has a brewing cycle of around 30 days, which is a significant length of time and something that should be celebrated and not sneered at. (How many craft lagers get four weeks in tank? How many macro lagers are smashed out in half that time?)

It's here that we see some beech chips. These aren't added for flavor, instead they're a traditional part of the Budweiser brew and essentially they are an addition to the secondary fermentation, where the chips give additional surface area that keeps the yeast in contact with the beer to help finish fermentation and produce carbonation.

There's one other element that interests me: high-gravity brewing. The beer is made to a higher alcohol level and then beer from different tanks is blended together. It's then checked against the required parameters and the water is added to get to the correct ABV before it's packaged. It's a way for breweries like this to help with their consistency and to negate the natural batch-to-batch variation that will occur (yeast, no matter how closely you manage it, can always do its own thing).

I'm surrounded by tanks of beer in these cold cellars and now I finally get the experience I've been waiting for: to drink Budweiser fresh and unfiltered from the tank. Dave attaches a tightly wound silver funnel into a tap on the side of one of the tanks and beer pours out fast into a small plastic cup. It's lightly hazy and pale with a rich white foam on top. It has a soft aroma, as clean as the air around me, with just a hint of fruity freshness from hops and yeast, like apricots and apples. It has a touch of malt flavor and then it ends with the characteristic clean, dry finish. It tastes just like Budweiser.

BREWING PERFECTION

I hear the word "perfect" a lot during my time in the brewery. Brewing Budweiser is about achieving perfection on one product, where perfect is defined as a very precise, definite flavor profile and set scientific parameters; the challenge is to always make Budweiser taste the way that it should taste; to make the most perfect version of Budweiser that they can.

In 2013, 16 million barrels of Budweiser were brewed. That's the equivalent of over 780 million 12oz bottles and each one of them will taste exactly the same. To produce Budweiser takes a lot of different people looking after many different interconnecting processes, where each process has to be exact or there will be a knock-on effect on the overall flavor. That's an astonishing level of precision for something made in such huge volume: the minutia in the massive.

The beer I drank in the cellar was the best version of Budweiser I've tasted. At the time I think I expected more of the beer—I wanted to be wowed and surprised—and when it didn't come I was initially disappointed. But in retrospect I was wrong to have expected something other than the classic taste of Budweiser because that's the point of this beer; it's just always exact, always precise, always the same. And that's what makes it so impressive. It might not have the huge flavor profile of an IPA or the romance of a micro-brewed beer, it might have such massive marketing ubiquity that we're desensitized to it, but the visionary industry advances made by the Busch family, the history, the scale of production, the worldwide consistency, and the worldwide renown all combine to place a crown on the King of Beer's head.

The idea of "the best" is challenging here because we have to shift our taste buds accordingly, but what's key is that Budweiser tastes like the best version of itself every single time. And while it's easy to think about the hundreds of millions of bottles that are brewed each year, that's the wrong mind-set because, as Dave tells me in the cellars: "It's not about how many you make, it's about how each bottle tastes, how perfect it is, because the drinker only experiences it 12oz at a time." And when I drink Budweiser I genuinely enjoy it and I think it's worthy of consideration as one of the best beers in the world.

The challenge is to always make Budweiser taste the way that it should taste; to make the most perfect version they can.

IPA HUNTING IN CALIFORNIA

IPA is a style defined by its huge hop aroma, where we expect citrus, tropical fruit, flowers, and pine. It's bold, bitter, and boozy, golden and orange in color, and gleaming on the bar top. It's the flavor antithesis of ubiquitous lagers as it shows new drinkers just how flavorsome beer can be. It's the best-selling craft beer style in America, it's the beer that breweries can be compared by, and it's the beer that so many drinkers hold up as their favorite. And the West Coast of America is where IPAs rule, so I'm on a road trip through California with my dad looking for the best IPAs in the country.

SAN DIEGO

To take a history lesson from Ron Burgundy, San Diego was discovered by the Germans in 1904. The name, in German, means "a whale's vagina." While we don't know for certain if those Germans brought beer with them over a century ago, we can say that today the name San Diego should really mean "City of Hops."

I'm starting at Stone Brewing because it was their beer that had such a profound impact on me. Considering the gargoyle images and the balls-out bravado of the brand, the Stone World Bistro and Gardens is a remarkably serene place, complete with elegant Japanese gardens. There is nothing serene or elegant, however, about Stone Ruination IPA (which has since been replaced by Ruination 2.0).

It hammers hops onto my tongue as it beats my taste buds with its bitterness, throwing all kinds of orange fruits, spice, pepper, roasted citrus, and tangy resins at me. It's a sensational beer and one that was worth traveling here to drink. But it's more than an IPA; at 8.2% and over 100IBUs (International Bitterness Units) this is a Double IPA and it was the first regularly bottled Double IPA in America. The Double part of the name really just signifies more of everything—malt, alcohol, and especially hops.

Their IPA is a deep gold color; it's herbal beneath the barrage of citrus pith, intense and bitter yet joyfully aromatic with citrus juiciness. And then there's Stone Enjoy By

LOVE AT FIRST TASTE

Never before had so many bitter oranges been driven through my nose, never had that dank resinous scent of pine forests been so powerful, never did I think I'd smell something more grapefruity than a grapefruit. This ferocious amber liquid wasn't like any other beer I'd ever had. I'd only been drinking beer for a few years, generally preferring dark, chocolaty Stouts. One taste and the bitterness exploded, gripped, stung, and was unrelenting as it invaded my senses. A second sip gave a sense of giddiness, of being more alert. By the third taste things had changed and there was a sadistic enjoyment as I went back for more of its painful pleasure. By the time the glass of Stone Ruination IPA was empty I knew my drinking habits would be changed forever.

IPA, a regular release that features on the label the date the drinker should consume it by, the idea being that it must be drunk fresh in order to get the best experience. These are the kinds of beers that have the ability to shock and delight and it's all down to the brewery's masterful use of hops.

At Ballast Point Brewery I'm all over their Sculpin IPA, a beer that's regularly held up as one of America's best. And it really is. Not far away at Alesmith and their IPA is another beauty. Both are gloriously aromatic, citrus fruit everywhere, tangerine and grapefruit, peaches and apricots, then bitter but with clean, dry bodies. It's the super-fruity aromas that make these so much fun to drink and already I want to move here to be able to drink beers like this all the time.

This sign is outside the Stone brewery... only in California!

The tap selection at Ballast Point, including the outstanding Sculpin IPA, one of the finest examples of the style.

In a bar one night I drink Alpine Brewing's Duet, which has one of the softest, lushest bodies I've had in a beer, all top-loaded with enormous amounts of orangey, floral hops. Then there's Nelson, a beer brewed with New Zealand hops, and it's unreal in how much tropical fruit aroma and flavor it has before a big kick of bitterness floors you. So good.

Before leaving the city I jump on a bus and head out towards the sea; I can't come all the way to the West Coast and not see the Pacific Ocean. I also couldn't leave without popping into Pizza Port at Ocean Beach, a bustling brewpub, where I go for their Jetty IPA and order a pizza. One mouthful of beer and I'm gushing all kinds of lupulin-laced love letters to this beautiful brew: glowing orange in color, it has a body that's a little sweet in the best way and that somehow enhances the fruitiness in the brew, all with a strong bitterness. Amazing. San Diego is definitely the City of Hops.

The beer flight at Firestone Walker. Visiting this brewery was a dream come true.

FIRESTONE WALKER

Since drinking a bottle of Union Jack IPA, Firestone Walker has been a brewery that I've always wanted to visit, so I've somehow managed to convince my dad that it's a good idea to take a 200-mile (300-km) detour from San Francisco just so I can go. It was a very good decision.

Sitting in their large beer hall I get all the IPAs on one four-beer flight board. I start with Easy Jack, a 4.5% ABV Session IPA brewed with German, Kiwi, and American hops, which give melon and mango, peach and tangerine. Not many Session IPAs are better. Union Jack is their core IPA, a 7.5% ABV West Coaster that's loaded with grapefruit and pine and backed up with honeyish malt. Double Jack is their 9.5% ABV Double IPA and it's the sort of beer you could drink a pint of, loving every gulp of the rich malt and fresh, fruity hops, without realizing quite how strong it is; it's a revelation of balance and big flavor. Then there's Hammersmith IPA, 6.7% ABV, a beer only available in the Taproom, and it's the best IPA I've had in a long time, with tangerine and peach, honey sweetness from malt, and a dry bitterness. It's so good I order a pint.

On the drive back to San Francisco, Hammersmith IPA leaves me thinking about the difference between good and great IPAs. What separates them in terms of quality?

For me, all the Firestone Walker beers stand out as great because they have a clarity of flavor. By this I mean that I can taste the hops perfectly, they are neither under- nor over-hopped, they are vibrant, fresh. I can taste a richness of malt but it's still light and not overpowering or sweet. There's balance in it and drinking beers like this is just a great experience.

SAN FRANCISCO

My first priority in San Francisco is finding Anchor Liberty Ale. In 1965 Fritz Maytag took over the failing Anchor Steam Brewery and brought it back to life—it was America's first craft brewery. In 1973, Maytag traveled to England to learn about local brewing techniques, including dry-hopping and the use of top-fermenting yeast. He used these finding to release Anchor Liberty Ale in 1975, initially dry-hopping it with the Hallertau variety before re-formulating the recipe to include American Cascade hops for bitterness, flavor, and aroma. They never labeled it an as IPA at the time but I don't think there's any argument about it being called America's first craft IPA.

Liberty Ale is a deep golden color and the Cascades give it a perfumy, grapefruity aroma with some bready malt backing it up. The bitterness back then would've seemed extraordinarily high at 40IBU, whereas today it tastes clean and simple. It's a classic American craft beer and something every drinker should taste, but it's not what we think of as IPA today—the style is always changing.

From the oldest to one of the newest: across town we drink in Cellarmaker, a small bar with the brewery out the back. They always have big hoppy beers on tap, like Dank Statement—a monstrous Triple IPA that's danker than a doobie and boldly bittersweet. It's astonishing that a powerful 11% ABV beer can be so drinkable.

Faction Brewing, across the Bay in Alameda (and with an insane view back into the city), was started by Rodger Davis, previously of other hop-forward breweries Triple Rock and Drake's. Rodger brews a wide range of hoppy beers, with Pale Ale being their flagship and rotating IPAs acting as its wingmen. Faction Pale Ale is a very fine example of a beer that's foremost about the hop aroma and flavor, throwing out citrus and dank pine, then softening it with fleshy fruit in the middle, and the kind of balanced bitterness that makes these beers so easy to drink.

Bottles of Liberty Ale fly along the conveyor belt at the Anchor Brewery.

Growler fills at the excellent Faction Brewing, one of the best breweries currently operating in San Francisco.

While drinking around the city, I have many different IPAs and what stands out is the variety in them. It also seems like IPAs taste different to how they were five years ago when I first came to America. Today there's a trend towards paler, drier beers that are full-on aromatic with hops, whereas back then the beers felt bigger, heavier, and definitely more bitter.

"I think the beers are paler, the bitterness levels are lower, and hop aroma is more prominent than ever. For me, a good IPA has, first and foremost, a fantastic hop aroma," says Kim Sturdavant, brewer at Social Kitchen & Brewery. "The basis for this is the new hop varietals brewers are favoring—we love these fruity, tropical hops and they work so well in paler beers... I like to blend these with other hops that are more piney and resinous. I'm looking for flavors of mangoes, limes, pineapple, and tree sap." And that's exactly what you get in The Smell, Kim's flagship IPA where the hops combine with a simple toasty sweetness and a big bitterness that ensures you know you're drinking an IPA. "IPA is a balancing act of malt flavor, malt body, hop flavor, bitterness, and high alcohol and there are so many ways to assemble these pieces. After all these years of being a serious beer maker and drinker, it's still my favorite style."

NORTH CALIFORNIA

It might dominate taps today but in the early 1990s there were only a handful of IPAs in America. It wasn't until 1995 that the first Californian brewery made an IPA their flagship beer, and that was Lagunitas. Despite the fact that I live in London, a city thousands of miles from California, Lagunitas IPA is one of the beers I drink most frequently and that's for one simple reason: it's really good.

Today Lagunitas is one of the biggest craft breweries in America and the fastest growing, thanks to a huge on-going expansion in Chicago and I genuinely wouldn't be surprised if one day Lagunitas IPA becomes the best-selling craft beer in

Patrons at the bar at Russian River Brewing Co.

10 OF THE BEST IPAs
OUTSIDE OF CALIFORNIA

- Maine Beer Co. Lunch
- Fat Head's Head Hunter IPA
- Trillium Congress Street
- Boneyard RPM
- Surly Overrated IPA
- Half Acre Senita
- Cigar City Jai Alai IPA
- Bell's Two Hearted
- La Cumbre Elevated IPA
- Odell IPA

the world. The version I drink at the brewery is like the beer I know so well, only now it seems to be in Technicolor brilliance: there's more hop flavor, it's crazily easy-drinking and balanced, there's all this orange, floral, and pine in there, some lemons and lime, a big bitterness but not a brash one, plus some chewier caramel flavor and, at 6.2% ABV, you can have a few of them. It's a beauty.

Next stop: Bear Republic. I love their Racer 5 which to me is a perfect IPA and one attached to good memories: before an awards dinner years ago I drank a pint of this in

London, the first time it had been available there on draft, then I won an award, drank more Racer 5 in celebration, and used the prize money to fly to California to drink even more Racer 5. The beer has a great golden color, a gleaming body, and a simple citrusy aroma unlike the smack in the nostrils of other brews. There's plenty of tangerine and grapefruit pith, a peachy flavor, then the malt has some balancing sweetness. It's just endlessly drinkable. It's not the hoppiest, not the most wow-inducing, nor even the best American IPA, but I love it.

THE ULTIMATE IPA?

Right between Bear Republic and Lagunitas is arguably the epicenter of American IPAs and a pilgrimage location for beer lovers around the world: Russian River Brewing Company (RRBC), in downtown Santa Rosa.

"I was a homebrewer making mostly IPAs. The goal was to open a small brewery that had an IPA in its line-up," says Vinnie Cilurzo, owner and brewer of RRBC. In 1994, Vinnie opened Blind Pig Brewing Company in Temecula, CA, with his IPA recipe up-scaled from his homebrew. "It had a modest alcohol content but a massive amount of hops added to it," including classic IPA hops like Cascade, Chinook, and Centennial. Alongside Blind Pig IPA there was Inaugural Ale—the first commercial DIPA brewed in America. "The beer was so bitter it was like licking the rust off a tin can," he says. "We found a market for the Inaugural Ale and our Blind Pig IPA but in general it was tough to sell much beer with 92IBUs."

In 1997 Vinnie moved to brew at RRBC, which was then owned by Korbel Champagne Cellars. Vinnie and wife Natalie bought the brand from Korbel in 2003 and in April 2004 they turned RRBC into a brewpub in Santa Rosa. Then in 2008, to keep up with the ever-growing demand, they opened a production brewery a few miles from the pub. Today RRBC is best-known for two things: superlative Belgian-inspired sour beers and some of the best hoppy beers in the world, where their 8% ABV DIPA Pliny the Elder gets people most excited.

"In 1998 we were asked to make a Double IPA for a new Double IPA festival," explains Vinnie. "I took a little inspiration from the Blind Pig Inaugural Ale and Anniversary Ale I had made previously at Blind Pig. But this time I didn't make the Double IPA as bitter and I used a lot more hops in the mid-boil, end of boil, and dry hop stages." This was the beginning of Pliny the Elder.

What makes Pliny stand out is the combination of epic hop aromas—hugely pithy citrus fruit, dank pine forest, some sweet tropical fruit—on top of a surprisingly light and dry body which barely gives any malt character before the bitterness powers in, long and clinging.

"I like IPAs to be dry with only a small percentage of crystal malt used," he says. "With less crystal malt you get more of the hop aroma and flavor pushing through." This creates a lighter-bodied beer which Vinnie also achieves through adding "a small amount of sugar in the kettle to ensure the beer dries out in fermentation," just like many Belgian brewers do. The beer is then built up on the base of tangy Simcoe hops with others added—Amarillo, Centennial, CTZ—to provide fleshy fruits and sweet citrus flavors.

Pliny the Elder is a beer that regularly gets held up as the best in the world. Every year **Zymurgy**, the magazine of the American Homebrewers Association, asks its readers to list their top 20 beers and in 2009 Pliny came out as number one. It repeated the trick between 2010 and 2015 as well. For seven consecutive years, it has been considered the best beer in America by knowledgeable, considered drinkers. Few beers challenge its reign apart from another one of their own: Pliny the Younger. Brewed just once a year, this Triple IPA is an absolute hop monster that has beer geeks rising at dawn and lining up outside the brewpub to get a glass of the super-rare beer.

"The beer was so bitter it was like licking the rust off a tin can."

"We are flattered and humbled that Pliny has been very well accepted by the consumers. Everything that has happened with Pliny the Elder and Younger has been consumer driven and that is the type of beer one dreams of having," Vinnie says.

RRBC also make Blind Pig IPA, a 6.1% ABV American IPA that shares Pliny's absolute dryness and huge, pithy aroma yet has more stone fruit and tangerine sweetness. I love Pliny the Elder, but Blind Pig is also a ridiculously great beer—so clean, so full-on yet balanced in its bold hoppiness. If I lived nearby I'd always have a six-pack of this on the go.

Sometimes hype doesn't match the expectation. Not so at RRBC where they've become so influential that beers with incredibly pale, light, and dry bodies, with tons of hop aroma and flavor, have become the standard for IPAs today.

We leave Santa Rosa the next morning and drive further north to Chico and the Sierra Nevada Brewery Company where we drink more IPAs (see pages 124–131), before continuing into Oregon. We discover that IPA is everywhere there as well, only now it's different: the hops are full-on for aroma but the bitterness is more balanced, where many are left lightly unfiltered to give the impression of soft richness in the mouth and have a juicier quality. IPAs dominate Oregon (see pages 132–141) just like they do in California. And just like they do in every other state because IPA is America's beer.

The infamous West Coast C-hops—the star of the show for American IPAs.

THE CRAFT BEER STYLE

We all know pizza: dough base, tomato sauce, cheese, probably some additional toppings. All pizzas are essentially similar yet all pizzas are different. Some are thin, some thick, some are loaded with cheese, others barely get a few tears of mozzarella; some toppings are spicy, others meaty. The best pizzas are made with the best ingredients and enjoyed as fresh as possible. And every individual eating a pizza has their own preference as to what they want. IPA is like pizza—all are similar yet different. Some are sweet and caramelly, others super dry with barely any malt flavor; some are painfully bitter, others are not; some smell like citrus, others like pine forest; some are light in alcohol and others are thick and strong.

IPA is my favorite style of beer. I love the amazing hop aromas, I love how the hop flavor fills my glass, I crave the bitterness, want that alcohol buzz, and I'm always hopeful that the next one I order will blow me away by being everything I want in an IPA. It's probably because it's so prevalent, because so many breweries make IPA, that I expect greatness from each one.

IPA is **the** craft beer style. It's also the most storied beer ever brewed and it continues to write new chapters in its ever-changing history where one thing is certain: we are in love with the smell and flavor of hops.

"STRONG AND HOPPY"

From India Pale Ale to IPA, the beer style has evolved more than any other ever brewed. From its 18th-century origins to the brash American IPAs that dominate craft beer bars today, it's a 300-year story of change.

Yet the thing with history is that we tend to look at the past with a halcyon stare and a storyteller's desire for the most interesting moment, which, through re-telling, gets stuck as misunderstood folklore. That's what happened with IPA: it has become this famous beer that was supposedly brewed very strong and very hoppy so that it survived six months at sea to arrive in India and be drunk with empire-leading gusto by thirsty British dignitaries. But that's an abridged version that's been pieced together to form the most soundbite-worthy snippet. Regardless of what's fact or fiction in that story, the simple idea of it being "strong and hoppy" is ultimately what has made IPA the most popular craft beer style today.

HERE'S HOW IT HAPPENED

In the 17th century, India was a key trade route for Britain. The English merchants based there would sip a potent spirit called arak and, underestimating the liquor's wallop, many died drinking it. As traders were joined by troops, the deaths continued to rise and the average life expectancy of a European in India was just three years—while disease was a factor, arak was a destructive drink. Beer would be a better choice.

The first Pale Ales were exported to India from at least 1784 but it would be George Hodgson's Bow Brewery, opened in 1752, which would become a significant name in the history of the beer. His brewery was located near the East India Company. Given their proximity, we can assume that Hodgson met with the captains who saw the potential to sell beer and make some extra income—it wasn't the East India Company that sold the beer, it was the captains. The first of Hodgson's Pale Ale and Porter (more Porter sailed to India than any other beer; Porter was drunk by the troops, paler beers were saved for officers) was sent at least by the early 1790s.

There is a common misconception that Hodgson "invented" IPA, or a beer suited to traveling to India, but that's not true. The beers he sent to India were more likely (because we can't be certain) just his regular beers, including Stock Ales and Porter. The Stock Ales, which were high in alcohol content, generally brewed with just pale malts, and then heavily-hopped, were aged, often for a year or more, in wooden barrels—this was the early incarnation of a "Pale Ale." With that maturation time the harshness of the bitter hops reduced and the flavor rounded itself out. Porters at this time were similar in many ways: strong, heavily hopped, and matured by the brewery, but were brewed with dark malts.

So "strong and hoppy" is what we associate with IPA and there is science to back that up: the natural preservative qualities in the hops and the alcohol helped to keep the beer from staling and brewers knew this. They also knew that hoppy beers survived better in warmer climes, so it made sense to send Stock Ales and Porters. What we don't know is at what point Hodgson and others started brewing recipes specifically for the Indian market, though it was likely happening by the 1820s.

Hodgson's Bow Brewery developed a virtual monopoly on exporting beer to India, but as they began to impose more restrictive terms on the Company, and as complaints came about the beer's quality, Campbell Marjoribanks, Chairman of the East India Company, contacted Samuel Allsopp of Allsopp's Brewery in Burton-upon-Trent. In 1822, Allsopp was asked to create an equivalent beer to Bow's India Pale Ale, which they started shipping to India in

1823. We can argue that this beer was brewed to suit the tastes of the Indian market, making it the first proper Pale Ale specifically for India. This Burton beer quickly became more popular than the London brews and other Burton-based brewers—Bass and Salt—started producing their own Pale Ales for India. It was soon after this, in 1829, that the name India Pale Ale was first mentioned.

Burton's beers were "very pale, brewed from only the highest-quality and palest malt. It was heavily hopped, both in the kettle and in the form of dry hops," and around 6–7.5% ABV, writes Ron Pattinson in **The Homebrewers Guide to Vintage Beer**, where English Golding hops were a preferred variety. One other thing that Pattinson points out is that compared to the other beers of the day, the Burton beers were very dry and didn't allow for much further fermentation in the barrel. Part of the reason for this was Burton's famously hard water that was especially suited to India Pale Ales.

By the 1840s, India Pale Ale was the name used for beer brewed for Indian export. It had also become a beer brewed around Britain and drunk locally, though domestic versions would've likely had adjusted recipes with lower alcohol and hop levels; the path of India Pale Ale had evolved. And it continued to evolve domestically as the beers gradually stopped being aged and began to be served as fresh "Running Ales."

As the 19th century ended, things changed again. Scientific and industrial advances saw golden lagers appear and artificial refrigeration made it possible to brew beer in India, plus those cool golden lagers were more refreshing than rich, hoppy ales. Back in Britain it was an established style but tax changes combined with World War rationing and a general shift in lifestyle and taste combined to see alcohol levels lowering to around 4% ABV during the first half of the 20th century. Beer wasn't being shipped to India, it wasn't being stored in huge barrels for months, it wasn't strong, and it wasn't really that hoppy. India Pale Ale was a different beer to the ones Allsopp or Hodgson were brewing.

THE AMERICANS ARE COMING

And the beer remained on the verge of extinction until craft brewers discovered the story. To these brewers, India Pale Ale was a new style to work with and one with an interesting history. It also came at a time when American hop varieties were being used in beers like Sierra Nevada Pale Ale, where India Pale Ale was the next logical step. Brewers started to make these beers which were "stronger and hoppier" than Pale Ale and attach romanticized stories of sea journeys and so on, firmly wedging the IPA myths into our heads.

But these new IPAs of the 1980s were nothing like the beers of 200 years before it. They were entirely new beers designed to be drunk as fresh as possible to get the maximum bitter and aromatic impact from the citrusy, floral American hops. They took India Pale Ale and they turned it into IPA.

As more drinkers ditched mainstream lagers for well-hopped beers, brewers became more comfortable with making bolder, more bitter brews that gave a hollering high-five to the high-alpha American hops. By the late 1990s IPA was becoming an important beer in craft breweries. And then it shifted again. A one-upmanship seemed to spur on more extreme, bitter examples, before they veered to a point where balance became a key quality and so recipes changed again. The beers became less bitter and more aromatic and the malt virtually disappeared.

Today the popularity is unending and the idea of the style—"strong and hoppy"—has seen an IPA-ization of beer which has given us Double and Triple IPAs, Black, White, and Red IPAs, Belgian IPAs, Session IPAs, and others. One thing is certain: it's all about the hops and that's unlikely to change any time soon.

India Pale Ale is a beer from history, a near-mythical thing that we'll never be able to taste. It has a brilliant story but it's not what we drink today; we drink IPA, a beer inspired by history but transformed into something new that's all about freshness and impact of hop flavor and aroma. No beer style has evolved more than India Pale Ale and IPA and it's still changing today.

SIERRA NEVADA PALE ALE

Other craft beers came before it. There was Fritz Maytag re-invigorating Anchor Brewing in San Francisco, and Jack McAuliffe's New Albion in Sonoma—forever romanticized as the first American craft brewery despite the fact that, or more likely *because*, it only survived a short time. But it was Sierra Nevada, and specifically their Pale Ale, that forever changed beer in America and then the rest of the world.

By using citrusy, floral American hops in a way to get as much aroma from them as possible, Sierra Nevada had a beer that hadn't been tasted before. Sierra Nevada Pale Ale is arguably the most important beer brewed in the 20th century while Sierra Nevada Brewing Company, based in Chico, California, is arguably the most important brewery of the 20th century *and* the 21st century.

MEETING A LEGEND

Sierra Nevada brewery was founded by Ken Grossman and Paul Camusi (who Ken eventually bought out in 1998) and they brewed their first commercial batches of beer at the end of 1980. But the story, or at least the important background information, begins years earlier in the town of Woodland Hills, outside of Los Angeles.

Born in 1954, Ken was a smart, curious kid, perhaps lacking academic focus in school but excelling in his own unconventional way outside of class, whether it was taking things apart and re-building them, his aptitude for fixing bikes, or indulging his passion for homemade explosives. As well as building, bikes, and bombs, there was brewing, which combined his interest in process, technology, and science. Inspired by his neighbor Cal Moeller, an accomplished homebrewer, Ken's first brew was in the summer of 1969.

After high school, Ken biked and hiked around north California, which is what took him to Chico. He clearly liked the town because he ended up moving there, taking a job in a bike shop. While in Chico, he continued to homebrew but also enrolled in college to study algebra and chemistry. As he became more serious about brewing he opened a homebrew supply store. By having the shop he got to brew a lot, learn a lot, and also taste a lot of different beers, including those by the few small breweries of the day. It was a visit to McAuliffe at New Albion that nestled the idea of opening a brewery in his mind.

"When I came up with the idea of opening a brewery... [I] realized that the level of technology that we would be able to cobble together with homemade equipment was really closer to what was being done in Britain, probably back in the 40s or 50s," says Ken. This essentially meant ales that were bottle-conditioned.

Sierra Nevada Brewing Company has a strong case for being the most influential brewery of the last 30 years, inspiring countless brewers to start making their own beers on a commercial scale.

When Ken says "cobble together," he means it literally: he built the brewery himself in an old warehouse, sourcing tanks and equipment from wherever he could—dairy farms, soda factories, metal brokers—and welded them together, wired all the electrics, and fit the refrigeration. This frugal resourcefulness was essential due to the tight finances but it also fit perfectly with Ken's ability to build and figure out processes. With the brewery coming together, next they needed the beer.

When Ken says "cobble together," he means it literally: he built the brewery himself.

"We started to work on homebrewing recipes in 1977 or '78, with the idea of perfecting an American Pale Ale. We didn't want to copy what the British were doing; we wanted to use American ingredients and do it with an American spin, so started to focus on American aroma hops."

On visits to hop farms in the Yakima Valley, Ken convinced a cooperative of hop growers to sell him one-pound hop samples known as "brewers' cuts"—these would be used by big brewers to assess the quality of bales before they bought them. These cuts were perfect to sell in his shop. Among the varieties was a hop called Cascade, which Ken picked out as being distinctively different to any other hop and something that "we could build our flavor on." And it was a decision that forever changed the flavor profile of beer.

Sierra Nevada's decision to experiment with Cascade hops was one of the most important innovations in craft brewing.

SEARCHING FOR CONSISTENCY

To begin with, Ken homebrewed 5-gallon (20-liter) batches of English-inspired and American-grown Pale Ale, trying to perfect the recipe using different ale yeast strains, different amounts of caramel malts and crystal malts, plus different water treatments. "We finally came up with what we thought was a really unique and interesting floral-focused Pale Ale."

With a brewery now in place and the recipes ready to go, Sierra Nevada started commercially brewing in November 1980. The first batch of beer was their Stout and then came the Pale Ale.

"We had already done dozens of homebrew batches [of Pale Ale], but once we did our first 10-barrel batch it took a number of months [to perfect]," Ken says.

"I remember the third Pale Ale, 'Pale Ale 3,' was pretty darn good and we thought 'This is it,' and we started sharing it with friends. The fourth batch was a little different and didn't ferment quite the same. The fifth batch was a little different again and then we were back to the drawing board, working out what we did wrong or what we needed to do to get the consistency back in our brewing."

> This dedication to quality has been in the brewery from day one.

The problem, it turned out, was understanding how their yeast behaved when scaling up from 5-gallon (20-liter) batches to 300-gallon (1,100-liter) batches, and then how to keep it happy generation after generation. It took three months and 12 brews before they finally figured it out.

"It was hugely frustrating," says Ken. "We were out of money and had been struggling for months, borrowing from family and friends to put the finishing touches on the brewery. We wanted to go to market so bad but we knew that if we couldn't make 'Pale Ale 4' match 'Pale Ale 3,' and 'Pale Ale 5' match 'Pale Ale 4' then we had a problem." Despite the initial frustration, this dedication to quality is something that has been in the brewery from day one and it's a major reason for their longevity and success.

With the recipe nailed and the brewery finally making beer, the next obstacle was selling it. "Our Pale Ale was probably at the time a bit extreme—we were 37 IBUs and bottle-conditioned and very aromatic. It did either get people to love us or hate us," he says. "I remember taking the beer [to tastings] and most people were like 'Woah, that's bitter'... but a few people were like 'that's fantastic.'"

On a hand-built brewery, making a recipe inspired by British beers and given an American influence through local ingredients, Ken Grossman essentially introduced the aroma and flavor of hops to the world and he gave birth to the American Pale Ale. In 1980 it was brave and innovative to make a 5.6% ABV amber-colored ale with a heady aroma of citrus and a powerful bitterness; today it's just how beer tastes. Now, four decades later, Sierra Nevada is one of the largest craft breweries in the world and their Pale Ale is one of the best-known beers in the world and the archetype of the style.

CASCADE HOPS

In 1956, as he did every year, Oregon-based hop breeder Stan Brooks crossed a few different hops and left them to grow. Come harvest time at the end of summer he evaluated each of these new crossbreeds by rubbing them in his hands and taking a good sniff. One in particular showed promise and so he progressed it along his breeding program. The hop, known as 56013, became commercially available in 1968, but received little attention from the large brewers who favored other already-established varieties, especially those from Germany.

Hop growers saw a future in this variety so continued to grow it despite the lack of interest from the big breweries. And then, in the early 1970s, by which point 56013 had been renamed after the Cascade Mountains of the Pacific Northwest, some of the most popular German hops were diseased by Verticillium Wilt, driving up prices. This forced American brewers to work with different varieties, including Cascade, though the big brewers used it because they had to, not because they prized it for its unique flavor.

But it wasn't the big breweries who would best utilize this hop, it was places like Sierra Nevada and Anchor who used Cascade in a way that really brought out all of those amazing aromas, showing American drinkers just how different beer could taste.

Today, floral, citrus, and pine aromas are so prevalent in beers that we almost expect them to be there but in the late 1970s this simply wasn't how beer tasted. The flavor profile of world beer shifted irrevocably when craft brewers used Cascade hops. And from there many more varieties have been developed to give similar bold characteristics.

AN OLFACTORY DELIGHT

My dad and I are booked onto one of the regular brewery tours at Sierra Nevada, which will walk us through the brewery following the order of the ingredients and the brewing process. After seeing the malt mill, we're led to the hop store. It was Sierra Nevada's use of American hops that changed beer so dramatically and I've heard that this is one of the largest hop stores in all craft breweries, so I'm excited to see it for myself, but nothing can prepare me for the reality.

It's freezing cold and the first breath is a shock to my lungs. The second breath is a shock to my senses as the most incredible smell of citrus encompasses us. The heady, hoppy aroma is incomparably fresh and fruity, it's like all of the IPAs I've ever drunk, blended with a hop farm during harvest, somehow vaporized into one super-condensed aromatic explosion. I've never smelt anything like this. And I've never seen anything like it, either.

An employee stands in the barrel room, where some of Sierra Nevada's special releases are aged.

Where most breweries use hop pellets, Sierra Nevada use the hop flowers—they are the largest user of hop flowers in the world. These come in huge rectangular bales, all bundled tightly together and stacked like massive green bricks. Before the hops are used, the bales are broken apart and raked. This separates the flowers back into their individual state, their crisp green leaves fluttering all around and their sticky, oily aroma making the air thick. If you could somehow use this aroma in the brewhouse then it would be the best-smelling beer in the world.

From the icy hop store we walk to the brewhouse and, shivering off the cold, we're now warmed by the humid air that's sweet with the smell of cookies and tea—this brewery is an olfactory delight.

Here in the brewhouse are two great copper tanks, squat and round and with pipes running all the way to the roof. Next to them are huge deep-green drums of hop flowers. On the walls all around are murals depicting brewing from field to glass. Our cheery tour guide explains that the people in the drawings are employees—she points out that Ken, who is shown adding the hops to the kettle, is painted considerably more muscular than the other men.

Next come the cellars where the pointed bases of huge silver tanks hang like upside-down pyramids and the sweetly fruity aroma of fermentation fills the air. After this we cross a bridge toward packaging and get a view over the whole, vast site, including rooftops covered in solar panels. Seventy to eighty percent of the brewery's power is self-generated, again highlighting Ken's dedication to doing things properly. It's astonishing to think that in 35 years a tiny brewery, cobbled together and built from old dairy equipment, could grow into a place where they can fill almost a million bottles a day.

The bottling room. Here the Chico brewery is capable of producing nearly one million bottles of beer a day. This makes it one of the largest beer producers in the United States.

TIME TO TASTE

The tour ends in the tasting room with seven or eight beers passed around in small glasses with nice explanations given about all of them. From there everyone moves into the Taproom—a large pub where stained-glass mirrors give an attractive burst of color above the busy bar. Here I can now finally have what I've dreamt about for a long time: a pint of Sierra Nevada Pale Ale fresh from the brewery.

I've never smelt anything like this. I've never seen anything like it, either.

They have two versions of Pale Ale here: Draught-Style at 5% ABV is the beer that's on tap all around the world; and there's a bottle-strength version at 5.6% ABV, which is only available on tap in the Taproom.

A beautiful-looking pint of Draught-Style Pale Ale is placed in front of me. It's a copper-golden color, a rich-looking brew with a thick foam on top. I lift the glass and have an immediate flashback to the hop freezer from earlier. Zingy, floral, grapefruity, grassy, and ridiculously fresh, it's an ode to Cascade hops. I've never smelt a beer like this before, a beer as evocative as pretty perfume and fruit fields during harvest. I'm inhaling deeply to capture that aroma and keep it in my lungs for as long as possible.

I take a mouthful. The malt depth gives a little toastiness, there's a distinctive subtle caramel, all balanced against the fruity-floral flavor of those hops, which grip hold of the grain and run right through the brew and into a dry, quenching bitterness, which immediately makes you want more. The freshness really makes it stand out and gives it a lightness, a waltzing kind of elegance, which is so good.

The 5.6% ABV Pale Ale comes the same deep golden color only it's a little hazier. There's floral, citrus pith, and pine. The yeast haze clutches onto more hop flavor, giving it a greater depth and body than the Draught-Style, making the malt more prominent with a little sweetness of caramel. It's more complex though less aromatic than the other, but it's the Draught-Style that gets me most excited.

"That's the best beer I've ever had," says dad.

Sierra Nevada Pale Ale has inspired so many brewers around the world. Pale Ales are made by almost every brewery today and each of those beers, in some way, can be traced back to this: the template of a classic Pale Ale, unchanged since 1981. The Pale Ale style, however, has shifted in that time, constantly evolving thanks to different influences and trends. Currently, Pale Ale is very pale, has very little malt character, huge hop aroma, and a dry, bold-yet-balanced bitterness. Sierra Nevada's is rich with malt and the hops are perfumy rather than punchy. All beer styles change but there can only be one original.

After the Pale Ales, dad and I start working through the other beers on tap, starting with the other two beers which Sierra Nevada have made since they opened: the Stout is clean and roasty with a dark chocolate depth, while the Porter is a little sweeter and more balanced—they are both, in their own rights, classic American examples of the styles. Nooner Pilsner is pithy and refreshing; Ruthless Rye is spicy with grain and zesty with hops; the latest Bigfoot Barley Wine is like bitter grapefruit-laced caramel; there's a Tripel and a Quad in the Ovila series, both reverential to the Belgian classics; a gorgeous malty Brown Ale; a Black IPA with its dusting of dark cocoa behind a wallop of hops; Torpedo IPA, another favorite of mine, is so fresh and aromatic, bursting with citrus, tutti-frutti and piney aromas; and then there's Celebration, a beer first brewed in 1981 and made with the fresh hops from that year's harvest—it was one of the first American IPAs and it's still a seasonal beer release which many look forward to each year.

There's one other beer I taste and it's so good I order a pint. Hop Hunter IPA was released just a few days before this visit in January 2015. Exemplifying Sierra Nevada's continuous, industry-leading innovation, this is a beer brewed with the distilled oil of green hops to enable them to brew a green-hopped beer throughout the year instead of just during the hop harvest.

You see, when hops are harvested they are dried as quickly as possible to preserve them, but the drying process knocks out many of the volatile aromatic oils. By distilling them while they're still wet or green, Sierra Nevada capture those fresh, elusive aromas and can use them whenever they wish.

Hop Hunter IPA smells like your hands after you've been rubbing fresh hops between your fingers. It's dank, grassy, and floral, with subtle citrus in the background, an indefinable spiciness, and a herbal freshness like cucumber and melon smashed with mint. And that's all captured in this glass of bright gold beer, which is super dry in the body like modern IPAs (and so very different to the chewier, richer body of the Pale Ale). It's bitter in the best of ways, making me immediately want another mouthful, and it's so fresh and evocative of the hop harvest.

"That's the best beer I've ever had," says dad. It really is very good.

When you arrive at the brewery, the first thing that catches your eye is the sunlight reflecting off these beautiful copper tanks that stand by the window of the brewhouse.

THANKS KEN

When Ken Grossman first brewed a heavily hopped Pale Ale it showed Americans, albeit on a very small scale to begin with, just how different beer could be from mass-produced lagers with no hop flavor. As his beer spread it became the flagship craft beer style, inspiring so many drinkers and brewers and changing the way beer tasted—who can say what the world of beer would look like today if it wasn't for Sierra Nevada Pale Ale? The brewery has always been at the forefront of craft beer and the levels of quality and consistency in their beers are industry-leading. They are a brave brewery, always trying to make the best beer in the best way, whether that's having great working environments or their dedication to being as self-resourceful as possible.

Ken, the father of craft beer, is still involved in everything day-to-day. He still buys the malts and selects the hops and he's still very into the processes and science of brewing. He's still building—he recently designed a second brewery in North Carolina—still fixing things, and still making others take notice of how the original craft brewery is still the most important craft brewery.

That pint of Draught-Style Pale Ale in the Taproom, after talking with Ken and touring the brewery, is one of the best beers I've ever had. Add to that its historic importance and continued relevance and Sierra Nevada's Pale Ale is unquestionably one of the best beers in the world.

PORTLAND

IN A STATE OF BEERVANA

Beer flows through Portland, Oregon. There are over 50 breweries for the 610,000 residents. Names we know from beer's vocabulary are literal things surrounding the city—the Cascade mountains, the Willamette River, the stunning snow-capped peak of Mount Hood. Half of the beer drunk in Portland is made by craft brewers, compared to the US average of 11%. Every kind of beer you can think of is made in Portland and you can find it wherever you look. *This is Beervana*.

Oregon is an enchanting, inviting state with tall mountain ranges and deep valleys, a craggy coastline, lush forests, and snowy peaks, plus enough drizzle to build a thriving indoor drinking culture. It's a state that's famously kooky, protectively so, preserving an edge of cool weirdness, of free-spiritedness, and a pride in all things local, which helps to account for that fact that 50% of all draft beer brewed in state, is drunk in state.

As for the beer itself, Oregon brewers have natural advantages: soft, pure water from snowmelt and clean rainfall; they're close to the main barley growing areas; the two top hop-growing regions of Yakima Valley, Washington, and the state's own Willamette Valley are nearby; while Wyeast, one of the world's foremost fermentation specialists, opened in Oregon in 1986. Beer just makes sense in Oregon and Portland in particular has been leading the way since the earliest days of American craft brewing.

IN THE BEGINNING

It was 1984 when it all began, with BridgePort, Widmer Brothers, Portland Brewing, and McMenamin Brothers all starting in Portland. Between them they managed to change legislature in 1985 to legalize brewpubs—they all celebrated their 30th brewing birthdays in 2014. Outside of the city there was Full Sail in Hood River, Deschutes in Bend, and Rogue in Ashland (now Newport), opening between 1986 and 1988, also all still around today. And that was just the beginning: in 2013, 30 new breweries opened in Oregon, helping the state total to pass 200, making it the fourth most-breweried state in America. Currently, it's the number one state in terms of breweries per capita (though they play leapfrog with Vermont on that statistic) and it's also top of the list in terms of the economic impact which beer has on the state.

In 2013, 30 new breweries opened in Oregon, helping the state total to pass 200, making it the fourth most-breweried state in America.

When Rob and Kurt Widmer started brewing in 1984 there were only 40-something brewing companies in the United States. Today **Widmer Brothers Brewing** (929 N Russell St; www.widmerbrothers.com) is one of the oldest of America's 3,500 craft breweries and by far the largest in Portland.

Rob Widmer, a charismatic, energetic man explains how, having German heritage in Dusseldorf, they "traveled to the city and really enjoyed the beer in Zum Uerige." They talked to the brewers who gave them a sample of their yeast, "So we decided our first beer would be an Altbier made with American ingredients."

At that time, this was not your typical kind of beer brewed in the US: it was brown, bitter, astringent; a hoppy ale unlike the light lagers. And it didn't do as well as they'd hoped. That's where Widmer Brothers Hefeweizen came from. Like the Altbier, it was inspired by a German style then given an American twist, this time using the same yeast as their Altbier instead of the classic German Hefewiezen strain (which characteristically gives banana and clove aromas), therefore creating its own, new beer style: American Wheat Beer.

"We've been called audacious for naming this a Hefeweizen," says Rob, "But in 1986 this wasn't audacity, this was practicality," meaning it was simply easier for them to manage one yeast strain instead of two. It's now their best-selling beer, sitting alongside their wide range of other beers that are all available at their smart taproom.

As a brewer who has essentially spanned the history of American craft brewing, while having their home in one prominent beer city, Rob tells me what's changed in that time. "In some ways beer hasn't changed at all," he says, with drinkers always having been receptive to trying experimental new beers in Portland. "It's just the sheer variety that's available now which is different."

And variety is exactly why I'm here in Portland, where my intention is to drink in as many breweries as possible.

ONE DAY, 10 BREWERIES

My dad has joined me on a road-trip up through California and into Oregon. We're staying on Burnside Street, which is the line that divides the city between north and south, with the Willamette River splitting it west and east, with roads beginning with their compass point locations (like SE or NW). I've plotted a brewery map and we can visit 10 breweries, or places linked to breweries, within just over a square-mile range of our hotel in the south-east of the city. And so there we have our challenge for day one.

As you cross over the Burnside Bridge, this sign welcomes you to Beervana.

In **Burnside Brewing** (701 E Burnside St; www.burnsidebrewco.com) the carnitas tacos are excellent with their Stout; both food and beer are very good in this open, bright brewpub and that sets us on our way as we head south to stop two, **Hair of the Dog** (61 SE Yamhill St; www.hairofthedog.com), a brewery with a reputation that's far bigger than their modest annual output. They've been around since 1993 and specialize in strong ales that are mostly bottle-conditioned. On tap there's an American Barleywine, a bourbon-barrel Quad, a strong English Mild, plus Adam, the beer you shouldn't miss: 10% ABV, full of body and endless depth: chocolate, leather, smoke, and burnt berries—it's dry, bitter, and extraordinary. Not many beers, or breweries, are like this and it's a must-visit place.

Sampling a few of the great beers made by Hair of the Dog.

Walking east, we get to **Cascade Brewing Barrel House** (939 SE Belmont St; www.cascadebrewingbarrelhouse.com)—they brew elsewhere but have around 18 of their barrel-aged sour beers on tap. Cascade coined the name "NW Style Sour" to differentiate their brews from other sours, where they have a whole range of different styles aging in different wooden barrels, many containing local fruits like blueberries, apricots, and strawberries. We have eight small glasses of beer which arrive like a rainbow in front of us. They are all brilliant—balanced, tart, fruity, aromatic, interesting—and if I wasn't on this 10-brewery quest then I'd be settling in for a long stay.

A block away is **Buckman Botanical Brewery** at the Green Dragon (909 SE Yamhill St; www.buckmanbrewery.com), a dive bar run by Rogue. Buckman are notable for their atypical approach of substituting hops with unusual ingredients, like their Apple Beer, which is a strange collusion of a Pale Ale, cider, and a Belgian Blonde.

A few blocks further south and we're in **Lucky Labrador's** brewpub (915 SE Hawthorne Blvd; www.luckylab.com), a family- and dog-friendly spot, where the Hawthorne Best Bitter is a superb rendition of the classic English style.

Stop number six is **Baerlic** (2235 SE 11th Ave; www.baerlicbrewing.com), the most recently opened of the breweries we're visiting, only pouring from the end of 2014. In their smart taproom we drink Primeval, a NW Brown, that is rich with dark malt and resinous with American hops, plus Noble, their lush and roasty Oatmeal Stout.

A couple of blocks away (everything is so wonderfully close together!) is **Commons** (1810 SE 10th Ave; www.commonsbrewery.com), a brewery focusing on Belgian styles. Urban Farmhouse Ale is their top brew, an

With its proclivity for alternative ways of doing things and its position close to one of the most prolific hop-growing regions on the planet, it's no surprise that the craft brewing movement exploded in the city of Portland.

orangey, earthy, spicy Saison, which we drink sitting right in the middle of the small brewhouse.

The most unique spot we visit is **Ground Breaker** (2030 SE 7th Ave; www.groundbreakerbrewing.com), America's first gluten-free brewpub, where they use things like buckwheat, lentils, and roast chestnuts instead of barley malt. Their IPA is bang-on with its citrusy aroma and clean malt body, though some of the other brews are less successful and strangely astringent. The food, however, is excellent.

50% of all draft beer brewed in state, is drunk in state.

Heading back north and powering into our ninth venue, we arrive at **Base Camp** (930 SE Oak St; www.basecampbrewingco.com), a brewery that focuses on lagers. In-Tents is a very nice India Pale Lager aged on oak. Their other beers include a hoppy black lager, a floral Helles, and a zesty rye Pilsner, all uniquely American in a good way and nothing like any bottom-fermented beers you'd find in Bavaria.

Foreseeing my drunken future, I deliberately left **Fire on the Mountain** (multiple locations; www.portlandwings.com) until the end. This place started out as a chicken-wing joint and as they expanded they built a new site with a brewery. Wonderin' Rye is pale gold, hazy, with the rye adding a sweet spiciness and a cracker-like savoriness that's a genuinely perfect match with wings as the beer's malty depth wraps around the hot sauce and cools it down wonderfully.

Stumbling home with sticky chicken fingers, I fall into bed a happy man because we did it: we drank in 10 breweries or brewery-linked venues in one day. And tomorrow we're doing it all over again.

RE-RUN THE FUN

Hopworks Urban Brewery (2944 SE Powell Blvd; www.hopworksbeer.com), or HUB as it's more commonly known, is a large brewpub with a bike theme. More people cycle in Portland than any other in the US and it is exceedingly bike friendly. Their main beer is a classic American IPA: citrusy, piney, and super with a stomach-lining sandwich.

Upright Brewing (240 N Broadway #2; www.uprightbrewing.com) is located a few blocks from the Willamette River in the north-east. "We were inspired by Belgian and French beers," says Alex Ganum, owner of the brewery. "When we started brewing Saisons there was almost no one else making them here," he tells us as we drink in the brewery's tasting room. As well as Saisons, Alex makes a number of barrel-aged beers using fruit from local growers, plus the wonderfully bitter Engelberg Pilsener.

McMenamins (www.mcmenamins.com) is one of the original Portland brewers and from one brewpub they've grown to a chain of 24, plus an estate of pubs, reaching into Washington State. What marks them out is the way in which they've turned interesting old venues into brewpubs—a ballroom, a church, a school, a railway depot—where a core range of brews are joined by local specials. Hillsdale Brewery (1505 SW Sunset Blvd) is the historic first in state, while downtown the Crystal Ballroom (1332 W Burnside St) is a fun bar with live music and pool tables. You can even sleep off the hangover at the Crystal Hotel just across the street.

Fat Head's (131 NW 13th Ave; www.fatheadsportland.com) is an Ohio-based brewery that expanded into Portland, building a large brewpub with one of the biggest beer selections in town. Head Hunter is their superlatively good IPA that's glowing extra gold in the reflection of all the medals it has won. And if you like sandwiches which are fatter than your head then this place will also leave you smiling like the jolly fella on the brewery's tap handles.

One of the busiest brewpubs in town is **Deschutes** (210 NW 11th Ave; www.deschutesbrewery.com), a third site beyond their Bend-based brewpub and production brewery. Their biggest-seller, Black Butte Porter, is my favorite of their brews and a malty sidestep from all the hops in town, though you should also order a Fresh Squeezed IPA because it's superb.

Over in Old Town is **Pints** (412 NW 5th Ave; www.pintsbrewing.com), a brewpub and coffee house with an industrial feel. Their Steel Bridge Stout is roasty, smooth, and rich, while the Seismic IPA is ground-shakingly good.

Ecliptic Brewing (825 N Cook St; www.eclipticbrewing.com) is run by Portland beer legend John Harris, who previously worked at McMenamins, Deschutes, and Full Sail before starting his own place, where his ever-rotating range of modern American brews are named after stars.

McMenamin's Crystal Hotel, which is on the National Register of Historic Places.

Ex Novo Brewing (2326 N Flint Ave; www.exnovobrew.com) is a "non-profit" place which donates all net profits toward organizations working to affect positive social change, which is surely good enough reason to stay for a second, though so is the cool wooden bar and decent food.

At **Breakside Brewery's** (820 NE Dekum St; www.breakside.com) busy brewpub I enjoy a cracking combination of their IPA, which won a gold medal at the 2014 Great American Beer Festival, with a great ahi tuna sandwich. Both are so good and it gives me a chance to pause and think about the time I've so far spent in Portland and the places I've visited, where I've already drunk so much great beer. I dream about having somewhere like Breakside near my house, or being able to walk a few blocks to Hair of the Dog or Upright or Fat Head's. And then it strikes me that these are just your typical neighborhood brewpubs in Portland. The name Beervana is beginning to make sense to me now.

The excellent IPA in Breakside also makes me think, and while I've seen every imaginable beer style, IPAs are everywhere. In fact, one-in-four beers drunk in Portland is an IPA.

"In Portland, they don't give you your brewing license unless you make an IPA," says Van Havig of **Gigantic Brewing Co** (5224 SE 26th Ave; www.giganticbrewing.com). He says this so completely deadpan that it takes a moment for me to register the joke. "This is Portland. If you're going to have one flagship beer then what the hell else is it going to be?"

Gigantic started making beer in April 2012. Their first brew was Gigantic IPA—one of the best examples I've had in a while—and for a long time it was their only year-round beer until they added Ginormous, a Double IPA.

"Why do people in Cologne drink Kölsch? Why do people in Munich drink Helles?" he says. "IPA is what beer is in this town. US hops have such a different, bright, punchy flavor that it made a big impression on people. We're American, we like big things and IPA just fits that."

"In Portland, they don't give you your brewing license unless you make an IPA"

We walk from the brewery and into the bar—a cozy space where all around people are relaxed and sharing beers, sharing stories. It might just be a little bar attached to the brewery but it has the atmosphere of a pub and that's rare. And this is a consistent thing I've felt in Portland. Sure, most of these places look like bars, but they feel like pubs, in the way a pub is welcoming like a second living room. Beer, breweries, and pubs are a fabric of life in Portland.

BEYOND THE BREWERIES

As for places to visit beyond the breweries, there are lots of these, too: **Horse Brass Pub** (4534 SE Belmont St; www.horsebrass.com) is the closest you'll come to an English pub on this side of the Atlantic; **Bailey's Taproom** (213 SW Broadway; www.baileystaproom.com) is modern and cool with a superb beer list; **Saraveza** (1004 N Killingsworth St; www.saraveza.com) has a small but perfectly picked tap list. Then there's **Belmont Station** (4500 SE Stark St; www.belmont-station.com) where you can find over 1,000 different bottles. Or find a **Fred Meyer** (multiple locations; www.fredmeyer.com) grocery store and you'll see long aisles dedicated to local brews and maybe a growler station with 20 beers on tap. In fact, growlers seem to be a fairly standard accessory for a Portlander, as essential as an umbrella, and ready to be filled at any time. There are dedicated growler bars, including perhaps my favorite name of any venue featured in this book: the **Big Legrowlski** (812 NW Couch St; www.biglegrowlski.com). And in a city famous for food trucks, you can also find beer trucks set up around the pods of four-wheeled cooks.

AFTER DARK

Now, if you're my mum and you're reading this, then know that nothing else happened after this apart from dad and I having a pint in a nice little bar where we discussed our favorite beers. We had a terrific time, enjoyed lots of good beers (but definitely didn't ever drink too much), and ate some lovely food. Weatherwise, it rained a bit and was foggy but it was also quite mild and sunny on one day, which was nice. Thanks for reading this far. You should ask dad about the Voodoo Doughnuts we had after the chicken wings on the first night. Oh, and ask about the brunch we had on the last day (yes, they eat bacon with their pancakes here!).

If you're anyone other than my mum, then it's important for me to tell you that in Portland you can also find great craft beer in places other than breweries or bars or pubs or growler stations or liquor stores or grocery stores. And that includes strip clubs.

Portland has more strip clubs per capita than any other city in the US. There's a karaoke strip club, a vegan strip club, and a steakhouse strip club that specializes in steak and has over 60 beers on tap. And there's **Mary's Club** (129 SW Broadway; www.marysclub.com). The oldest still-operating strip club in the city, it's a dark and small spot that's great for a late-night beer. It's a strip club so you can guess what's happening on that stage, but with an even mix of guys and girls sliding their dollar bills to the dancers, it's a fun, friendly place to enjoy a beer. If you're interested then pints are $5 and Eugene-based Ninkasi's Total Domination IPA is bloody nice, or have Topless Blonde, a house beer brewed for them by Cascade.

Portland really is one of the greatest cities to drink in. I now get why they call it Beervana.

The bike-themed bar at Hopworks Urban Brewery.

BEERVANA

"I think that if you're a beer lover then this is the best place to be in the world," says Rob Widmer, the man who has been brewing and drinking in Portland for over 30 years. "You're always close to a brewery, you can find world-class examples of every type of beer, it's compact and easy to get around, and there's a good quality of life; you're an hour from the beach or an hour from the mountains." He points outside at the heavy, gray skies for which the city is also famous. "The downside is you have days like today where it's raining, but that helps our pub culture."

In town you can drink almost any type of beer imaginable and because of the prevalence of beer and the brilliant atmosphere, it really is one of the greatest cities to drink in; one where the overall quality is astonishingly high. I now get why they call Portland Beervana.

You can even buy craft beers at one of the many food-truck locations dotted all over the city.

CITY GUIDE

PORTLAND

Beards and bikes, food carts and fresh-ground coffee, sunshine and showers, hipsters and hops. Portland is a quirky, fun, and welcoming city in the North West of America where, thanks to having over 50 breweries and countless bars, it's taken the name Beervana.

Sacaveza
Breakside Brewery
Ex-Novo Brewing Co
Upright Brewing
5
84
E SANDY BLVD
HAIR OF THE DOG
ADAM
Burnside Brewing Co
Fire on the Mountain
E BURNSIDE ST
Belmont Station
Base Camp
Cascade Brewing Barrel House
SE BELMONT ST
Hair of the Dog
Buckman Botanical Brewery
Horse Brass Pub
SE HAWTHORNE BLVD
Lucky Labrador
Commons
Portland, Oregon.
Baerlic
SE DIVISION
Ground Breaker
Hopworks Urban Brewery
26
GIGANTIC
Gigantic Brewing Co.

IS VERMONT HOP HEAVEN?

It's only a small state but beer is huge in Vermont. Drawing drinkers in from far away with the promise of stunning sights and perfect pints, there are two names lighting the way for incoming beer tourists: The Alchemist and Hill Farmstead.

HEADY HEIGHTS

John Kimmich only makes one beer but when it's as good as Heady Topper, his Double IPA, one is all you need. "I remember one day a guy was sitting at the pub and he'd flown in from Florida because he'd seen a tweet that said [Heady Topper] was on tap," says John. "And he sat all day and drank a dozen of them. That was one of the first times when it was like, this is crazy."

On November 29, 2003 John and Jen Kimmich opened The Alchemist Pub and Brewery in Waterbury. John had been in the industry for years and had saved up to open his own place. In January 2004, the first batch of Heady Topper was tapped. "I was amazed at peoples' reception of it; people who said they didn't like hoppy beers said "I like this beer!" He kept brewing it simply because he liked to drink it "And then it just slowly created this groundswell of people wanting to try it and then trying it and loving it."

Things were going well so they decided to build a new brewery, adding a canning line to package their beer. And then one night in the summer of 2011 things changed dramatically when Hurricane Irene blasted through and destroyed the pub. It gave John and Jen a chance to reflect on what was right for The Alchemist and they decided that they would simply focus on perfecting one thing—brewing Heady Topper and putting it in cans. Judging by the reactions of drinkers he achieved his goal because on BeerAdvocate.com, Heady Topper is the world's highest-rated beer.

"I put way more in [ratings websites] than those," says John, pointing to competition medals on the wall in the brewery office. "If you are getting this random sampling of people that are collectively considering this to be delicious it means way more than 10 dudes sitting at a table swirling, sniffing, talking, tearing it apart." From over 10,000 ratings, Heady Topper averages 4.73 out of 5 (as of July 2015).

As we walk around the brewery, John grabs two empty cans from a pallet. He takes them to a conditioning tank and pours beer into each, handing one to me. When he takes a mouthful his eyes light up and he smiles. When I take a mouthful I immediately laugh. "It's like juice!" I say—it's astonishingly fruity. The hop flavor is so deep within this beer, while the body is full, yet not sweet or malty, and the bitterness has this wonderful savory quality that makes me crave more of the citrusy hops. Rarely does a beer get me as excited as this one. I can see why it's so highly rated.

Stunning beers in a stunning location make a visit to Hill Farmstead an essential addition to any beer fan's bucket list.

WORTH THE TRIP

RateBeer.com lists over 19,000 breweries on their site and in 2013 and 2014 Hill Farmstead was rated the number one brewery in the world. On the same website, Hill Farmstead brewed seven of the 100 best-rated beers in the world for 2014. It's mecca for beer geeks.

Shaun Hill turned the Farmstead, which has been in his family for over 220 years, into a brewery. Getting there is part of the fun because it's miles away from anything. It's impossible to convey just how remote it is. You just have to trust your satnav and keep on going, winding through tiny country lanes, hoping that at some point a brewery will appear through the trees.

When you finally arrive you'll first be astounded by the number of cars there, then you'll spot the long lines of people waiting to snag the latest bottle releases. Where did they all come from? As you join the lines you'll hopefully get a chance to notice the beauty of the location as it looks out from atop a hill over the surrounding green countryside. It's in a great spot.

The excitement of arriving—of simply finding it—is made better when you get a beer because they really are superb. The Pale Ales and IPAs share huge fruity aromas and the bodies keep a remarkable lightness; the dark beers have a deep, wonderful richness, with a magic balance; the Saisons have an elemental mystique about them, something vibrant, alive, elusive. There is something special about Hill Farmstead beers. Sure, their rarity adds to that, as does the location, but the brews are genuinely great. However, once you've got to the front of the line and got your beers (you're limited to four samples and a couple of growlers), there's nothing else to do there, so head to Waterbury.

BEYOND THE BIG TWO

Waterbury is home to Ben & Jerry's ice cream. If that's not enough for you then this town of 5,000 people also has a lot of good beer. Prohibition Pig is a brewpub serving BBQ food plus some of the best Vermont brews, including Lawson's Finest Liquids (drink anything from them—it's all good), Fiddlehead who make excellent IPA, and Lost Nation who brew a great Gose. Also in town is Blackback Pub with over 20 taps, The Reservoir has 38 taps, and Arvads has 10 taps. Book a B&B—you'll want to stay.

Also go to Burlington. Begin at Vermont Pub & Brewery with some cask ales and British-style pub food. VPB—everyone just calls it VPB—is where craft beer started in this state thanks to local legend Greg Noonan, who wrote books on brewing and also changed legislature to legalize brewpubs in Vermont. Elsewhere in town, The Farmhouse Tap and Grill has 24 taps of mostly local beer plus superb food, again sourced locally (there's a genuine love of local produce in Vermont and more so than anywhere else I've visited they support their state's products). Nearby is American Flatbread, home to Zero Degrees beers, where you can get the house beers with fantastic flatbread. Walk south for a few kilometers and you can visit Queen City, Switchback, and Citizen Cider (who use beer yeast and hops in some of their excellent ciders).

If Portland, Oregon, is known as Beervana, then could Vermont be Hop Heaven?

THE VERMONT IPA?

Drink Pale Ales, IPAs, and Double IPAs from The Alchemist, Hill Farmstead, Fiddlehead, Lawson's Finest Liquids, and others, and you'll find beers that are luminous orange-gold in color and hazy from being unfiltered, which gives a fullness to the body. They are bursting with sweet citrus, tropical fruit, and tangy floral hops, with less of the danker, piney aromas of the West Coast. The malt seems to be there simply to hold onto the hops and they finish with a balanced, dry bitterness. With the standout combination of being unfiltered and hugely aromatic with juicy-fruity hops, has Vermont developed its own kind of IPA?

THE REGIONAL IPAS OF THE UNITED STATES OF AMERICA

It might be America's—and craft beer's—flagship style, but drink around and you will likely taste regional variation, meaning what we think of as an IPA can vary, depending on where we are geographically. Here's a loose-fitting categorization of IPA. It's important to bear in mind that wherever a brewer is based they can be inspired to make any kind of IPA they most enjoy. Consider these a discussion point.

The Original American IPA (mid-1990s-onward)
Try: Lagunitas IPA, Bear Republic Racer 5
Toffee-like malt in the background with a burst of floral, grapefruity hops in the aroma and the flavor. The moderately high bitterness is balanced against the malt sweetness, though still punches hard. These are the early defining American IPAs and still stand up today.

The West Coast IPA: The Early Years (2000-onward)
Try: Green Flash Palate Wrecker, Stone IPA
The hugest of hop hits, resinous, pithy, citrusy, with a very high bitterness, often completely unbalanced. The use of caramel and crystal malts bulks out the body but you probably won't notice more than the brutal hops.

The West Coast IPA: The Less-Bitter Middle Years (circa 2007-onward)
Try: Ballast Point Sculpin IPA, Firestone Walker Union Jack IPA
The huge hop aroma remains, it still gives all the qualities you expect, with lots of dank pine and citrus pith, only now there's some balance in the beers, even at the extreme top end—less bitterness, less malt, but still some toasty sweetness.

The West Coast IPA: The Next Years (circa 2010-onward)
Try: Stone Enjoy By IPA, Societe The Pupil
Seemingly the hops have shifted from being the bittering addition and have instead been added as late or dry-hops. Bodies have slimmed, bitterness reduced, aromas use more recent hop varieties than the classic C-hops (Mosaic, Citra, etc), but flavors are still big and bold.

The East Coast IPA
Try: Dogfish Head 60 Minute IPA, Brooklyn East India IPA
An early form of the style, but still around today. These are maltier than the West, some caramel and toasty depth, less of the harsher crystal malts), more floral and grapefruity instead of resinous and juicy (maybe from British hops), rounder mouthfeel, and less pronounced bitterness.

The Northwest IPA
Try: Deschutes Freshly Squeezed, Gigantic IPA
These are all about the hop aroma and flavor where the beers are top-heavy with fruity, citrusy, piney hops. Importantly they are also often unfiltered which adds to the simple grain bill and gives body and a general malt richness without sweetness.

The Midwest IPA
Try: Bell's Two Hearted IPA, Goose Island IPA
Think oranges, marmalade, orange soda, and floral, where a sweetness of malt gives a caramel richness to the brew and balances the bitterness. These likely use the classic American C-hops rather than newer varieties.

The Colorado IPA
Try: Oskar Blues Gubna, SKA Modus Hoperandi
Lots of caramel malts pack the body with a lip-sticking sweetness and a toasty, toffee-ish flavor, while the hops aggressively come in to balance that bitterness and then throw out some dank, pithy aroma.

The Vermont IPA
Try: The Alchemist Heady Topper, Fiddlehead IPA
Similar to Northwest IPAs, these are very aromatic, fruity with citrus and tropical, lots of floral aroma, and the hop flavor is loaded throughout. Expect a hazy and relatively full body because they're unfiltered, where there's a juicy mix of hop and malt to balance the brews.

The Russian River IPA
Try: Russian River Blind Pig, Russian River Pliny the Elder
This arguably stands alone as one brewery's defining impact on the style. Loads of hop aroma, zesty and fresh, piney and floral, citrus, then a very dry, pale, clean body of malt. In many ways this type of beer is becoming the standard of American IPA today and reflects back to the current West Coast IPA.

10 OF THE BEST IPAS AROUND THE WORLD

Eisenbahn Bison IPA is an astonishing Brazilian IPA that's bright gold, really dry in the malt profile, totally bursting with juicy, piney hop aroma, and then has a deep bitterness to finish.

8 Wired HopWired IPA uses just New Zealand hops giving a beer that's bursting with mango, pineapple, passion fruit, and grapes above a sturdy base of New Zealand malt. It's a tropical fruit delight.

Feral Hop Hog is one of Australia's top brews and it's the combination of toasty malt, in-your-face fleshy stone fruit, and tropical hops that makes it so good to drink.

BrewDog Jackhammer is a brutal, bold British IPA that punches grapefruit and pine cones right into your nose and mouth, never relenting yet always pleasurable in its power.

Nomád Karel is an amazing IPA that uses only Czech hops, though you'd never guess that given the outrageous aromas of oranges and lemons. The body is clean and smooth and the ideal base for launching those lesser-known Czech hops at you.

Jing-A IPA is everything you could ever want in an American-style IPA. It's balanced yet has a huge flavor, there's so much hop aroma and it's laced with flavor throughout, going big on tangerines and tropical fruit. It's worth flying to China to drink it.

Dieu du Ciel Moralité is so good it's hard to ever buy another IPA again after drinking it. I have no idea how so much orange, mango, and grapefruit aroma can get into a beer with such gorgeous balance, or how they made a beer with the softest, lushest mouthfeel ever.

Galway Bay Of Foam and Fury comes at you like a hop cannon; it's explosive, it's a riot of citrusy flavors, oily, lime-like, grapefruit, and a kick of dank resin all wrapped in a strong body of malt.

Toccalmatto Zona Cessarini has all kinds of glorious things going on with lemons, limes, oranges, and passion fruit combining with a smooth malt body to be a beautiful IPA with style, balance, and brilliance.

Omnipollo Nebuchadnezzar IIPA is a muscular Double IPA that's bulging with tropical fruits and citrus pith, underpinned by dank resin and a stick-in-the-gums kind of bitterness.

THE IPA FAMILY: 10 TO TRY

Beavertown's Black Betty is a beer which smells like an IPA and looks like a Stout. The malt darkness is just a shadow and barely influences the taste that's all about citrusy, piney hops—for me that's the defining quality of a great Black IPA.

Boulevard Brewing's 80 Acre is a Wheat Beer hopped like an IPA giving a smooth, dry texture in the base and a hint of spice, which works wonderfully with the tropical fruit aroma from the hops. They also have Tank 7, a hoppy Farmhouse that's a wonderful mix of hops and yeast.

Dogfish Head's Aprihop has all the fruity hop aromas you expect of an IPA then the addition of apricot juice adds an extra fruitiness plus a creamy, sweet texture. Another fine fruited example of an IPA is Ballast Point's Grapefruit Sculpin.

8 Wired Tall Poppy is an "India Red Ale" where the redness from the malt is giving some bready, toffee flavor before the familiar floral, citrusy hops come in alongside some berries. If we see the words "Red Ale" today we expect them to be hoppy.

Jack's Abby Hoponius Union is a particularly piney and dank India Pale Lager made using lager yeast, giving a subtle malt sweetness.

Chouffe Houblon is a Belgian Tripel IPA that's gloriously fruity with peachy, orangey, floral hops and the peppery kick of Belgian yeast, all with a dry body that helps enhance the hops.

Founder's All Day IPA is already a classic Session IPA, the biggest-growing craft beer style of the mid 20-teens, which packs in all the hops of a big IPA into a lower alcohol (sub-5% ABV) beer, meaning you can drink more of it.

Boneyard Notorious is an astonishing 11.5% ABV Triple IPA which is more bangable than most beers half its strength. Monster hop aroma, sticky roasted citrus and tropical fruit, loads of mango, then somehow a body that's big but not sweet.

Wild Beer Co Evolver IPA is fermented with the wild yeast Brettanomyces that adds its own fruitiness, plus a peppery bitterness, to the tropical aromas of the hops.

Urban Chestnut Hopfen gets its grassy, lemon, barley sugar, and apricot aroma from just German hops, while the influence of lager's clean malt bill and body provides the perfect base brew to enhance those aromas.

CITY GUIDES:

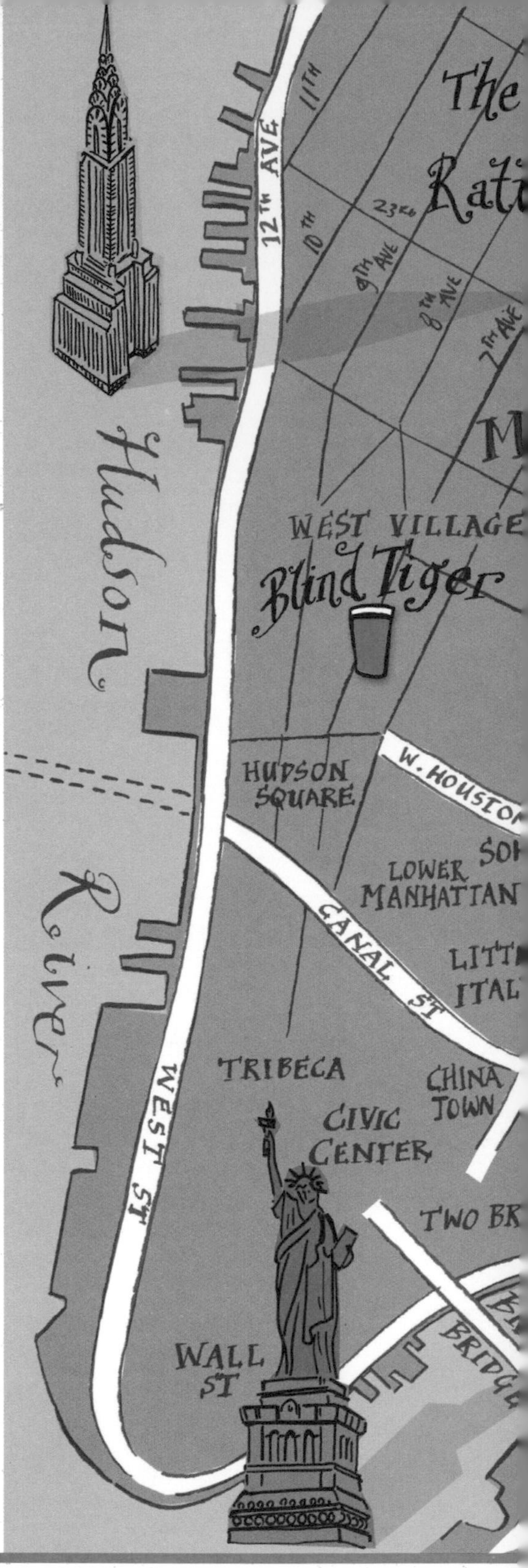

CITY GUIDE

NEW YORK

We go there for the sights of one of the world's greatest cities, to explore Manhattan in the shadows of skyscrapers, to walk in Central Park after seeing it from the top of the Empire State Building. We see the Statue of Liberty, pay respects at Ground Zero, hop around the hip Brooklyn streets, feel like movie stars as we stand in the bright lights of Times Square. And when we're done with all of that there are great bars and breweries in all five boroughs of New York City (though Brooklyn and Manhattan are where you'll hang out most of the time) where you can expect well-chosen tap lists, tasty bar snacks, good pub fare, lively atmospheres, smart staff, and late closing times befitting the city that never sleeps.

THEATER
DISTRICT

42ND

The Jeffrey Craft
Beer & Bits

ger Man

Hum

5TH AVE

PARK AVE

MURRAY
HILL
34TH

QUEENS

NOMAD

23RD

KIPS BAY

LONG

HATTAN

2ND AVE

1ST AVE

23RD

14TH ST

STUYVESANT
TOWN

East River

McGUINNESS BLVD

BROOKLYN
B
BREWERY

BROOKLYN
BREWERY

BROOKLYN
BREWERY

Jimmy's
No 43

EAST VILLAGE

EDR DRIVE

Brooklyn
Brewery

MANHATTAN AVE.

Tørst

278

GREENPOINT

E. HOUSTON ST

p Hops
eer Shop

DELANCEY STREET

Mugs Alehouse

BROOKLYN-QUEENS EXPY

MORGAN AVE.

WILLIAMSBURG

METROPOLITAN AVE.

Spuyten Duyvil

NY TOP NY
HOPS
BEER
SHOP

BRIDGE

MANHATTAN

Fette Sau

UNION AVE

Barcade

BROOKLYN

BROADWAY

NEW YORK

BROOKLYN BREWERY

79 N 11TH STREET, BROOKLYN;
WWW.BROOKLYNBREWERY.COM

You have to visit Brooklyn Brewery. A large open space with lots of picnic bench tables, fill your pockets with beer tokens, pick from the 10 beers on tap or special bottles in the fridges, get on one of the free 30-minute tours, then go back and work through the rest of the taps and bottles while enjoying the buzzing atmosphere.

The beer scene in New York always lives up to expectations.

TØRST

615 MANHATTAN AVENUE, BROOKLYN;
WWW.TORSTNYC.COM

With one of the best, most interesting, and certainly geekiest beer lists you'll find anywhere in the world, Tørst is run by Jeppe Jarnit-Bjergsø who owns Evil Twin Brewing. In the back you'll find Luksus, a small restaurant specializing in new Nordic cuisine, pairing the food with different beers—go for a special occasion because the tasting menu isn't cheap but it is superb and elevates food and beer appreciation many levels beyond what anyone else is doing.

MUGS ALEHOUSE

125 BEDFORD AVENUE, BROOKLYN;
WWW.MUGSALEHOUSE.COM

I'll never forget the Ithaca Flower Power IPA I drank here on my first visit—it was the most juicy, fruity, perfect IPA I'd had—and now I always return when I'm in town. It feels quintessentially American as you enter: tap handles dominate the bar, TVs are tuned to sports, the beer list is large and excellent, brewery flags and signage all around.

BARCADE

388 UNION AVENUE, BROOKLYN;
WWW.BARCADEBROOKLYN.COM

Collect up your quarters and then go to Barcade, one of my favorite beer bars in the world. The bare warehouse-like open space is lined with bright old arcade games, the draft list is always varied and great, the atmosphere is fun, and the whole place just has a great feeling about it. I'm shockingly bad at all the games but I don't care because this place rocks. There are also two other locations in Manhattan: 148 W 24th St and 6 St Marks Place.

SPUYTEN DUYVIL

359 METROPOLITAN AVENUE, BROOKLYN;
WWW.SPUYTENDUYVILNYC.COM

Let me be straight with you: I've only been to Spuyten Duyvil once and I was so drunk that I don't really remember it. I also left here and walked for about an hour in the wrong direction. What I do remember is sitting in a cool seat by the window, loving the Belgian beer vibe and ogling the rare beer list.

FETTE SAU

354 METROPOLITAN AVENUE, BROOKLYN;
WWW.FETTESAUBBQ.COM

I still dream about the meat in this impossibly cool Brooklyn BBQ joint. You'll have to wait in line but it's worth it. Tap handles are old butchers' knives and cleavers and the beer behind them is a meat-friendly mix of local brews. The bourbon selection is also awesome (and the reason I can't remember my visit to Spuyten Duyvil).

RATTLE N HUM

14 E 33RD STREET;
WWW.RATTLENHUMBARNYC.COM

With 40 draft beers, all of which you'll want to drink, this lively, busy bar is a fun place to hang out. It's narrow as you enter but pass the bar, checking out the chalk board tap list on the right, and find a seat wherever you can, then order a pint and a bowl of IPA fries—they are brined in beer and seasoned with hop salt.

GINGER MAN

11 E 36TH STREET;
WWW.GINGERMAN-NY.COM

Not far from the Empire State Building, Ginger Man and Rattle N Hum will sort you out for your Midtown boozing. This place has a large dark wood bar top, lots of space to sit, a menu of good beer food (sandwiches, sausages, and pies), and 70 taps to choose from.

BLIND TIGER

281 BLEECKER STREET;
WWW.BLINDTIGERALEHOUSE.COM

Blind Tiger is one of the city's original beer bars and still one of the best places to visit. Work through the long, interesting draft list that's a mix of New York brews and some of the better breweries from around the country. They also have a few cask beer lines and hold different events every week.

THE JEFFREY

311 E 60TH STREET;
THEJEFFREYNYC.COM

Head to the Upper East Side, find The Jeffrey and then choose the right door—quite literally the door on the right—as that leads to 30 taps of beer. If you pick the door on the left you find coffee and cocktails, plus growlers to go. If the weather's good then out the back is a nice patio for some outdoor drinking. It's a cool place.

TOP HOPS BEER SHOP

94 ORCHARD STREET;
WWW.TOPHOPS.COM

With over 600 bottles and 20 taps, this is your go-to place for to-go beer. Sit and have a glass of something local while you work out which bottles to stick in your bag or which drafts to fill a growler with. They have a lot of really interesting rarities as well as all the classics and the staff know their stuff.

JIMMY'S NO. 43

43 E 7TH STREET;
WWW.JIMMYSNO43.COM

This place looks like a German beer cellar, with arches and old wooden barrels. While it's not a 50-tap emporium, it does consistently have one of the best-chosen beer lists in town. The meaty beer snacks are a great addition to your pint.

TOP 5 BEERS IN TOWN

Brooklyn Lager
A classic craft beer

Ithaca Flower Power IPA
One of my favorite IPAs

Captain Lawrence Captain's Reserve
One of the best Imperial IPAs

Other Half Hop Showers
A banging Brooklyn-brewed IPA

Brooklyn Sorachi Ace
Stunning Sorachi-hopped Saison

• CITY GUIDE

CHICAGO

You'll be blown away by the beer scene in the Windy City. With a mix of brewpubs and brewery taprooms, loads of great bars, and really good food, Chicago is definitely one of the best beer towns in North America—and there's loads to do and see while you're there. Have deep-dish pizza, drink Intellegensia coffee, go to Al's Beef for a sandwich, eat a Chicago hot dog, and try to see a baseball game at Wrigley Field. And if you want to check out tap lists before you arrive, most keep www.beermenus.com updated.

GOOSE ISLAND CLYBOURN

1800 NORTH CLYBOURN; WWW.GOOSEISLANDBREWPUBS.COM

A big, square wooden bar sits in the middle of this classic Chicago venue where brewing started in 1988. You can get all the classic Goose beers plus a range brewed on site. It's an institution and you shouldn't skip it. Have a house beer then find something from the Goose barrel program—those beers are world class.

The taps at Goose Island Clybourn.

REVOLUTION BREWING TAPROOM

2323 N. MILWAUKEE AVE; WWW.REVBREW.COM

The Revolution Brewpub was such a success that within no time they'd opened a production brewery close by to add more capacity (it's 3340 N. Kedzie Ave and you can drink there, too—if you've seen the movie Drinking Buddies then you'll recognize it.) At the Taproom you'll find classic pub food and good American beers.

HAYMARKET PUB & BREWERY

737 W. RANDOLPH ST; WWW.HAYMARKETBREWING.COM

This busy brewpub has a really interesting range of their own beers. When I went they were being poured from serving tanks, which is always nice to know. Typical bar food, lots of TVs tuned to sports, and a lively atmosphere.

HALF ACRE TAPROOM

4257 N. LINCOLN AVE; WWW.HALFACREBEER.COM

One of my favorite breweries in Chicago. Don't miss Daisy Cutter as it's a superb Pale Ale, while there are always some really interesting specials. You can order food in as you drink and there are tours every Saturday at 11am.

PIECE BREWERY AND PIZZERIA

1927 W. NORTH AVE; WWW.PIECECHICAGO.COM

Eschewing Chicago's famous deep dish, in Piece you'll get great thin-crust pizzas to go with excellent house-brewed beers. The wheat beers and Pale Ales are recurrent medal winners and rightly so because they rock. It's a fun place and who doesn't love the combo of beer and pizza?

LAGUNITAS CHICAGO TAPROOM
2607 W. 17TH STREET;
WWW.LAGUNITAS.COM

You'll be repeating the word Lagufuckingnitas when you leave this enormous new brewery in a massive warehouse. Make sure you get on one of the free tours and enjoy the Willy Wonka experience then work through the great range of fresh beers on tap. There's often live music but it kicks out at 9pm. It's a fun place.

LOCAL OPTION
1102 W. WEBSTER AVE;
WWW.LOCALOPTIONBIER.COM

This is a good-time dive bar with a large and excellent tap list, including a range of their own-branded brews, like the oaked Kellerbier Die Königin and Exorcist, their satanic Export Stout. Expect tacos and po boys on the menu—good to go with whatever brew you choose.

HOPLEAF
5148 N. CLARK ST; WWW.HOPLEAF.COM

One of the best beer bars around. At Hopleaf you'll find friendly staff, a great crowd of locals, a warm vibe, a seriously good draft list (which includes lots of Belgians as well as great US taps), excellent bottles, and really good food, including the naughtiest sandwich I've seen: CB&J which is cashew butter, fig jam, and Morbier cheese—it's unreal with a Stout.

MAP ROOM
1949 N. HOYNE AVE; WWW.MAPROOM.COM

I bloody love maps. And I also love rooms filled with maps and lots of beers from around the world. Therefore I love Map Room. Expect some hop-forward US craft brews, like Three Floyds, alongside lesser-spotted Belgian and German drafts.

BANGERS & LACE
1670 W. DIVISION;
WWW.BANGERSANDLACECHICAGO.COM

The bangers part refers to the wonderfully extensive selection of sausages on the menu (it's a good chance to tick-off a Chicago-style hot dog) while the lace is all about how the foam of a beer leaves its lacing down your glass. With over 30 taps of really interesting beers, again with many from Europe, you'll see more lace than in a lingerie store.

SHEFFIELD'S BEER AND WINE GARDEN
3258 N. SHEFFIELD AVENUE;
WWW.SHEFFIELDSCHICAGO.COM

Not far from Wrigley Field, Sheffield's specializes in good beer and good BBQ. It's a varied place with different spaces and a great beer garden out the back—if it's sunny then you'll never want to leave. A fun crowd and a broad beer list with lots of local brews on—those in the know go to the Beer School bar for something more interesting or rare to drink.

LINKS TAPROOM
1559 N MILWAUKEE AVE;
WWW.LINKSTAPROOM.COM

With bare brick walls and clean lines of tables, Links has a chilled out atmosphere that makes you want to order a hot dog and hang around and work through the 36 lines of beer. They have an electronic beer board which updates to show how much is left in each keg—if it goes red then get to the bar quickly.

WEST LAKEVIEW LIQUORS
2156 W ADDISON ST; WWW.WLVLIQUORS.COM

This is the place to go to buy bottles. There's a phenomenal beer choice from the US and way beyond, including lots of Belgian brews, and the staff are excellent. Simple as that.

TOP 5 BEERS IN TOWN

Half Acre Daisy Cutter
One of the best US Pale Ales

Pipeworks Ninja vs Unicorn
Delightfully named Double IPA

Three Floyds Hop Zombie
Not from Chicago but close enough and awesome

Revolution Eugene
A rich and robust Porter

Any Goose Island barrel-aged beer
Because they are extraordinary

• CITY GUIDE

BOSTON

Boston is a city with cool beer bars, a lot of breweries, and some great food. Many breweries are outside of the downtown area but they're worth visiting if you don't mind wandering around ugly industrial estates looking for them. Head into Cambridge, where Harvard University is located, for the best pubs and a more chilled out atmosphere.

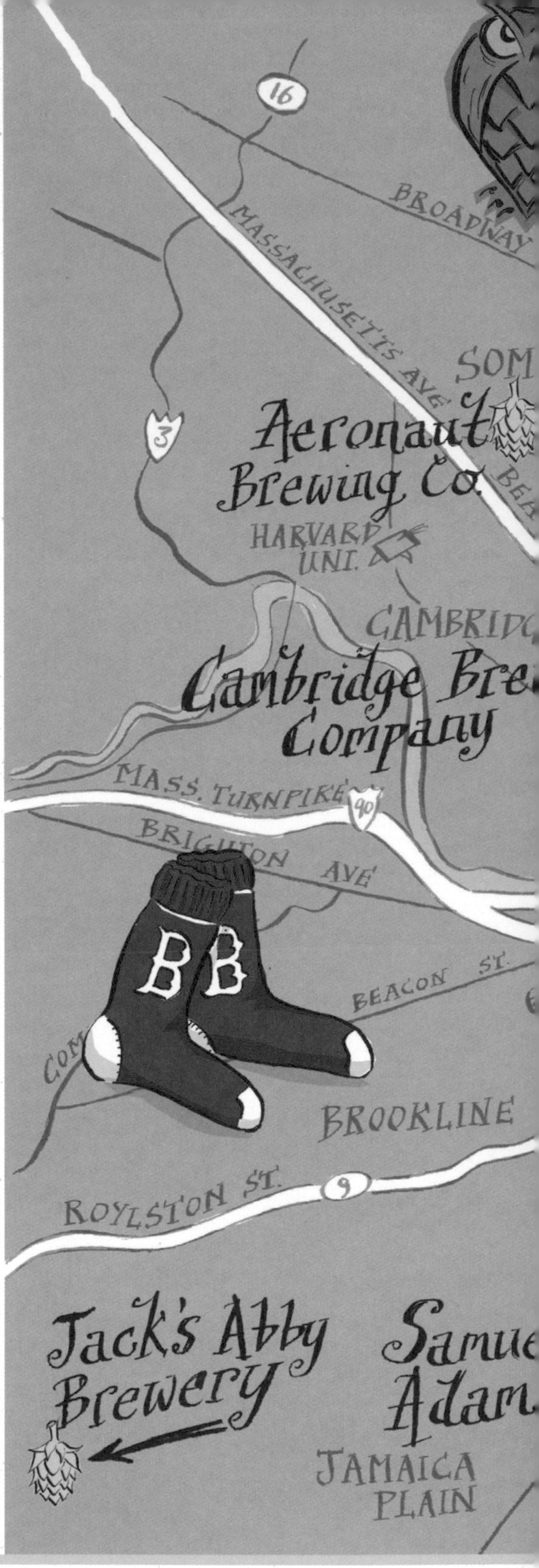

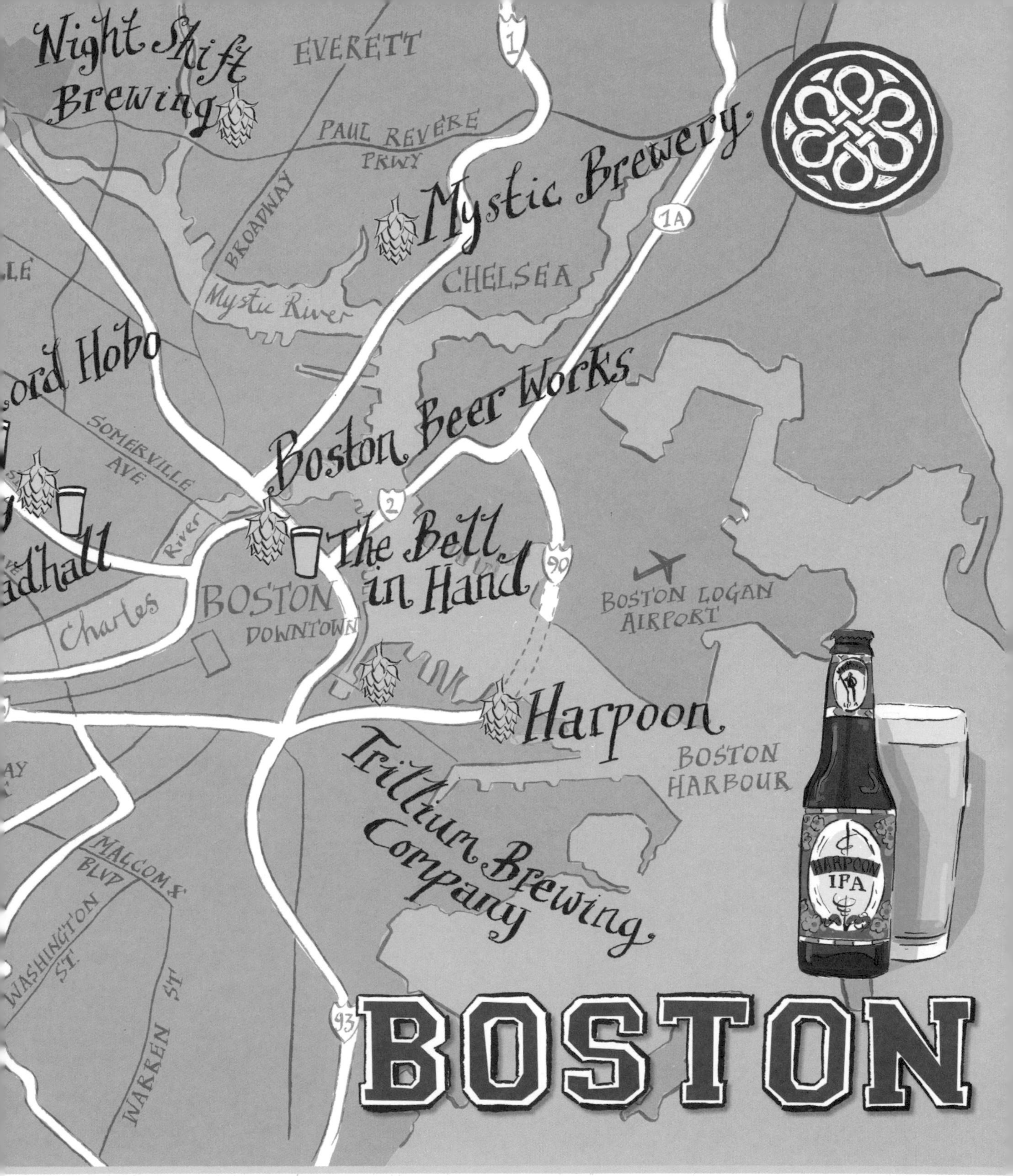
Night Shift Brewing
EVERETT
PAUL REVERE PRWY
Mystic Brewery
1A
BROADWAY
CHELSEA
Mystic River
Boston Beer Works
SOMERVILLE AVE
The Bell in Hand
River
Charles
BOSTON
DOWNTOWN
BOSTON LOGAN AIRPORT
Harpoon
BOSTON HARBOUR
Trillium Brewing Company
HARPOON IPA
MALCOM X BLVD
WASHINGTON ST.
WARREN ST
BOSTON

SAMUEL ADAMS BREWERY

30 GERMANIA STREET; WWW.SAMUELADAMS.COM

Go here for the popular and busy tour which is free, entertaining, and focused around the biggest-selling craft beer in the US. You'll get three beers at the end, before (in the most American of ways) you're directed into the gift shop.

LORD HOBO

92 HAMPSHIRE ST, CAMBRIDGE; WWW.LORDHOBO.COM

Prepare to spend a lot of time here because the tap list is bloody great and the food is the best in the area. Walk in through the velvet curtain into a handsomely rugged bar that's cozy and cool. You'll find loads of local beers plus some big names from around the US.

JACK'S ABBY

81 MORTON ST, FRAMINGHAM; WWW.JACKSABBYBREWING.COM

If you don't visit Jack's Abby then you're an idiot. Sure, it's an hour out of town but don't let that put you off because it's worth getting on the train to West Natick. They only ferment with lager yeast and you'll find everything from the simple, gulpable Jabby Brau to soured lagers to their biggest-seller Hoponius Union, an IPA-styled lager. Unmissable.

AERONAUT

14 TYLER STREET, SOMERVILLE; WWW.AERONAUTBREWING.COM

It's more Brooklyn than Boston with a huge projector linked to old-school Super Nintendo, bands playing in a canteen, and food trucks outside. Good fun.

HARPOON BREWING

306 NORTHERN AVENUE; WWW.HARPOONBREWERY.COM

One of Boston's biggest and oldest breweries, opening in 1986. They have a busy taproom down by the docks with 12–15 beers on tap and a selection of pretzels to snack on plus regular tours around the brewhouse.

CAMBRIDGE BREW CO

1 KENDALL SQUARE, CAMBRIDGE; WWW.CAMBRIDGEBREWINGCOMPANY.COM

Cambridge is where much of the best beer is. Cambridge Brew Co is your central, essential brewpub to stop at. Classic brews plus some unusual seasonals and good food.

NIGHT SHIFT BREWING

87 SANTILLI HWY, EVERETT; WWW.NIGHTSHIFTBREWING.COM

Jump on the Orange Line and head to Wellington Station. It's worth the walk around busy roads and quiet industrial estates to get to this place because they make some of the best beers in town. Essential drinking.

MEADHALL

4 CAMBRIDGE CENTRE, CAMBRIDGE; WWW.THEMEADHALL.COM

If Lord Hobo didn't sate your thirst then the 100 taps at Meadhall should do it. Clean and polished, it doesn't have the atmosphere of other bars but the beer range is brilliant.

BOSTON BEER WORKS

MULTIPLE LOCATIONS; WWW.BEERWORKS.NET

With one brewpub by Fenway and another downtown, plus others spaced further around the state, Boston Beer Works is a reliable if unexciting beer stop. You'll find loads of taps of house-brewed beer.

THE BELL IN HAND TAVERN

45 UNION STREET; WWW.BELLINHAND.COM

If you want to drink in America's oldest tavern then find the Bell in Hand. It doesn't necessarily feel that old today with polished wood beams and shining TV screens, but it's one to tick off for historic value and they have some good local craft beers on tap.

Acorn Street in the historic Beacon Hill area, round the corner from The Bell In Hand Tavern.

MYSTIC BREWERY

174 WILLIAMS STREET, CHELSEA;
WWW.MYSTIC-BREWERY.COM

A fun little taproom with a good mix of beers, mostly in the farmhouse style. It's good for grabbing a flight or filling a grower.

TRILLIUM

369 CONGRESS STREET;
WWW.TRILLIUMBREWING.COM

Based in the Fort Point Channel part of town, Trillium run a tiny taproom area which, when I visited, was just for tasters and growler fills.

TOP 5 BEERS IN TOWN

Anything from Pretty Things
Because they are brilliant

Something sour from Night Shift
Because they nail sour beer

Jack's Abby Hoponius Union
The best hoppy lager in town

Jack's Abby Smoke & Dagger
The best smoked beer in town

Trillium Fort Point Pale Ale
Superb Pale Ale

CITY GUIDE
DENVER

I like to drink at breweries when I travel and Denver is an ideal city for that, with many places all within walking distance of each other. There's a great culture and attitude for beer in Denver—you will find great beer choices wherever you look.

Memorabilia on display at Falling Rock.

FALLING ROCK TAP HOUSE

1919 BLAKE STREET;
WWW.FALLINGROCKTAPHOUSE.COM

One of America's best beer bars, with so many taps pouring such a great range of beers. Always busy, always a good crowd, a fun outside space, cozy booths inside, pool tables, and filling food.

CROOKED STAVE @ THE SOURCE

3350 BRIGHTON BOULEVARD;
WWW.CROOKEDSTAVE.COM

The Source is an indoor collective of artisan producers including a baker, coffee roaster, and brewer. And not just any brewer; Crooked Stave makes some of the best Wild Ales in the world.

GREAT DIVIDE BREWING CO

2201 ARAPAHOE STREET; WWW.GREATDIVIDE.COM

With 16 taps of their own beers, this small taproom is home to some big beers like the Yeti Imperial Stouts. Great food trucks stop outside.

JAGGED MOUNTAIN

1139 20TH STREET;
WWW.JAGGEDMOUNTAINBREWERY.COM

In an industrial building a couple of blocks from Great Divide, Jagged Mountain makes a wide range of American beer styles, all well executed and interesting, so be sure to order a flight.

RIVER NORTH

2401 BLAKE STREET;
WWW.RIVERNORTHBREWERY.COM

River North specializes in beers brewed with Belgian yeast, whether that's Belgian styles like Witbier or funked-up American styles like IPA. Not a big space but a good place to hang out. It's near the ballpark so can get busy on game days.

OUR MUTUAL FRIEND

2810 LARIMER STREET; WWW.OMFBEER.COM

Worth a stop as it's in the middle of a brewery crawl in the River North district, this is a hip spot with a few of their own beers on tap and a decent atmosphere.

EPIC BREWING

3001 WALNUT STREET; WWW.EPICBREWING.COM

This is the kind of taproom I like: big and open, a range of around 25 beers, plus you can see the brewery working while you drink. Their IPAs are very good.

PROST BREWING

2540 19TH STREET; WWW.PROSTBREWING.COM

Prost specializes in German-style beer, made in good-looking copper tanks, served in a beer-hall environment. The Pils is good and hoppy and the other brews are legit German iterations. There's a good view back into the city if you drink outside.

SANDLOT BREWERY

2161 BLAKE STREET;
WWW.BLUEMOONBREWINGCOMPANY.COM

This is where Blue Moon was born. Whatever you think about that beer (I like it!), this is an important American brewpub for that reason. It's also worth visiting because they have a range of different beers on tap, including a White IPA. It's at Coors Field so go when there's a game on.

FORMER FUTURE

1290 S BROADWAY;
WWW.EMBRACEGOODTASTE.COM

This is a great little industrial place that, as the name alludes, is about recreating some classic old styles—Cream Ale, English IPA—and bringing them into the present. All good, all interesting, and worth visiting to drink them.

TRVE BREWING

227 BROADWAY STREET #101;
WWW.TRVEBREWING.COM

They make some really interesting styles in this dark, small brewpub. There's a Table Beer, a Mild, American Stout, Dry-Hopped Wheat, and others, all with a backing track of heavy metal.

LOWDOWN BREWERY + KITCHEN

800 LINCOLN STREET;
WWW.LOWDOWNBREWERY.COM

A varied food menu, including good pizza, and a lot of decent brews, LowDown is an underrated stop in the south of the city. I genuinely loved every beer I drank, especially the Pils, Wit, and IPA.

VINE STREET PUB & BREWERY

1700 VINE STREET;
WWW.MOUNTAINSUNPUB.COM

Go here and eat the chicken wings—they are huge and delicious. The beers they brew in this neighborhood joint are good, too. If you love hops then try the FYIPA.

EUCLID HALL

1317 14TH STREET; WWW.EUCLIDHALL.COM

This is one of the top beer restaurants around. The food is really high quality and the beer list is very good with plenty of choices to match the meals (try the chicken and waffles with a glass of Left Hand Nitro Milk Stout).

FRESHCRAFT

1530 BLAKE STREET; WWW.FRESHCRAFT.COM

Expect lots of local taps, a great bottle range, plus really good food. There are many bars in town but this is simply better than most and you should go.

TOP 5 BEERS IN TOWN

Left Hand Nitro Milk Stout
The best Milk Stout there is

Crooked Stave Hop Savant
Beguiling combo of hops and Brett

Odell IPA
Classic American IPA

Oskar Blues Ten Fidy
The mighty canned Imperial Stout

Great Divide Oak Aged Yeti
An oaked beast of a Stout

OUT OF TOWN

It's definitely worth traveling outside of Denver for a day. The must-visit town is Fort Collins, home to some unmissable breweries. One of the best experiences I've had is at **Odell Brewing** (800 East Lincoln Avenue; www.odellbrewing.com)—their IPA is a favorite and a flight of everything will show you how good this brewery is. Just around the corner is one of the biggest craft breweries in America and **New Belgium** (500 Linden Street; www.newbelgium.com) is another must-visit place with a great tour and great range of brews. Completing a convenient triangle is **Funkwerks** (1900 E Lincoln Avenue; www.funkwerks.com) where you should start on their Saison and order some cheese on the side. If you want a choice of 100 beers on tap then visit **The Mayor of Old Town** (632 S Mason Street; www.themayorofoldtown.com).

Over in Boulder, a mountainside college town, the big draw—big enough for you to dedicate the whole journey to it—is **Avery Brewing Co** (4910 Nautilus Ct; www.averybrewing.com), which is one of my favorite breweries to drink in (White Rascal, their Witbier, and Maharajah, their Double IPA, are two of my favorite beers). You can also visit **Mountain Sun Pub & Brewery**, **Fate Brewing Co**, **West Flanders Brewing Company**, and **Boulder Beer Co**, which was Colorado's first craft brewery, opened in 1979.

CITY GUIDE

SAN DIEGO

This is one of America's must-visit beer cities as it's home to some of the best names in craft brewing (plus good weather, a long coastline, and great food). The only downside is that many places are out of town so require you to drive or be driven, so keep that in mind and be safe and legal behind the wheel.

STONE BREWING WORLD BISTRO

1999 CITRACADO PARKWAY, ESCONDIDO; WWW.STONEWORLDBISTRO.COM

Go to Escondido for one of craft beer's finest locations: a magnificent garden, a restaurant with delicious food, and a busy brewery making some amazing beers. Nearer to the city they have a similar set up at Liberty Station (2816 Historic Decatur Rd #116) where they have a 10-barrel brewery. There's even a bar at San Diego airport.

ALPINE BREWING

351 ALPINE BLVD, ALPINE; WWW.ALPINEBEERCO.COM

If you like hops (and you only really go to San Diego if you like hops) then this is definitely worth the short trip out of town. You'll want to drink Duet, Pure Hoppiness, Nelson, and Exponential Hoppiness—they are awesome. The pub is slightly unusual and a bit like an old diner but it has its charms. Order a sandwich because you'll need it.

ALESMITH BREWING

9368 CABOT DRIVE; WWW.ALESMITH.COM

It's a small, bare tasting room but who cares when you've got a glass of their IPA in your hand? It's a quintessential West Coast IPA and seriously good. Also don't miss Speedway Stout, the coffee Imperial Stout.

GREEN FLASH

6550 MIRA MESA BOULEVARD; WWW.GREENFLASHBREW.COM

Right in the middle of the brewery is a fun tasting room. I love how beer is being made all around and all are high quality, particularly Double Stout and Mosaic Session IPA.

PIZZA PORT

MULTIPLE LOCATIONS; WWW.PIZZAPORT.COM

This is a group of brewpubs plus a production brewery (2730 Gateway Road, Carlsbad). I love Pizza Port Ocean Beach (1956 Bacon Street) that's a few blocks back from the sea in a hip, laid-back part of the city. The beers are really good here (have The Jetty IPA). Get a pizza, too.

LOST ABBEY AND PORT BREWING

155 MATA WAY #104, SAN MARCOS; WWW.LOSTABBEY.COM AND WWW.PORTBREWING.COM

Two breweries in one, so pick which side of the shared tasting room you want first: Lost Abbey is where you'll find Belgian-style beers and brilliant barrel-aged brews, whereas Port Brewing is an all-American hop-fest. Obviously you'll have beers from both because both are great.

SOCIETE BREWING

8262 CLAIREMONT MESA BOULEVARD; WWW.SOCIETEBREWING.COM

At Societe you'll drink in a wood-clad tasting room looking into the brewery. They have four ranges: Out West is their hoppy lot (try The Pupil), Old World are Belgian styles (The Madam is a strong Belgian Golden Ale), Stygian are the dark brews (The Butcher is a bold Imperial Stout), and Feral are barrel-aged brews.

BALLAST POINT BREWING

MULTIPLE LOCATIONS; WWW.BALLASTPOINT.COM

They brew and distil at Ballast Point and they have four locations to choose from. I say go to Miramar (9045 Carroll Way) for the production brewery and optional tour, or in the city to their Tasting Room & Kitchen (2215 India Street).

MIKE HESS BREWING COMPANY

3812 GRIM AVENUE;
WWW.MIKEHESSBREWING.COM

This modern brewery in the hippest beer hotspot is one of the most impressive places to visit as you walk on a gangway over the brewhouse to get into the tasting room. Great staff, great atmosphere, and great beers. Order a flight and work through their range of brews with the added bonus that you'll get a souvenir glass when you're done. Food trucks outside.

MONKEY PAW PUB AND BREWERY

805 16TH STREET;
WWW.MONKEYPAWBREWING.COM

In East Village you'll want to hit up Monkey Paw where you'll choose between their own house brews (which are really varied and good) and some great guests. The menu is simple but all you really need after a few pints: wings, waffle fries, and cheesesteaks.

MODERN TIMES

3725 GREENWOOD STREET;
WWW.MODERNTIMESBEER.COM

A bar made of books, a wall of comics, murals made from Post-It notes... Modern Times is a seriously cool place bursting with good beers. Black House is a great Coffee Oatmeal Stout. They also have a tasting room in North Park (corner of 30th Street and Upas Street).

WHITE LABS TASTING ROOM

9495 CANDIDA STREET; WWW.WHITELABS.COM

This is the place for the homebrewers and hardcore beer nerds. White Labs supplies the brewing industry with yeast varieties and to showcase their many strains they have a small brewery and on-site Tasting Room. If you're at all interested in yeast or fermentation then this is the single-most interesting bar you can visit anywhere in the world.

HAMILTON'S TAVERN

1521 30TH STREET; WWW.HAMILTONSTAVERN.COM

With a large tap list of California-brewed beers, plus some classic imports, Hamilton's is the sort of tavern many non-US beer lovers imagine when they think about American craft beer bars: dark, lots of taps, brewery neons, sport on TV, friendly staff, and all-American bar food.

BLIND LADY ALE HOUSE

3416 ADAMS AVE;
WWW.BLINDLADY.BLOGSPOT.CO.UK

In a city with so many good places to drink, this is one of the few to go out of your way to get to—the large list is excellent. Automatic Brewing Co. beers are brewed in the back of the bar.

TIGER! TIGER!

3025 EL CAJON BOULEVARD;
TIGERTIGERTAVERN.BLOGSPOT.CO.UK

Similar vibes and style as Blind Lady Ale House because they are owned by the same guys. Expect great beer and sandwiches.

TORONADO

4026 30TH STREET; WWW.TORONADOSD.COM

Sister to the San Francisco beer institution, this is a less-divey bar with a similarly excellent beer list where all your hoppy wishes will come true.

O'BRIEN'S

4646 CONVOY STREET; WWW.OBRIENSPUB.NET

The 28 taps are some of the best selected in the city with a focus on hops. It's a bit out of town, and in a shopping mall, but don't let that deter you—it's worth the trip. The pub is run by Tom and Lindsey Nickel who own Nickel Beer Co.

TOP 5 BEERS IN TOWN

Stone Brewing Enjoy By IPA
One of the best, freshest Double IPAs

AleSmith IPA
Just a banging West Coast IPA

Alpine Nelson
A juicy, fruity NZ-hopped IPA

Modern Times Fortunate Islands
Summery smashable American Wheat

Lost Abbey Deliverance
Because you can't just drink hops

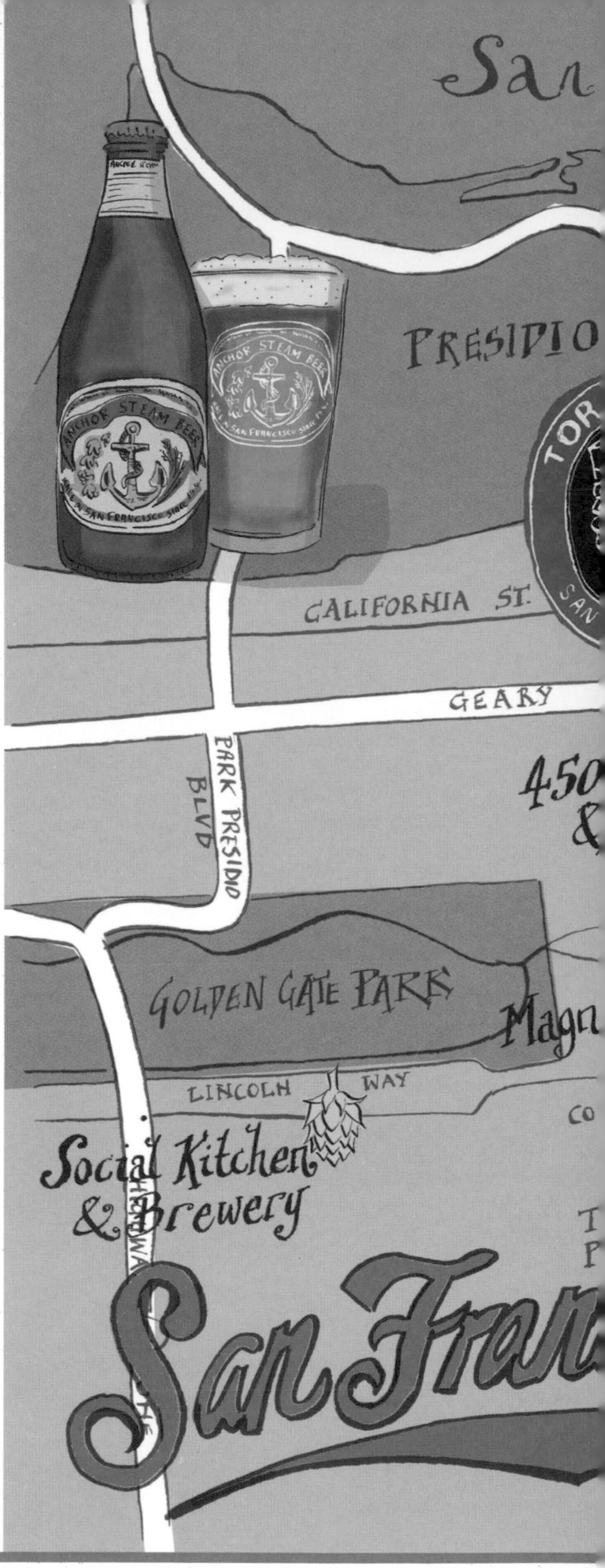

CITY GUIDE

SAN FRANCISCO

With its mix of many breweries, cool bars, awesome food, stunning sights, and general great vibe, San Francisco is a brilliant beer town and a great central base in Northern California to allow you to explore a little further.

Francisco Bay
FISHERMANS WHARF
COIT TOWER
TELEGRAPH HILL
RUSSIAN HILL
LOMBARD ST.
VAN NESS AVE
BROADWAY STREET
CHINATOWN
DIVISADERO ST.
Mikkeller Bar
GEARY BLVD
MARKET STREET
FOLSOM ST.
SF-OAKLAND BRIDGE
80
Faction Brewery
CELLARMAKER BREWING COMPANY
WEBSTER ST.
MISSION ST
Cellarmaker Brewing Co.
SOUTH OF MARKET
21st Amendment Brewery
4TH ST
Toronado
OAK ST.
City Beer Store
MISSION BAY
DUBOCE TRIANGLE
Zeitgeist
The Monks Kettle
Southpaw B.B.Q.
Triple Voodoo Brewery & Tap Room
STREET
GUERRERO ST
S. VAN NESS AVE
MISSION DISTRICT
Anchor Brewing
280
Smokestack
THE CASTRO
DOLORES ST
FOLSOM ST
101
DOGPATCH
Pi Bar
CESAR CHAVEZ ST

TORONADO

547 HAIGHT ST;
WWW.TORONADO.COM

Unquestionably one of the best-known beer bars in America. Walk in, check out the beer board, swoon, swear, and then order your drink (Russian River is always a good choice here). Then sit back and take in the beating, busy atmosphere of the place. If you want food then go next door to Rosamund's for a hot dog.

MIKKELLER BAR

34 MASON ST;
WWW.MIKKELLERBAR.COM

Right in the roughest part of the Tenderloin is Mikkeller Bar, one of the smartest spots in the city. The Danish brewer has built a big, clean space that has an oh-my-god good beer list. Many of the house beers are brewed at Faction and they're superb.

CITY BEER STORE

1168 FOLSOM ST #101;
WWW.CITYBEERSTORE.COM

This is a great bottle shop across the street from Cellarmaker. They also have some very good beers on tap, so you can sip a brew while you choose what bottles to take home.

TOP 5 BEERS IN TOWN

Russian River Pliny the Elder
Damn good Double IPA

Moonlight Death and Taxes
World-beating black lager

Anchor Steam
The classic craft beer

Social Ramsgate Rye
English-inspired, American bravado

Faction Pale Ale
Simple, hoppy perfection

SOCIAL KITCHEN & BREWERY

1326 9TH AVE;
WWW.SOCIALKITCHENANDBREWERY.COM

My favorite beers in San Francisco are brewed at Social. Whether it's a wonderfully balanced British Bitter, a zesty-floral lager, a superb IPA, or something Belgian, all of the brews are absolutely brilliant and I wish I could drink them daily. The food is also excellent. Don't miss this place.

CELLARMAKER

1150 HOWARD ST;
WWW.CELLARMAKERBREWING.COM

If you want to know where the local beer geeks are getting their growler fills, then check out Cellarmaker. Always busy and with big hype behind them, they don't disappoint with their range of brews, especially their big-hitting IPAs. Also look out for the rarer barrel-aged beers.

21ST AMENDMENT

563 2ND ST;
WWW.21ST-AMENDMENT.COM

A cozy brewpub by the ball park, stop in here to drink some classic American beer styles. You'll want the Watermelon Wheat, an unusual yet deliciously refreshing beer. I also love Down to Earth, their Session IPA. And look out for specials brewed out the back.

ANCHOR BREWING

1705 MARIPOSA ST;
WWW.ANCHORBREWING.COM

A beer trip to San Francisco technically doesn't count unless you go to Anchor Brewing, the original craft brewery. The tour costs $15 and sells out months in advance, so book ahead. You'll see the handsome copper brewhouse and loop through the whole building before a full tasting at the end. It's excellent.

Well-stocked shelves at the City Beer Store.

MAGNOLIA BREWPUB AND SMOKESTACK

WWW.MAGNOLIAPUB.COM

Magnolia has two spots in the city. The brewpub (1398 Haight St) has lesser-seen hand-pulled ales, many in the British style, plus some great pub grub classics done really well. Smokestack (2505 3rd St) is their production brewery and BBQ joint in the Dogpatch district, where they have their mix of British styles and American brews alongside a lot of meat.

TRIPLE VOODOO

2245 3RD ST, SAN FRANCISCO;
WWW.TRIPLEVOODOO.COM

A couple of blocks from Magnolia Smokestack is Triple Voodoo, a small bar with the brewery out the back. They have some Belgian-inspired brews, all with an American edge to them. If you want food then you can order in from nearby restaurants.

ZEITGEIST

199 VALENCIA ST;
WWW.ZEITGEISTSF.COM

A cool bar, a big beer garden, and over 40 beers on tap. It's a good place to get Moonlight beers, a brewery in Sonoma that makes some amazing lagers. There's a good, lively vibe to Zeitgeist and there are often events and tap-takeovers held here.

PI BAR

1432 VALENCIA ST;
WWW.PIBARSF.COM

Craft beer and pizza in the Mission. The beer list is tight and well chosen (more Moonlight, some Russian River) and the pizzas are really tasty. I probably don't need to say more than that, right?

SOUTHPAW BBQ

2170 MISSION ST;
WWW.SOUTHPAWBBQSF.COM

There's BBQ food, there's house-brewed beer, and there's whiskey. The food is very good, the house beers include the superb Irish Exit Stout, which is great with the meat, and the whiskies make for a fine way to end the night.

MONK'S KETTLE

3141 16TH ST;
WWW.MONKSKETTLE.COM

Monk's Kettle is one of the top spots in the city for beer and food together. The food is some of the best quality that you'll find to go with a stellar beer list, which is always smartly selected with some rarities that you won't want to miss.

4505 BURGERS AND BBQ

705 DIVISADERO ST;
4505MEATS.COM

Fancy more great BBQ meat? This is probably the best place in the city for satisfying that craving. Amazing meats, seriously great sides, and a small but very good beer list all chosen from local breweries. Brilliant.

FACTION BREWING

2501 MONARCH ST, ALAMEDA;
WWW.FACTIONBREWING.COM

Faction isn't the easiest place to get to, but make the effort because they brew some of the best beers in the Bay Area, plus you get a stunning view back across to San Francisco. Drink the Pale Ale because it's probably the best made nearby. There'll be food trucks outside if you're hungry.

CITY GUIDE

MONTREAL

Montreal is a city of brewpubs. Explore it on foot because it's a great looking place with plenty of interesting things to see at walking pace as you pass between pubs. You'll mainly find a mix of Belgian and US styles, reflecting the city's cultural mix of French and Canadian. And check opening times before you go because bars can serve until 3am but might not open until 3pm.

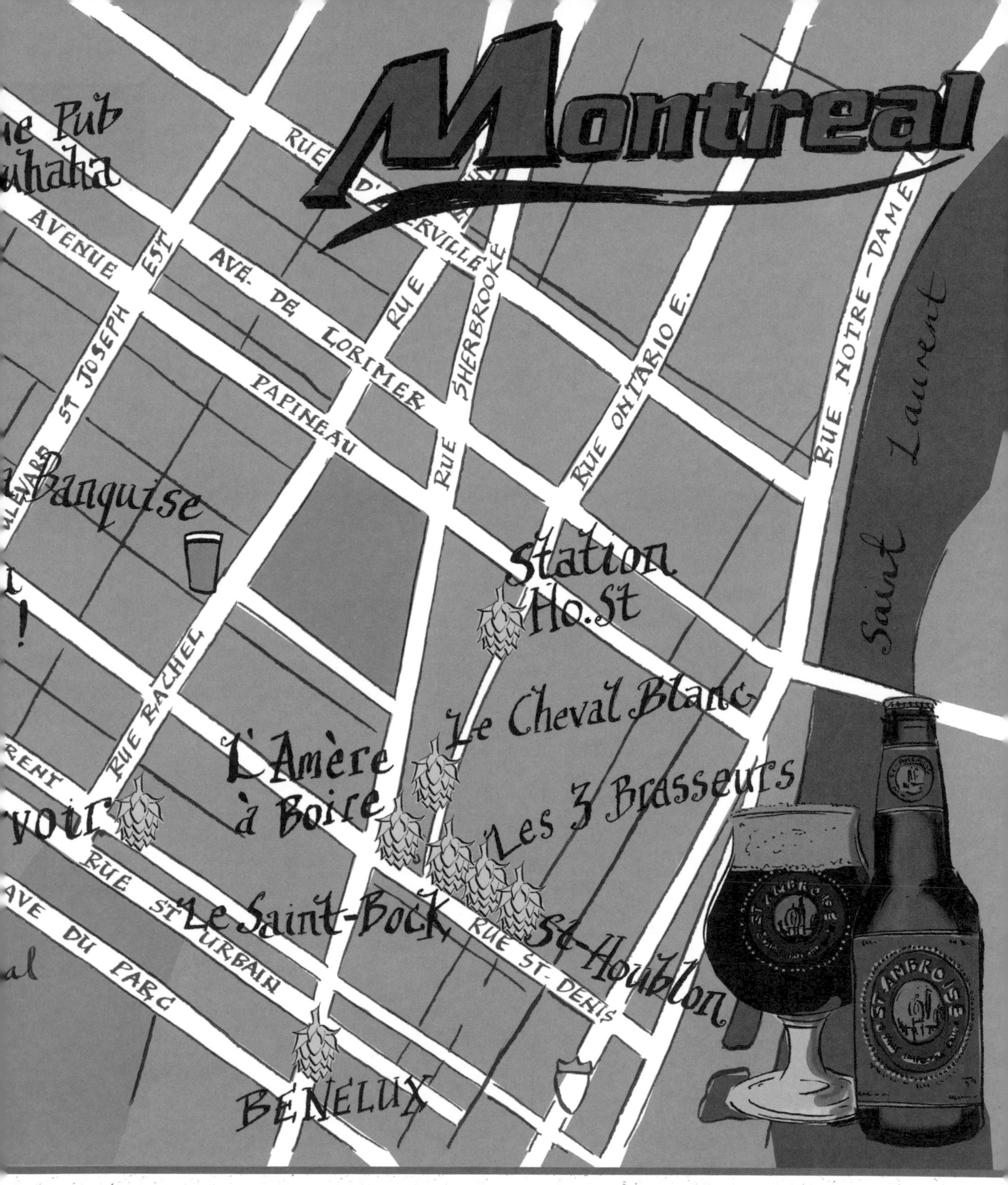
Montreal
RUE D'IBERVILLE
AVENUE
RUE SHERBROOKE
RUE ONTARIO E.
RUE NOTRE-DAME
Saint Laurent
ST JOSEPH EST
AVE. DE LORIMER
PAPINEAU
RUE RACHEL
Station Ho.St
Le Cheval Blanc
L'Amère à Boire
Les 3 Brasseurs
Le Saint-Bock
St-Houblon
RUE ST. DENIS
RUE ST URBAIN
AVE DU PARC
BENELUX
ST-AMBROISE

DIEU DU CIEL!

29 LAURIER WEST;
WWW.DIEUDUCIEL.COM

One of the best brewpubs in the world and a must-visit when in Montreal. A warm and cozy bar, you'll find up to 20 beers on tap and you won't find a bad one to drink. Péché Mortel is perhaps the beer they're best known for—a cracking coffee Imperial Stout. The IPAs are superb as are their interpretations of classic Belgian brews, so plan to spend plenty of time here. Also plan a detour to Fairmount Bagels (www.fairmountbagel.com) either before or after the beer—they are sweet, dense, and delicious.

LE SAINT-BOCK

1749 RUE SAINT-DENIS;
WWW.LESAINTBOCK.COM

They might as well rename Rue Saint-Denis "Brewpub Street" because it's home to no less than four small breweries, all situated very close together. Le Saint-Bock has 45 taps, most of them from their own brewery, plus many from around the rest of the country. You can get small pours of all the beers, so this is the perfect place to sample some of Canada's best brews.

L'AMÈRE À BOIRE

2049 RUE SAINT-DENIS;
WWW.AMEREABOIRE.COM

A simple brewpub with a very good range of beers, L'Amère à Boire has a good vibe for you to enjoy while sipping from their choice of very good lagers, Pale Ales, and Stouts. In particular look out for La Muesli, an Oatmeal Stout that's rich, smooth, chocolatey, and laced with berry fruits—it's exemplary of the style.

SAINT HOUBLON

1567 RUE SAINT-DENIS;
WWW.SAINTHOUBLON.COM

With beer-infused food, you could come here just to eat. Happily there's also the bonus of some good house-brewed beers and a fun, cool atmosphere.

At the end of Rue Saint-Denis, location of L'Amère à Boire, Saint Houblon, and Les 3 Brasseurs, stands this statue. When you see it, you'll know good beer is close by.

LES 3 BRASSEURS

1658 RUE SAINT-DENIS (PLUS OTHER LOCATIONS); WWW.LES3BRASSEURS.CA

An ever-growing chain, there are a few of these in Montreal. Go and you can expect to see their line-up of Blonde, Wit, Amber, and IPA, plus specials. At the Saint-Denis site, the smart copper brewkit can be seen as you pass down the street. Pop in for a half on the way to the other places nearby.

CHEVAL BLANC

809 RUE ONTARIO EST;
WWW.LECHEVALBLANC.CA

This dark, cool brewpub has a central bar and around 10 house beers to choose from. Their Oatmeal Stout is one that you shouldn't skip, the hoppy beers have a great freshness to them, and there'll always be something different and interesting to taste.

BENELUX

245 RUE SHERBROOKE OUEST;
WWW.BRASSERIEBENELUX.COM

A bustling brewpub by night, it's quieter during the day. The Blanche is smooth and creamy with a nice spiciness, the IPAs are properly hoppy and good, while you'll find some style-shifting Saisons of various strengths.

RESERVOIR

9 AVENUE DULUTH EST;
WWW.BRASSERIERESERVOIR.CA

A cozy bar packed with small tables, this is a smart little brewpub off the cool Boulevard St-Laurent. The Pilsner is snappily bitter and aromatic, the Brown Ale is somewhere between classic British and hoppy American in a very good way, but it's the IPA which you want to drink—soft-bodied, smooth, and lushly fruity. The food is also great.

HELM

273 RUE BERNARD OUEST;
WWW.HELM-MTL.CA

Houblon, Eau, Levure, et Malt is what the name stands for. There are around 15 house-brewed beers to choose from, and you'll happily stay for a while and work through them in this cool place to sit and drink with friends.

VICES ET VERSA

6631 BOULEVARD ST-LAURENT;
WWW.VICESETVERSA.COM

The city's premier beer bar with all Quebec craft brews on tap. Good crowd and atmosphere, and a tasty menu including some really good sandwiches and local cheeses. Don't miss it.

BROUE PUB BROUHAHA

5860 AVENUE DE LORIMIER;
WWW.BROUEPUBBROUHAHA.COM

They have their own beers here plus some of the best from the region. The smoked meat is good, especially with the hoppy house beers.

STATION HO.ST

1494 RUE ONTARIO EST;
WWW.STATIONHOST.CA

This is the tasting room for Hopfenstark. A long bar, it's sparse but smart and a good place to hang out and sip through the various brews, including classic styles and innovative Saisons.

LA BANQUISE

994 RUE RACHEL EST;
WWW.LABANQUISE.COM

Poutine is a Montreal speciality—fries, a thick gravy and cheese curds in one plate of ultimate belly-filling comfort food. La Banquis is very good; they have around 30 versions of poutine to choose from and some decent beers in bottle.

TOP 5 BEERS IN TOWN

McAuslan St-Ambroise Oatmeal Stout
Few Oatmeal Stouts are better than this

Dieu du Ciel! Péché Morte
A world class coffee Imperial Stout

Brasserie Dunham Black IPA
a brilliant hoppy black brew

Les Trois Mousquetaires Kellerbier
A superb unfiltered lager

Dieu du Ciel! Moralité
One of the best IPAs you'll find

THE REST OF THE WORLD

Great beer is everywhere and going beyond the better-known countries, like Germany, Belgium, and America, reveals so many interesting stories and different types of beer. Take Australia's amazing craft beer scene, for example, or Blumenau, the small town in the south of Brazil that holds a huge Oktoberfest every year. Then there's China, the world's largest beer market, and Vietnam, where you can get the cheapest beer in the world. If you want to drink good beer then the world is yours to explore.

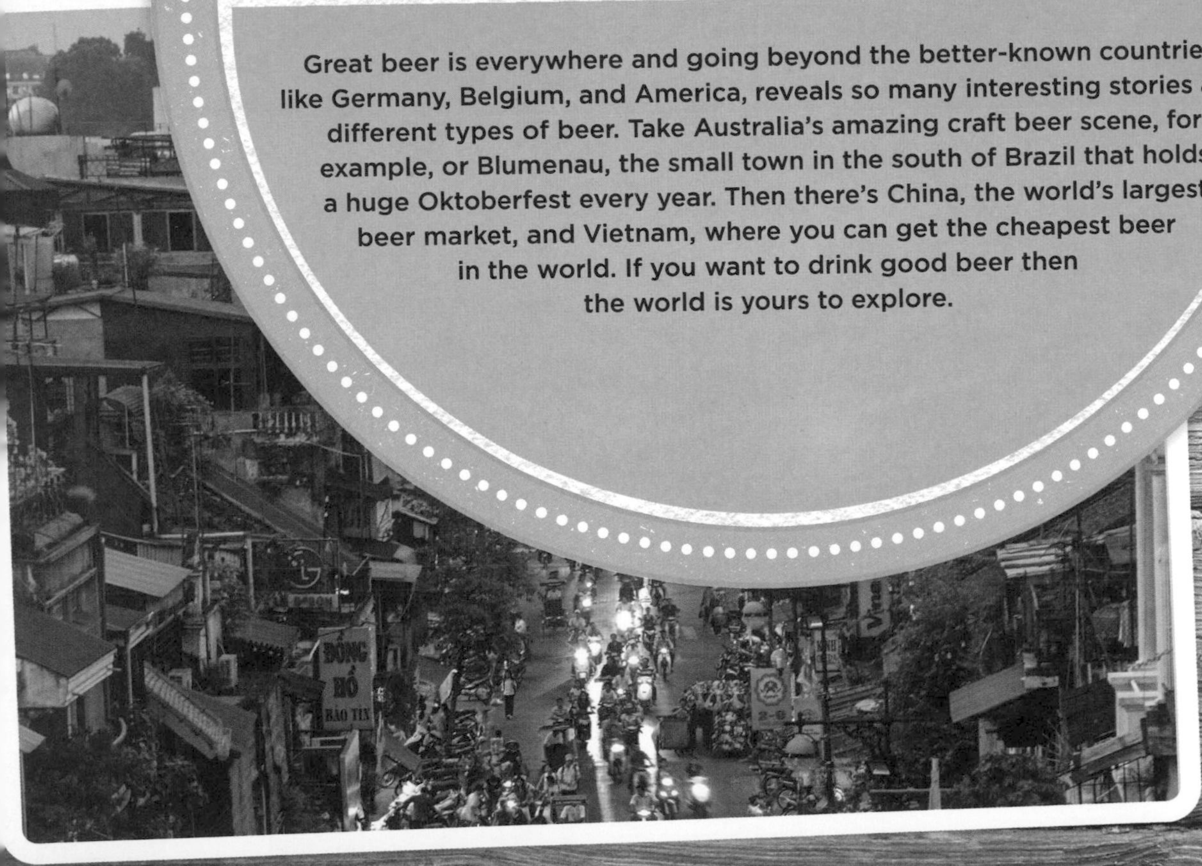

BIA HOI
COOL BEER

CHUNG-BICH

TRADIÇÃO
TODOS OS DIAS.
Bradesco

IS THE BEST-SELLING BEER IN THE WORLD THE TASTIEST?

Matt and I are in a cold, fluorescent-bright restaurant down a dark hutong in Beijing. There's a family of eight with dozens of plates and scraps of food messily spread everywhere. A group of guys barely have space to eat their dumplings because of all the empty beer bottles on their table. We're shown to two small stools in the back corner. Next to us staff are cleaning chopsticks and pushing them into paper packets.

We point at the fridge and we're given two bottles with shiny blue labels, the liquid almost as clear as the glass it's in. They come with two tiny plastic beakers, the sort you drink milk from at pre-school. We toast our final night in China, excited to finally have the beer we traveled halfway across the globe to drink. This beer is called Snow. Unless you've been to China then it's unlikely that you've ever tried a glass because none of it leaves the country. But that's not to say that it's a rare, obscure brew: Snow is the biggest-selling beer in the world. And you won't believe how hard it was for us to find it...

THE BEST-SELLING BEERS IN THE WORLD

1. Snow
2. Tsingtao
3. Bud Light
4. Budweiser
5. Skol
6. Yanjing
7. Heineken
8. Harbin
9. Brahma
10. Coors Light

THE SEARCH BEGINS

We land in Beijing and head straight out for beer. Matt and I have both enjoyed all kinds of different drinks all around the world, so have a decent understanding of bars and boozing. As this is the first time either of us has been to China, we want to find a bar, somewhere we can sit and take in the drinking culture.

"Where shall we stop?" Matt says, after we've been walking for half an hour on a cold November night.

"I have no idea. I just figured there'd be a bar somewhere around here."

Endless red neon lights make the street glow in a strange way as it blurs through the smoggy haze. The unusually silent streets make it feel like a dirty Las Vegas with the volume set to mute. We're in the Dongzhimen area, which we chose because of Gui Street, a one-kilometer strip with around 150 restaurants located along it. This should be the perfect place to find a drink but as we walk up and down the full stretch of the street we don't see a single bar that we can just stop in for a beer. Our drinking radar is usually well attuned to finding a pint wherever we are, but it doesn't seem to be working too well here in Beijing.

With so much going on in the city, it will be easy to track down the world's best-selling beer, right?

We shrug our shoulders; it's alright, but doesn't really taste of anything.

"I'm pretty hungry for dumplings. Shall we just eat and then try somewhere else later?" says Matt after we've been walking for an hour. We choose one of the busier restaurants on the street, figuring if it's full then it must be good, and it certainly smells good as we walk in: the air is warm with broth, sweet with shellfish, fragrant with Szechuan peppers.

On all the tables are large green bottles of beer. We order two pijiu, which is a name derivative from the Czech pivo, and we're given the same as everyone else. The label is simple, swirled with Chinese symbols in deep green and in bright red are the words "Yanjing Beer.'"This is one of the top-10 best-selling beers in the world and it's Beijing's brew, so it makes sense that this is what we get. It's one of the palest beers I've ever seen. The body is thin; it's dry, clean, and presumably uses a significant proportion of rice in the grain bill, which contributes to its lack of flavor. We shrug our shoulders and agree that it's alright, but doesn't really taste of anything. It's also very light in alcohol at 3.4% ABV.

Our attention is now on the food and as we drink we start pawing through the huge menu. Which is when I see the words "frog wang." I turned 30 three days ago and still that made me guffaw like a 13-year-old.

Matt sees it, too: "Frog wang is on the menu! They also have something called 'old vinegar sting head' and 'spicy beauty shoes!' And how can we not order 'husband and wife lung slice,' that sounds delicious!"

When we finally finish giggling we manage to place our order by pointing at the pictures in the menu. One by one the dishes arrive and cover our table. The prosaically named "dry rot know of the shrimp" is outstanding, with whole shrimp steaming in a dish with garlic, chilies, and tongue-numbing Szechuan peppers. We have one dumpling so soft that I could nap on it and another filled with broth that bursts when I bite into it. Both types are so good our chopsticks battle over the last ones.

In comparison to the great food, the Yanjing is really boring. The bottle holds 660ml, so it's big and we only want one through the meal, plus at such at low ABV it won't even get us drunk. It's also the only beer choice on the menu, but at least it's cheap at under $1 per bottle.

We deliberately under-ate so that we can have another meal later, which is what we go in search of next, this time in another busy part of town where we explore some cool hutongs. These hutongs are narrow alleyways, which are like a complex web joining the whole city, and are where people live and socialize. Many have shops and restaurants, making them perfect for backstreet bars, which makes it especially frustrating when we can't find anywhere to drink.

We pick a restaurant that looks interesting and I ask for Snow. I get a blank stare back so I say it again. Still they have no idea what I'm saying. After repeating the word Snow about 10 times, each with a different pronunciation and intonation, I give up and point to the bottle of Harbin sitting on the table next to us.

The famous Quanjude restaurant is celebrated for its roast duck but not its beer selection.

SNOW IN CHINA

One in every 20 beers drunk in the world is Snow. In 2013, 10.3 billion liters of the stuff were brewed and drunk in China. No size comparison really makes this figure easier to understand (4,200 Olympic swimming pools?), but it's more than all of the beer brewed in Germany in a whole year and you can add together the total volume of beer brewed in the UK, Belgium, and the Czech Republic and there's still more Snow in the world.

Snow, which is actually a collective of a few different beers totaled under one name, is brewed in a joint venture between China Resources Snow Breweries Ltd and SABMiller. It was only founded and first brewed in 1993, so the brand's ascent to become the biggest-selling beer has been fast, and today around 90 breweries across the country combine to produce that much Snow. China may have a relatively modest per capita consumption of 9 gallons (35 liters) a year, but between them the population of 1.35 billion people helps to make the country the largest overall producer and drinker of beer in the world, with one beer out of every four brewed on the planet made there. This enormous brewing output sees that four of the 10 best-selling global beers are also Chinese: Snow, Tsingtao, Yanjing, and Harbin.

Harbin was first brewed in 1900 in the north east of China, making it the oldest Chinese brand, though today it's owned by AB-InBev. It's better than the watery Yanjing, with a little more malt depth and a dry bitterness that has a hint of hops, but it's still pretty plain. We eat zhajiang mian, a bowl of wheat noodles topped with pork in a soybean paste plus some chopped radish, and the beer is simple, refreshing, and nothing more.

On the walk home we keep looking for bars, for anywhere to just get a beer and sit for a while like we would in the west. Finding nothing we bail on the boozing, hoping that tomorrow we'll do better.

> We pick a restaurant that looks interesting and I ask for Snow. I get a blank stare back.

HIGH HOPES

Day two begins with the tourist stuff. As this is a beer book, I'm not going to describe how we walked through the Forbidden City, explored old temples, and stood in Tiananmen Square. Instead you'll know that if you go to Beijing then you're going to want to see this stuff because it's really interesting.

Lunch is at Quanjude, a place famous for Beijing duck, probably the city's best-known meal. Like last night, the menu is huge, and again everyone around us is drinking beer—Yanjing and that's all. We eat a whole duck between us, wrapping the rich meat in soft pancakes and topping it with sweet hoisin sauce, and it's delicious. The beer, however, is as bland as it was last night.

Being in the tourist area, we search again for Snow. There are restaurants everywhere and we look through all the windows, trying to see through to the fridges. We pick a busy Mongolian hot pot place where the steam from the soup makes the windows foggy and the air warm, thick, and meaty.

"Snow pijiu?" I ask and after a momentary blank stare the server nods and heads to the fridge.

"Did she understand that right? Is she actually going to get Snow?" says Matt, which is when I see her turn with two large green bottles in her hands. More bloody Yanjing. The waitress expects us to order food, which we politely decline on several occasions. On her fourth attempt to show us the menu we give up, quickly drink our beers, and make an exit, waving goodbye to the confused-looking waitress.

In planning this trip we mostly thought about the food—the beer, we assumed, we'd find everywhere (I probably should've been more prepared for that, I now realize). Because duck is the famous dish, we wanted to try a couple of different versions so we went double-duck for the day, having dinner in Da Dong. Again, the menu is extensive, and the food here of a finer quality, yet there's just one beer, this time it's Tsingtao. Pronounced 'ching-dao,' this bottle has more depth of flavor than the other beers but it's still uninteresting. It works fine with the food without offering anything more than simple refreshment.

For locals, beer doesn't get much better than a bottle of the ubiquitous Yanjing. We're not so convinced.

After dinner we get back on the hunt for Snow, wandering around endless hutongs looking in the restaurants, focusing on the smaller back-street places that a working class local would go for some cheap food and beer. We figure that's our best option to find the somehow-elusive brew.

We spy a restaurant with a large fridge at the back, the many bottles on the shelves giving us hope. We barge in and walk straight to the fridge, scanning for that one beer that we want. "Why the hell does nowhere have it?!" The frustration is kicking in.

As we turn, a table is presented to us with the staff smiling and pointing at the pictures in the already-opened menus. We can't leave now so we order two beers and close the menus; we're so full from the duck that we can't face another dish. We can barely face another beer, especially the Yanjing that's coming our way, and once again through the whole bland bottle we attempt to explain that we only want a drink to the confused staff.

A POOR FORECAST

Into day three and I'm getting concerned about the lack of Snow, so I make the call to check out some supermarkets to see what they have; I can't come all the way to China specifically in search of one beer and then not drink it. If it means drinking bottles in the hotel room then that's fine, I just have to find Snow.

In a small shop, we find the fridge at the back. Next to brightly colored bottles of soda, the beers are given a small space, with Yanjing having its own shelf, Harbin beneath it, Tsingtao to the side, plus a few brands we haven't seen so far. But no Snow.

We find a larger supermarket with a huge selection of wine bottles, spirits, and crates of beer all randomly stacked. Bottles and cans are lined up; a wall of green, white, and blue with Chinese characters etched into them. We scan the shelves, past many types of Yanjing, past a variety of Harbin in different colors, past the Tsingtao… still nothing.

That afternoon we explore some more and while we can't find Snow, we can't escape smog; my throat hurts, my lungs wheeze. When I get WiFi, I check the Air Quality Index (AQI). On the AQI scale, 0–50 is fine and there's no risk—around 50 is what you'd expect in London or New York; 150 is unhealthy for sensitive people, though ok for most of the population, while 300 is dangerously hazardous and the entire population can be affected. Today it's over 500, which explains why many people are wearing masks in the city. If ever there was a day to find a bar to sit in for a while then today is it.

Even the supermarkets in Beijing failed to stock the world's best-selling beer.

And then, wonderfully, while walking down another winding hutong, we see a dirty window with hundreds of bottles of Belgian beer lined up. The lights are on so we go in. It's like a furnace with a space heater blasting into our faces. And it's loud as a movie plays on a small TV above two large fridges. It's tiny; there are a couple of chairs and tables, what looks like a small kitchen at the back, and that's all. But it does have beer and it is a bar. We found one!

We're the only customers. The guy working there turns the TV down and shows us the fridges. They have lots of Belgian and German bottles, but we want Chinese beer, which is the next challenge because we can't see any. We ask the guy for a local beer and thankfully he understands, opening the fridge and pulling out a bottle with no label on it. He offers it to us and after we try and confirm that it's local, he opens it and gives us two glasses.

"Pale Ale," he says smiling before he returns to his movie, turning it up to an obnoxiously high volume.

"I think this is homebrew…" says Matt as he pours out the lively, cloudy liquid.

It's not very good, unfortunately, and we're in one of the weirdest places I've ever drunk beer, but at least we're in a bar and out of the smog.

For dinner Matt and I meet up with Alex Acker, who owns Jing-A, a great Beijing craft brewery. He suggests we go for chuar, a traditional fast food where everything is cooked on skewers. With our meal we drink Yanjing (we checked: they don't have Snow here) and talk about our experiences in Beijing so far, Alex helps us understand Chinese drinking culture. First up, bars are just not a thing in Beijing, apart from in fancy hotels or connected to more Western-inspired venues. Instead beer is

"Why the hell does nowhere have it?!" The frustration is kicking in.

what the Chinese drink when they eat. And eating is what they do to socialize. People don't drink alone here and they don't drink without food, which helps to explain why we've been getting strange looks for drinking in restaurants without ordering food.

Beer is something that everyone can afford and so it doesn't have any status to it. However, Alex is seeing a shift and people will order his beer specifically because it's strong or expensive, to suggest an elevated personal status; the Chinese are beginning to see beer differently. This makes sense when we see how well wine has done in recent years—China is the biggest consumer of red wine in the world, something partly attributed to the color red being associated with joy and good fortune in Chinese culture.

Another drink that's popular in China, and also reflects this status shift, is baiju. It's a strong Chinese spirit, somewhere between vodka and rocket fuel, which ranges from very cheap to very expensive. We finish our meal with baiju and I have no memories beyond that bottle.

Scorpions on sticks, just one of the many local delicacies available at Wangfujing Street night market.

A LOST CAUSE

Our final day in Beijing means one last chance to get Snow. So after a lunch that saw us pass on the Yanjing (partly because we know it's rubbish, partly because of the baiju hangover), we walk to Wangfujing Street for its famous night market.

Passing under tall red gates, it's busy with tourists taking photos of all the unusual foodie things, most of them impaled on long wooden skewers: there are whole squid stretched out like linen-white sails; pink shrimps, brown bugs, fat grubs, seahorses, and star fish; there are large pointy-tailed scorpions next to smaller versions still wriggling on the stick; there are tarantulas with round bodies and crispy legs; kidneys, liver, and veiny pink testicles; flaccid snakes wrapped around the stick; and the weirdest thing I've ever seen on a stick ready to be grilled and eaten—a whole baby shark.

After some crunchy, salty scorpions we want a beer and there's a guy selling drinks on the side of the road—he has more Yanjing, Tsingtao, and even Budweiser, but still no Snow. It's late and we're tired after four days in the city and three days in Vietnam before that. We walk off with no destination in mind, happy to simply have a decent dinner somewhere and enjoy our last evening.

By now I'm prepared for the fact that we are unlikely to find Snow, which is incredible. How could we not find the world's—and China's—biggest-selling beer in the country's second-largest city? And we've looked hard to find it. That's when we walked down another dark hutong and into a bright, busy restaurant. That's when we were directed to the table at the back by all the dirty dishes. We passed the fridge without even taking notice and when we were asked for our order we pointed at the fridge and simply asked for two beers. It was only then that we looked at the stack of bottles. It was only then that we saw the clear bottle with the shiny blue label.

"THEY'VE GOT SNOW!"

In front of us now, in little green plastic beakers, is the world's best-selling beer. I've never had this beer before but surely by virtue of it being the bestseller it has to be good? We toast our tiny cups and we celebrate finally finding Snow. We drink the beer, placing our beakers down at the same time.

"Well?" says Matt.

"It's dreadful."

After four days of searching Beijing for Snow I got my answer: the best-selling beer in the world is definitely not the best-tasting beer in the world.

RIGHT: Mission accomplished—we finally found Snow in China.

CRAFT BEER IN BEIJING

I didn't travel all the way to China to just drink mass-made lagers and the beer geek in me was in search of the best of the craft brews. It's interesting to see how craft beer is growing here. And much of it is genuinely good, too. A city like Beijing or Shanghai picks up trends very quickly, so while you might not go to China specifically for the beer, in the big cities you can always find something great to drink.

Great Leap Brewing is Beijing's best-known craft brewery. The brews have a Chinese twist, with many using Chinese hops plus local ingredients like rice, honey, and cinnamon. And did you know that China is one of the leading hop growers in the world? They are almost exclusively used domestically, so aren't well known. If you want to try some then have Great Leap's Pale Ale #6. It's brewed with Chinese hop flowers which give a subtle spicy, grassy, fruity fragrance. It's also made with Chinese barley.

Jing-A is brewed in a BBQ restaurant, where the meaty meals are perfect with the hoppy brews. The brewery also has a Taproom in the city pouring American-style beers that also make use of local ingredients, such as roasted chestnuts, Szechuan peppercorns, mandarin zest, sake rice, and wasabi. Their Flying Fist IPA is a superb beer and there's also a brew dedicated to Beijing's infamous smog. Called Airpocalypse Double IPA, the beer's price fluctuates depending on the day's smog levels—the worse the air quality, the cheaper the beer, so stay in and drink it.

Slow Boat is tricky to find but it was worth the search for their Monkey's Fist IPA. Panda Brewpub is an urban-chic space that feels more Brooklyn than Beijing with the shiny silver tanks visible behind the bar. They have a Witbier, Pale Ale, Honey Ale, Brown Ale, and Stout among their offerings and all are decent.

NBeerPub has loads of taps and bottles and the biggest selection in town, including plenty of Chinese craft beers. Pass By Bar has a decent range of brews in a cool part of town.

THE FRESHEST, CHEAPEST BEER IN THE WORLD

Winding in and out of the never-ending traffic, the scooters are so fast and there are so many of them, flying at me like a swarm of giant mechanical bees, blasting their horns. The atmosphere is alive and vibrant, colorful, the air warm and fragrant with mint and basil. There are people everywhere; people carrying baskets balanced across their shoulders, people selling doughnuts and skewers of meat, people standing around talking in their tonal tongue, sitting on chairs with huge steaming bowls in front of them.

I can read the names on the storefronts but they make no sense, accented with all kinds of unusual hooks. There are tables of the darkest coffees I've ever seen, trays of brightly colored fruits which I can't name, fish being filleted, grills smoking, wicker baskets bulging with leafy greens, stock pots bubbling and making the humid air smell like pork. The buildings look like they're toppling, like they've been squashed in so tightly that they're being squeezed down on top of each other, their balconies heavy with laundry. And the scooters, they never stop. The constant blaring of horns is always there.

"We need to cross here," says Matt, who couldn't resist the chance to come back to Hanoi in Vietnam, where he'd been before on his honeymoon. "I'll let you go first."

I'd been warned about the bikes in Hanoi but that doesn't prepare me for the reality of the impenetrable wall coming at me at different speeds and from different directions. Remember the game Frogger? Well it's like that only it's real life. There are no traffic lights, no crosswalks, and seemingly no way to get across the street. I look back at Matt and he's laughing—he's done this before, he knows what to do. "Just walk," says Matt. "Trust me. Don't stop, just walk and they'll drive around you."

THEY LOVE BEER IN VIETNAM

In 2013, Vietnamese breweries produced 3.13 billion liters of beer, putting them 12th in overall world beer production, and that production level has grown year-on-year for over a decade. To put their annual output into perspective, Vietnam brews almost as much beer as Belgium and the Czech Republic combined, though the 10 gallons (39 liters) per capita consumption in Vietnam doesn't compare to the mighty 38 gallons (143 liters) that Czechs chug a year.

"Look at how many bikes there are! Can't we just stay on this side of the street. It looks the same as that side."

"Nope, Bia Hoi Corner is that way."

"Bollocks. Ok. Let's do this." I look again and still there's no gap in the bikes coming at me, whizzing and winding left and right, turning off down tiny streets. I take the first step, then another. The riders all look ahead, veering from side to side, passing

Crossing the road in Hanoi amounts to stepping out into the middle of hundreds of bikes and hoping for the best.

me on the inside and out. With each step I feel like my toes are going to get run over, but I keep on stepping, no hesitation. Against all childhood advice on crossing streets, against all adult instinct to not get hit by a fast-moving scooter carrying three people and a giant sack of fruit, I just walk. One more step—more of a run and a jump—and I make it to the other side. Looking back the traffic still flows, unending.

"Easy!" says Matt, laughing.

A LITTLE DONG GOES A LONG WAY

Around a few more winding roads and we arrive at Bia Hoi Corner, a crossroads of four streets, lined with bars and surrounded by hundreds of people sat drinking glasses of light golden beer. It's hard to tell where one bar becomes the next as they spread out from the street corners so we just find a couple of free seats and order two bia hoi. The chairs here are little plastic stools like those you sat on in the classroom as a five-year-old. We sit with our knees up near our chins and our feet in the road. Behind us on the curb are four silver kegs, battered and stacked. Our server squats beneath the lowest keg and opens a tap, pouring out the liquid into two plastic mugs. I can see across to the bar opposite and they have the same set-up: pouring beer straight from the keg and hurriedly serving them to drinkers packed around nearby tables.

The beers arrive and Matt hands over a 10,000 Vietnamese Dong bill. "I just gave her a lot of DONG," he says.

"My dong is literally bulging out of my trousers," I laugh, pointing at my bill-filled wallet. As we tap our glasses and say cheers to Vietnam and another beer adventure, we both know that what follows is three days of drinking, eating, and dong jokes.

This is my first taste of bia hoi, a beer unique to Vietnam and the reason we're here in Hanoi. The name translates as "gas beer" but more simply it means "draft beer," with the "bia" part deriving from the French "bière." It's a very light lager, gently carbonated, soft bodied, a little sweet and caramel-like, reminiscent of classic Czech lagers, then refreshingly dry at the end. What makes it special is that it's probably the freshest beer in the world.

Bia hoi is relatively low in alcohol, typically 3–4% ABV, and the grain bill uses a significant portion of rice, making it light and crisp. What makes it different from other Asian rice lagers is that it has a surprising richness of malt similar to Czech Světlý Ležák, only it's a little more watery. There might also be some banana and bubblegum fruitiness, and even a hint of butterscotch.

It is brewed typically as a light lager, but once fermentation has finished it doesn't go through lager's usual long, cold-conditioning period (which would help to cover up the natural fruity flavors known as esters, or the buttery diacetyl flavors produced during fermentation, hence they are still present in bia hoi). Instead the beer is packaged right away and sent to bars, meaning brewing takes place only a few days before you drink it. Additionally, because it's unpasteurized and Vietnam is a hot country, a barrel of beer will only stay fresh for 24 hours, so it's drunk the day it's delivered.

A woman pours us a couple of bia hoi in her tiny store.

As well as being the freshest, bia hoi is also one of the cheapest beers in the world. It costs a mere 15p (¢25) to buy a glass, which holds around 14 oz (400 ml). In other words, it's bloody cheap. Matt and I both live in London and don't flinch at handing over £5 ($7.50) for a pint. Here, for that same amount we can get 33 beers.

After a day of traveling, the first beer is followed by satisfied "ahhs" as the stresses of airplanes and taxis are replaced with the freedom and buzz of being somewhere new. And this is immediately an exciting and unusual situation: our feet are literally in the road, there's hawking and beeping and yelling all around, people are pushing carts of food which smell so tasty, the beers are different to anything I've tasted before. There's constant activity, noise, speed; it's unrelenting and crazy.

In the humidity of Hanoi the first beers are gone in just a few minutes, so when we spot a couple of stools free in the bar down the street we run across to them and order two more.

This bia hoi—the name refers to both the drink and the bar, so you can say "I'll see you at the bia hoi" and "let's have a bia hoi"—is tiny with just a little old lady inside. Through a dark-green door, past a counter of cigarettes and bottles of cola, one keg stands on its own with a sheet hanging above it saying "Bia Hoi 5,000VND." I've never seen beer served like this before, in a place that's really just a gap between bigger bars. This beer tastes different, too; a little warmer, a little more carbonated, a little sweeter.

The mission tonight is to go to all the bars on Bia Hoi Corner, eating Vietnamese street food snacks as we drink.

We spot another bar: "Let's do that one next and also get some food—I want spring rolls and fried chicken!" This place is right on the junction of Bia Hoi Corner, so it's the busiest; a bustling space where elbows and knees knock against strangers all sitting on the tiny stools. The beer here is 10,000VND each, which already seems outrageously expensive to our fast-adjusted sense of prices.

The staff carry red trays topped with plastic tankards, while one woman sits inside pouring constantly from the large tilted barrel. This beer is different again—colder, drier, and more refreshing, perfect with the fried snacks and spicy dipping sauce we order. The food here comes from the bar's own kitchen, but across the corner there seems to be a second kitchen supplying food for a number of the bars, with platefuls continuously appearing and going to different places. Then at the side of the street there are skewers of meat grilling, a cart stir fries corn with chili and scallions (spring onions), and you can eat all of these while you drink in the bars—it's a very open, shared place.

As the night goes on the atmosphere changes with more and more people around, spilling further into the streets that have now become pedestrianized, halting the cacophony of scooters. There's a mix of locals and tourists, sitting side by side, all drinking and eating, with the buzz of the bikes replaced by the chorus of conversations. It's social, friendly, fun—like a big street party, with everyone outside in the warm night enjoying these small glasses of pale lager.

Moving from bar to bar, all the beers are similar yet still different. Temperature varies, carbonation varies, some are clean and dry, others fruitier, some more bitter. The glasses are different, too: tankards, pots, tumblers; some plastic, some glass.

Hanoi is a remarkable, colorful, vibrant city with surprises at every turn.

It might all be called bia hoi but it's not all the same beer from the same brewery. Also, not all the draft beer here is bia hoi and you'll find pasteurized, filtered beer, which is typically more expensive, served colder and of a more consistent quality—we have a glass of Larue to compare and it's good. If you want bia hoi then you need to specifically ask for that, especially toward the end of the night because bars will run out of bia hoi and stop serving it. We also see all the local bottles, names like Saigon, Bia Ha Noi, Halida, Hanoi, and 333.

We stumble back to our hotel, somehow avoiding the bikes that are still flying around, and fall into our beds. I think we've had 12 beers each, eaten a lot of food and spent around $23 (£15) between us, or, because it makes us sound more badass, about half a million Dong. "HA! Dong!" is the last thing Matt says before passing out.

It might all be called bia hoi but it's not all the same beer.

Poured straight from the keg, beer doesn't come much fresher (or cheaper) than this.

OFF THE BEATEN TRACK

Day two in Hanoi is my 30th birthday. Getting into the hotel last night I thought that I'd found beer and food heaven. This morning, with a head-spinning hangover, I'm almost certain that I've stepped into hell. The noise, oh god the noise, the bikes, the horns, the cars, the impenetrable language, the speed of it all. We have to cross the street and it leaves me getting spun around like a cartoon character, my brain feeling like it might explode.

We grab a breakfast of Vietnamese coffee—the thickest, richest, most delicious coffee I've ever had—and a fortifying bowl of pho, the country's famous noodle soup, then we wander the food markets and randomly wind our way through the active streets. On one road you'll see nothing but people slurping noodles, another will be lined only with silks or kitchenware, another with mechanics. We see men getting a hair cut on the side of the street, groups huddled over board games, we walk in the road because all the scooters are parked on the curb, we see foods that we can't identify. Each new turn reveals itself as you walk down it, a constant surprise of a city.

Bia hois are a consistent sight, standing out with their red and yellow signs. Like the concept of a local pub in other parts of the world, the Vietnamese have their own bia hoi where they go to meet friends and family, to have a beer and some food, to relax after work. Bia Hoi Corner is the famous central place but there's more than just one of these and the beer can be found all around the city. And that's today's challenge: find bia hoi beyond Bia Hoi Corner.

We start in a tiny bar called Bia Hoi 39 on Duong Thanh. Two large kegs are stacked inside and three are on the street outside, each spray-painted with "Haso" in red. The plastic mugs look like small German beer tankards, the foam is light and fluffy, the beer has a handsome haze to it, a full, creamy texture, and bitter lemony finish. In front of us two young guys drink and smoke, sitting inside the back of the bar are tables of men in their 60s, sipping on beers, sucking on cigarettes, picking at peanuts. Just a casual Sunday lunchtime.

The relentless high-pitched buzz of scooters provides the soundtrack to a night drinking at Bia Hoi Corner.

Up the street, on the corner of Duong Thanh and Bat Dan, are two bia hoi opposite each other, both large and packed with people. In one, which has the least sturdy stools we find—so un-sturdy that they bend and crack when our heavy British arses sit on them—the beers are the most bitter, refreshing, and clean so far, showing again how varied bia hoi is. The bar opposite has large 26-gallon (100-liter) drums of beer lined up, racked on a metal shelf with a tray of glasses beneath it. I have no idea what's in those drums… could it be kegs, could they just be filled with beer? Either way the beer here is very good.

We bounce from bia hoi to bia hoi all day. In one place the server and people inside laugh at us, presumably because we've just been charged the "tourist" price of 9,000VND and then given them 20,000VND as we leave, waving away the change. They laugh because we paid so much, yet we're laughing because we paid so little. What we do notice is that unlike the mix of people at Bia Hoi Corner, it's almost exclusively men who drink in the bia hois around the city—the only women are the ones working. But no one drinks alone here; they're always in groups, always talking, and always eating. That's another great thing about Vietnam—the beer is affordable for literally everyone, making it a very sociable and achievable drink, while the food is also so cheap and so good that people eat out all the time.

We eat as much as we can: amazing bun cha with pork patties, rice noodles, and a garden of fragrant herbs; cha ca la vong, a dish of white fish cooked in turmeric and dill; spring rolls and summer rolls; the best rice I've ever tasted served with omelette and hot sauce; banh mi baguettes filled with pork and herbs. There are more coffees because they're so gloriously addictive. There's fresh coconut water to stay hydrated. And there's a never-ending rally of jokes every time we get our dongs out.

It's this type of relaxed, communal scene that makes the experience of drinking bia hoi such a memorable one.

KICKING THE KEG

We return to Bia Hoi Corner late at night when the bars are packed. It's lively and loud but there's no drunkenness, just people having a good time. Some bia hoi have run out of fresh beer and are closing but we find a bar that's still serving bia hoi and set ourselves the challenge of kicking the keg before we leave. They won't serve this beer tomorrow so it seems like a decent thing for us to do, plus it is my birthday.

Beer after beer comes and goes. We eat the most delicious deep-fried pork and hot sauce, plus morning glory greens cooked in garlic, soy, and chili that is as perfect a bowl of food as I've ever tasted. With the keg now well tilted and pouring slowly, we know we're close to achieving our goal as we say "cheers" over another glass. What we don't realize is that it's nearly 12pm and that's not a good thing because bars in Hanoi have a midnight curfew. Confident we're about to kick the keg, we order our next beer but the server says: "Police come. No more beer." And that's it. We're kicked out and can't drain the barrel.

We failed the bar and ourselves, though falling into the street we immediately forget that at the shock of seeing literally no one nearby. Ninety minutes ago this was the busiest junction in Hanoi, now it's empty. It's a strangely calming experience to walk through the deserted streets after the chaotic rush of the last few days.

Bia hoi is about the experience of freshness and of place.

What strikes us on the walk home is how bia hoi is an everyman experience which is remarkably low status. Around the world people are obsessed with names and brands, whether it's a brewery, a designer, a chef, or whatever. Bia hoi is different. It's made by different breweries and typically you don't know who made the one that you're drinking, you just know that you are drinking a type of beer—one that's totally unique to Vietnam. Each glass is a bit different with some being lighter, some sweeter, some fruitier, others more bitter. They also change through the day as the beer gets older and the barrels empty. Each glass of beer is different and each is good. It doesn't have the same beer geek appeal as other brews on this search, but I'm increasingly seeing that beer is about way more than just how it tastes. And that's especially true here because bia hoi is about the experience of freshness and of place: a simple drink served in the simplest of ways, drunk just days after it was made and enjoyed with simple, delicious food in busy no-frills bars. That's what makes it so special.

Not many places have an indigenous beer type that is theirs alone. Bia hoi is Vietnam's unique beer and you can't find beer served like this anywhere else in the world. It's the world's freshest, cheapest beer and while it might not be best brew I've ever tasted, it's a must-have beer experience. I'll definitely be getting my dong out in Vietnam again.

THE BREWPUBS OF HANOI

There's more to Hanoi than just bia hoi—it is also home to over 20 brewpubs, some independent and others part of a larger chain of pub-based microbreweries like Legend and Goldmalt. The first thing to know is that they are almost exactly the opposite experience of being in a bia hoi: the brewpubs are all ornate Czech-styled brewhouses, mostly indoors, mostly lined with copper, seemingly shrines to Pilsner Urquell in their décor. They all make a dark lager and a pale lager that's richly malty with the caramel sweetness and hoppy finish of a Czech Pilsner. You can expect to pay 30,000–40,000VND ($1.50–$2.00) per glass so it's also considerably more expensive, meaning the clientele is also different and includes many more businessmen. While it's interesting to visit some of these brewpubs, and they take you to different parts of the city, for me they don't have the fun factor of sitting out on the streets at a bia hoi. If you want to know more about the beers and brewpubs of Vietnam then read www.beervn.com.

3 BREWPUB RECOMMENDATIONS

Step into Hoa Vien Brewhouse (1A Tang Bat Ho, Hai Bà Trung) and you could easily have slipped through a wormhole to Prague because it's ostensibly a Czech beer house. The two beers are very good and the best examples I found. The menu (which is expensive) is in Vietnamese, English, and Czech and the dishes are almost all Czech classics.

The brewhouse at the Windmill Brewery (31 Dang Trân Côn, Dông Da) can be seen from the street before you walk into its leafy courtyard. The beer is deep gold with a good full body and nice bitterness. It's a relaxed environment to drink in and a calmer experience than being out on the street.

There are over 10 Goldmalt brewpubs in Hanoi and the one I liked most was at 65 Ngo Thi Nham, Hai Bà Trung. With a copper kit in the corner and a stack of silver fermenters, it was busy with locals and had two beers on tap: pale lager and dark lager.

THE WORLD'S SECOND BIGGEST OKTOBERFEST

Munich's Oktoberfest is the biggest beer event in the world, the most famous drinking festival in the world, something that transcends beer lovers and non-drinkers and attracts people from all over the world. And I've never been.

"You've never been to Oktoberfest?" comes the response when people learn this. "Surely you have to go?!" they say. "I just assumed you would've been."

They're right. I should've been by now. But you know what? I don't really want to go to Munich's Oktoberfest. Plus every other beer writer has been there, done that, and told tales of crowded tables, long lines, large glasses of lager, lots of drunkenness, and nearly being sick on a merry-go-round. What more could I actually add to that boozy book of stories?

Regardless of all of that, Oktoberfest is too important a beer thing to overlook in my quest to find the best. And that's why I'm 6,000 miles (10,000 km) from home. It's why I've been traveling for over 24 hours and why I'm on a very small airplane that's bouncing and rocking into Navegantes–Ministro Victor Konder International Airport. If I'm not going to the main Oktoberfest in Munich then I'm going to the world's second biggest Oktoberfest and that's in Blumenau, in Brazil's southern state of Santa Catarina.

BOUND FOR BLUMENAU

The hour-long bus ride from the airport to Blumenau involves weaving around dusty roads with little to look at apart from dark-green trees, high rolling hills, and the occasional collection of weary-looking red-roofed shacks.

As we approach the outskirts of the city we pass squat apartment blocks, stores where the white paint is cracking, tropical trees growing in front of pastel-yellow tower blocks. There's a wide, open expanse of river, dark brown and turbid, and fringed with thick forest on the opposite bank. But there's also something curiously different: the sunshine yellow that dominates the colorscape of Brazil is joined not by the usual flashes of green and blue, but by red and black. We stop next to a building with a pointed orange roof that looks like a gingerbread house. It's not what I expected to see in Brazil. As we get closer to the center we pass more and more buildings like this. It looks like a postcard of Germany was used in the town's planning.

Getting off the air-conditioned bus is like walking into an oven—it's 95°F (35°C) and so humid I'm immediately covered in sweat. I can see dark-green mountains reaching up in to the blue sky; the muddy river makes me think of the Amazon (though it isn't); tall, thick trees hang low all around me, plus there's tanned skin and dark hair and I can't understand any of the Portuguese being spoken. I'm definitely in Brazil, but none of the buildings look very Brazilian to me...

I walk along Rua XV de Novembro (which used to have the far more fun name of "Wurststrasse," or "Sausage Street" because of its narrow curves) and through the small town center where the German influence becomes increasingly apparent:

stores selling dirndls and lederhosen; German flags attached to everything; silver beer steins in every window; yellow, red, and black balloons. There's even German Oom-pah music, albeit with a Brazilian beat in the background.

Then I spot Castelinho da Havan, the most German-looking building I've ever seen: pretty pointed steeples, tiny windows wrapping all around, a crisscross of dark wood on white, small arches holding up the weight of the "little castle." Surrounding the Castelinho are hundreds of people, most wearing German clothes, all swinging steins of beer and singing in both German and Portuguese, while flags form a sun-shielding canopy above them. These people are here for the annual Oktoberfest. The festival doesn't start until 6pm, but they are already a few beers in before lunch.

With the combination of heat and travel-weariness, I don't really know what's happening right now and I've seemingly stepped into a hilarious parody of Germany. I knew I was coming to a place famous for its German heritage but this is unreal.

THE GERMAN CONNECTION

I've arranged to meet Luiz Koerich at the Cultural Foundation of Blumenau—he's showing me around some museums and then we're going to the city's archives. Fair-skinned and with a wave of strawberry blonde hair, he doesn't look classically Brazilian, but I guess his surname gives that away. "Yes, I have German heritage. It goes back many, many generations," he says. Just like the history of the town.

Blumenau might be thousands of miles from Germany, but the town is very proud of its German heritage.

Dr. Hermann Bruno Otto Blumenau (1819–1899) was a pharmaceutical chemist from Hasselfelde in central Germany. Following his studies, he worked in a few pharmacies, including one in Erfurt, where he met Alexander von Humboldt, a renowned geographer and explorer who traveled extensively in Latin America and studied biological geography. In the early 1840s, Blumenau traveled to London where he met Johan Jacob Sturz, the German Consul-General of Brazil, before returning home in 1844 to study for a doctorate in chemistry.

Via these connections and qualifications, in 1846 Dr. Blumenau traveled to Brazil at the behest of the government to check upon the wellness and living conditions of the already-established communities of Germans in Brazil. His trip took him to Santa Catarina in the south where in São Pedro de Alcântara (100 miles/150 km south of what's now Blumenau) there were over 500 German immigrants, while a significant community had settled in Gaspar (9 miles/15 km east of Blumenau).

Luiz introduces me to Professor Sueli Maria Vanzuita Petry, Director of Blumenau's Historic Archive, and translates the story of Dr. Blumenau. "When he came here he was enchanted by the region. He had no initial interest in settling in Brazil but he left and then returned in 1848 and decided to buy land," she explains. Dr. Blumenau knew of a Brazilian law that said German immigrants could get land for free to encourage them to colonize different areas, but there was a fairly strict condition involved: "He had the possibility to own the land for just 10 years and if he didn't succeed in building a colony then he had to sell the land back to the government."

Volkswagens, steins of beer, and lederhosen—what could be more Brazilian?

In 1984, six years after planning began, the first Blumenau Oktoberfest took place.

Dr. Blumenau bought some land and was given more for free, choosing an area next to the Itajaí-Açu River, in a valley surrounded by forests and hills. The official founding date of Blumenau is 2 September, 1850. His vision was to bring 250 people with him from Germany to Brazil, but he only managed to convince 17 people to make the first trip—at that time many Germans were emigrating to North America, so it was a challenge to encourage them to this strange, hot country.

When his initial 10 years was up the town's population had grown to 947, which seems a decent growth in a decade. Despite this, it was deemed to have been unsuccessful and Dr. Blumenau was forced to sell the land back to the Brazilian regime. In 1865, Dr. Blumenau returned to Germany to try and convince more people to move to Brazil. While home, Dr. Blumenau married and started a family before returning to Brazil in 1869, where he stayed until 1882, by which time the town's population had grown beyond 15,000 and had become well-established, with a mix of Germans, Italians, and Brazilians.

THE PARTY ORIGINS

So the town was of German origin, the first people to move to the colony were German, yet as the town grew it became more Brazilian and more removed from its roots. So what's the link to today's Oktoberfest, the event for which the town is known?

"People started to try and market Blumenau as a place to visit," explains the Professor. "They produced postcards with pictures of the church, the streets, the harbor. Then in 1967 they produced a leaflet," which the Professor produces from her desk drawer. "What country is this?" it reads. Various bucolic European-like pictures are shown with pretty buildings and lush forests, and beneath them are listed European countries: "Switzerland? France? Germany?" Then comes the surprise reveal: "No, it's Brazil!" The idea was to draw in Brazilian tourists who wanted to see Europe but couldn't afford to go. It was a big success. To maximize on Blumenau's newfound awareness from outside of the town, they decided to throw a party, something that might also attract more people. The government helped to promote it, and it was so good that they repeated it for three consecutive years.

With more visitors arriving, it became a catalyst for Blumenau to focus on their heritage and this saw further buildings raised in the German style, including Castelinho da Havan, which was only built in 1978 and is a replica of the city hall in Michelstadt (and here's a good fact: it's the second most photographed thing in south Brazil after the Iguaçu Falls). Next, the town began work on a bigger project, a party that would highlight Blumenau's German heritage. In 1984, six years after planning began, the first Blumenau Oktoberfest took place, inspired by the Munich version. It has taken place every year since.

There's another story told in town about the origin of the festival: the Itajaí-Açu River frequently floods, and did so particularly badly in 1983. The alternative tale suggests that the town decided to throw a big party to make people feel better after that flood, thereby starting the Oktoberfest tradition. There is some crossover between the two stories as the first Oktoberfest was planned for 1983, but had to be postponed to 1984 because of the flooding.

"She will show you some pictures," explains Luiz as we follow the Professor to the kind of computer I haven't seen since the early 2000s. She clicks away, searching through virtual folders until she pulls open one sepia photo of three women on a procession cart with crowds of people lining the street. She says something and Luiz seems shocked.

"That is the Professor there!" he says, pointing to the pretty brunette on the left. It's a photo from the first festival.

"That year we had..." Luiz stops and again gets the professor to repeat herself, "They had over 100,000 people. Wow, I never realized it was that many!" he says. "And it lasted for seven days." The Professor reads out some more statistics: 102,000 in the first year, 362,000 in year two when it was also extended to 17 days, like the one in Munich. It continued to grow and in the fifth year over one million people attended. In the first year, 103,000 liters of beer were drunk, jumping to 721,000 liters in year five. Recently, the numbers have been deliberately controlled and constricted to ensure a better, less hectic experience for everyone there, but they still expect over 450,000 attendees this year.

The party put Blumenau on the map while simultaneously encouraging the citizens to celebrate their German ancestors and bring back the traditions of years ago. The city itself evolved into an increasingly German-looking place as the festival developed. And this helps to explain why so many people were standing outside a little German castle, dressed in dirndls and drinking steins of lager, singing in German in this sultry city thousands of miles from Munich.

DRINK LOCAL

Blumenau has a good history of small breweries, which is no surprise given their heritage: the first brewery opened in the **back of Dr. Blumenau's house in 1858, and** by the end of the 19th century there were 12 **breweries in town. Currently, it has 10 small** breweries, including Eisenbahn which is one **of the original Brazilian microbreweries,** opening in 2002. The town also holds a huge craft beer festival in March, which pours **over 600 beers from the country's** microbreweries.

The micro-brewed beers here are a nice **counter to the massive volumes of beer brewed in Brazil: it's the third-largest** market by volume produced in the world **(13.5 billion hectoliters in 2013, which** accounts for 7% of all world beer **production) and two of the world's 10 best-**selling brands are Brazilian: Skol and Brahma (Skol, by the way, is probably the **worst beer I had while looking for the** world's best... it's weak, thin, tart, and just **not nice to drink).**

Spending the evening partying with my hosts: Joanna, Vinicius, and Luiz.

TIME TO PARTY

I left it too late to book a hotel—I hugely under-estimated how busy Blumenau gets during the festival—but managed to find a room on AirBnB staying with a guy called Vinicius who's invited me to join him, his girlfriend Joanna, and his friend Luiz at the Oktoberfest tonight. At 10pm we set off for the party, it doesn't get busy until midnight and runs until 5am, so there's no hurry. As we get to the main street leading away from Vinicius' apartment, still 10 minutes from the venue, it's already a carnival of people drinking and dressed in Bavarian outfits.

"Does everyone dress up?" I ask.

Shops in town selling anything Germany-related that you can imagine—from steins to Bayern Munich soccer shirts.

"A lot of people," says Luiz. "They used to get in for free if they dressed up. Now it's half price." This explains why there are so many stores in town selling these clothes.

The closer we get, the louder it becomes and the more people we see, already singing and dancing as the whole town converges on Vila Germânica. Given the name of this place, and given what I've already seen in the city, I probably should've known what to expect but I can barely believe what I'm seeing as we walk up to a complete replica German village. There's a castle-like drawbridge leading in, plus rows of huge Bavarian-style buildings, a tall clock tower in the middle, steeples stuck on the side of orange buildings, open courtyards... and tonight it all comes with a backing track of loud German music. It's unbelievable. Especially with all the German flags, mugs of beer, and German outfits. I can't stop smiling as I walk through a Disneyland-like village on this hot evening. It's surreal and brilliant. The village, which is open year-round, is attached to a huge indoor space that houses three massive interconnected pavilions, each so big I can barely see from one side to the other. Every pavilion has a stage with live music, and each is ringed with bars decorated like German beer gardens. There are some tables and benches around but mostly revelers stand, walk, and dance—and there are already thousands of people doing just that. Passing through the packed pavilions and back outside, the center of the German village has small stores selling clothes and festival memorabilia. There's a craft beer shop selling Brazilian and German beers, there are restaurants... and they are all in Bavarian-style buildings.

Back inside and we line up to get the tokens we need to buy the beer and food, meaning we have to choose in advance what we want to eat and drink. The main beer here is Brahma and you can get 10 tokens for R$55 (or 10 14 oz/400 ml beers for US$20). There are also four Blumenau craft breweries—Eisenbahn, Das Bier, Bierworks, and Wunderbier—with each having an "Artesanal Pilsen" (R$7, US$2.50) and "Artesanal Especial" beers (R$8, US$3). The specials include Dunkel lagers, Hefeweizens, Pale Ales, Red Lagers, and Ales. I go for five Pilsen tokens and five Especial beers, plus a token for a baked potato.

"Every pavilion has different music and a different atmosphere," says Luiz as we order a Das Bier Pilsen. "One is quieter, one is for dancing, one is for really partying." There are young and old here, all drinking and having a great time. Nearly everyone has their own silver tankard instead of drinking from plastic cups, and when my first beer is gone I go back into the village where I buy one for myself—a half-liter handled tin with the green-hat festival logo on it. I fill this with Eisenbahn's Dunkel before cashing in my food token on a head-sized baked potato filled with a creamy sauce, bacon, and some crunchy cheese pieces—perfect belly-filling food.

We work through our tokens and through the different beers. The micro-brewed Pilsens are all very good and fresh, the dark lagers are toasty, the Hefeweizens are smooth and bananary, some of the red beers are as hoppy as Pale Ales. I came expecting to drink Brahma all night, so it's great to be able to try something else instead. The beer store outside is selling 10 different craft beers, so we pick some of those; we eat bratwursts; we sing along to German drinking songs played by Brazilian ska bands; we drink more beer. It's Friday night, everyone is having a great time, and as every beer festival goes, we all get drunker and sillier and enjoy the party.

In 2014, Oktoberfest attracted 458,550 people.

As it gets later, people stumble around, they fall, their friends laugh at them, they get back up and they carry on drinking. I see a guy passed out until the chant of "Zicke Zacke, Zicke Zacke, Hoi Hoi Hoi!" begins and he jumps up and into the song like he's leading it. Another guy has fallen asleep on a bench with half a beer in one hand and half a hot dog in the other while his friends take photos of him. Groups hug and dance together, they laugh together, sing together, drink together. But one thing really stands out here—beyond the fairytale vision of Germany, beyond the dressing up, beyond the booziness, beyond being in Brazil—and that's the unexpected sexually charged energy in the place. It's like being at a drunken school disco, with strangers making out all over the place. It's not just young people, either. I see couples in their 50s just getting at it on the dance floor!

During the day, a parade passes through the streets of the town.

It's not just the young people in the town who enjoy the party, the older residents are more than happy to sink a few steins.

A SHARED EXPERIENCE

Blumenau's Oktoberfest is a huge event. In 2014 it attracted 458,550 people, drinking over a million pints of beer (I can claim about 12 of those pints over the two nights I was there). It's put the town on the map, like it originally intended, and people continue to visit every year. I went expecting a beer festival, but that's not what it is. It's a party where everyone is drinking beer. Events like this are all about the shared experience and in this instance the whole town is involved. There's a huge build up—everyone talks about it, everyone is excited about it, and they all go to it. The fact that Blumenau's Oktoberfest has good beer is an excellent bonus but it's not the reason they're there. And Munich's Oktoberfest is the same—you go for the fun experience. You happen to drink steins of superb beer while you're there, but that's secondary to the event itself.

Every beer festival is different. Some are super-geeky where you'll be able to drink the world's rarest beers on tap, some have thousands of brews to choose from, some focus on different beer styles, some on beers from different places. But what connects them all is that ultimately we get drunk with friends and have a good time. The beer in our glass might be amazing or it might be "meh" but that doesn't really matter because we're there for the universal experience of being with others, and it's that which makes us want to go to beer festivals.

So the second-largest Oktoberfest celebration in the world was a grope-fest of good beer and Germanesque cheer, and it was nothing like I expected it to be, in the most unforgettable of ways.

BUILDING BLACKMAN'S BREWERY

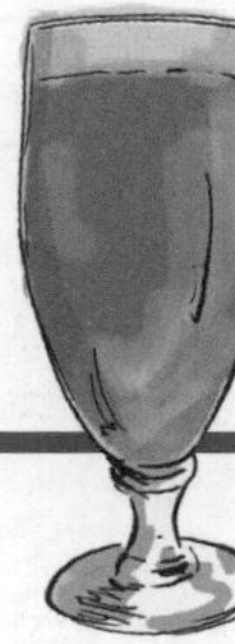

"G'day mate, howya going. Ready to brew some beer?" says Renn Blackman in his ever-chirpy voice.

A few minutes ago I was shocked awake by a 6.30am alarm clock, jarred by the jetlag of being 10 time zones from home. I rolled out of bed, threw on some old clothes, and walked downstairs into the brewery where I'm spending the day learning more about what it's like for a young couple to open up their own brewery.

I'm at Blackman's Brewery in the surf town of Torquay, an hour's drive outside of Melbourne, Australia. It's a cool brewpub, a few hundred yards from the sea, started by Renn and his wife, Jess, in August 2014. They brew and cook downstairs and they live upstairs.

Renn is working out the exact details for today's recipe when I get there. He's brewing a new beer today; it's a wedding gift for his friends Ben and Anna, and it will be named after their dog, Mervyn.

A chilled-out surfer dude, Renn is wearing ripped-up old shorts and a tatty and faded Yeastie Boys Brewery t-shirt, while sitting on a keg and punching numbers into his phone. There are brew sheets stuck on the wall alongside a whiteboard that lists everything currently in tank and the upcoming schedule.

"Going to the Czech Republic and Germany was an inspiration"

At the back of the brewery is the brushed copper kit where two tanks sit side by side, a control panel is on the front with steps leading to a platform between them. Renn has already laid out the sacks of malt he's using in the brew.

In front of the brewhouse is a bank of fermentation tanks; six tall, thin silver vessels neatly lined up like dots on a dice and with thick, snake-like hoses attached to their conical bases. Opposite is a water tank and there's a kegging area that doubles as a desk. The door behind me leads through to the brewpub's kitchen, passing a small lab-come-outside bar, and the door to my left opens out into the beer garden.

The restaurant is large and comfortable, perfect for both cold nights or hot days straight in from the surf. Jess looks after the restaurant, marketing, and some bookkeeping, and together they've designed everything, choosing the beers they love and the best food to go with it. From deciding they were going to open their wn brewpub to pouring beers for the public for the first time, it was 12 months of hard work, "But we did it and it's awesome to have our own place!" Renn says.

Renn Blackman in front of his brewkit.

THE BACKSTORY

Having studied for an undergraduate business degree in Perth, Renn realized that he didn't know what he wanted to do. "I was interested in beer but was never really a homebrewer. I saw it was a growing industry and that it was a different kind of job, I suppose." So he took a side step and studied for a graduate diploma in brewing. From there he spent some time keg washing at Sail and Anchor Brewery in Fremantle, Western Australia and then moved to The Monk Brewery and Kitchen nearby, where he got to brew a range of different beers on the pub's small brewkit.

Renn and Jess met in 2008, aged 21 and 23 respectively, while working a ski season at Mount Buller, 130 miles (200 km) outside of Melbourne. In 2011 they moved to London where Jess worked in marketing and Renn started working at Camden Town Brewery. They stayed in London for 18 months before spending six months working their way back home, via most of the rest of the world, and orienting by way of major brewing centers like Bamberg, Pilsen, and Cologne.

"Going to the Czech Republic and Germany was an inspiration, as was working at Camden Town learning about lager," he says. "A lot of those beers have a good drinkability factor and I like beers that go in that direction. That work and travel definitely influenced my beers today."

GRAFTING

When the water has warmed, we're ready to start the brew and milling the grain is the first job. "We're going just Maris Otter and a touch of wheat in the mash. I want something real simple and clean to show off that great Maris flavor," he says, opening a white sack of malt and crunching on a few kernels. He then effortlessly throws the sack onto his shoulder and tips the golden grains into a large opening at the top of the mill, where they are crushed.

Now it's my turn and seeing Renn do this makes me think that it'll be no problem. Lift a sack and pour grain into a big hole. Easy, right?

First of all these sacks are 55lb (25kg) each and the same size as my body from neck to waist. I go to the gym but I can't shoulder press a 55lb (25kg) dumbbell with one arm. I also can't quite work out how to bear hug this thing or how to maneuver it from ground to shoulder. I wrap my arms around it and hoist it upward, making it as far as my thigh and almost toppling over in the process. Another heave and it's chest high, one final push and it's almost on my shoulder, high enough that I can tip the open end into the hole. The grain flows out, with a significant amount missing the mill.

"Reckon you can manage the rest?" Renn asks. There are a dozen sacks of malt at my feet, my arms already hurt, I'm making a mess, I'm out of breath after one, and I feel a bit sick.

"No problem!" I say hopefully, as I grunt and groan lifting the second sack.

Renn checks on the beers in his fermentation tanks while I continue my struggle to get the grain in the mill. When all the sacks are empty Renn goes to the control panel on the front of the tank, which is decorated with lots of inputs and outputs for hoses. One of these is attached to the hot water tank. "Go over there and turn that lever," he says. We need to get the water to 162°F (72°C), so have to balance the hot tap and the cold tap, just like running a big bath. As water surges into the mash Renn jumps back and forth, over hoses and buckets, checking a temperature gauge as water surges into the mash.

"Mate, we're in Australia, of course we've got Vegemite!"

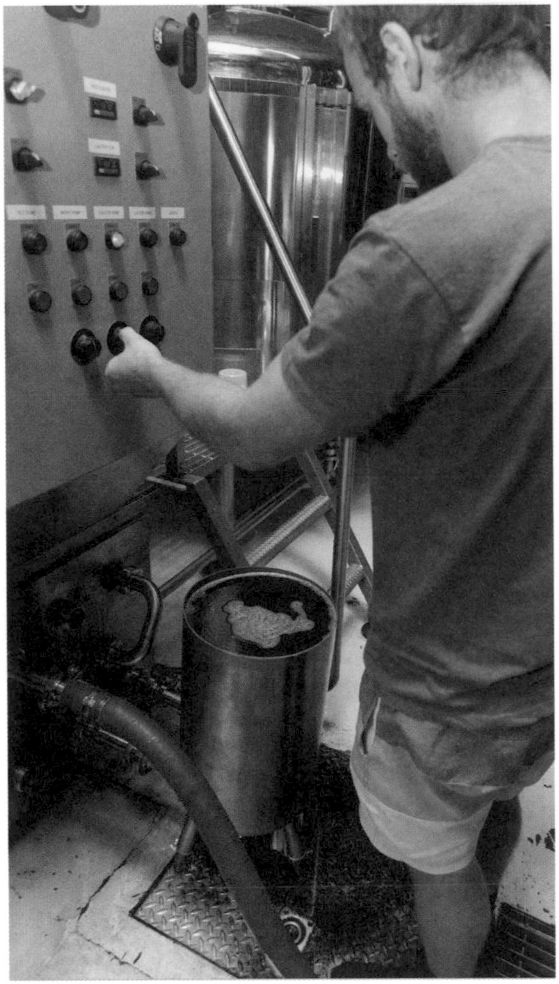

Throughout the brewing process, Renn fastidiously checks to make sure everything runs exactly as it should.

"Come up here," he says, climbing the small ladder and opening the tank. It's filling with hot water and steam billows out. He tells me to press a big button on the panel and that moves the milled malt into the mash. Now we're brewing. For the next 15 minutes we monitor the temperature and flow, balancing everything to get the right pace and fill in the tank, leaving us with a thick, sweet mix of water and grain.

"Smells like delicious toast!" I say.

The beach town of Torquay, where Blackman's Brewery is based. There can't be many better spots to brew beer.

"It's about time for brekkie, eh? We've got a few minutes while we're mashing."

"You got any Vegemite?!"

"Mate, we're in Australia, of course we've got Vegemite!"

Like the British Marmite, Vegemite is made from brewers' yeast extract along with some additional flavors and spices. It's thick and dark brown with a strong, umami richness. He spreads it thick on fresh toasted sourdough and it's delicious.

So far this is Renn's daily routine—getting up, starting a brew downstairs, having some breakfast upstairs, getting back into brewhouse, making his beers, and so on. I'm impressed and even a bit envious of him, though I'm not envious of all the hard work it takes physically to brew and run two businesses at the same time.

ON TAP AT BLACKMAN'S

Unfiltered Lager
A great beer inspired by Czech lager and Renn's time at Camden Town. There's a super-clean malt body made smooth by being unfiltered, then a fresh hop aroma, lemons and peaches, all balanced with the kind of bitterness that demands you drink more.

Bob
A smooth-drinking Witbier with just a hint of yeast playing with the floral-orangey depth of coriander seed and a sweetly toasty touch of coconut.

Ernie
A juicy Golden Ale that you could drink all day with Aussie hops giving grapefruit, mango, and pineapple.

Reginald
A piney, peachy IPA with a kick of bitterness at the end to balance the chewy malts.

Arthur
An amazing Smoked Porter that's rich, roasted, smoky, and smooth.

THE SET UP

When Renn and Jess arrived back in Australia in early 2013, Renn started brewing at True South in Melbourne while Jess continued to work in marketing, but they always had ideas to do their own thing.

"Being in Perth with great brewpubs like Little Creatures and The Monk, then living in the UK and going to places like Germany, seeing all of the awesome spots to drink beer over there, it was very inspiring to make your own brand," Renn says. A few months after getting home they began properly planning and six months after that it all started happening. But not as they originally thought.

"The plan was always to open a cool bar with a 200-liter kit out the back and brew like crazy," but then things changed at True South, who were considering removing the brewery. Renn and Jess discussed the possibility of buying the kit for their own place. True South agreed, with Renn promising to continue brewing beer for them once they found a home for their brewpub. Eventually they came across a site and took the entire brewery from True South, putting it on the back of a big truck, and moving it over 60 miles (100km) away to a former restaurant in Torquay.

"It's a pretty awesome spot," Renn says. "It's a coastal town with a relaxed vibe and it just fitted with where we wanted to live and where we wanted to make beer."

Setting up wasn't easy, as Renn describes, "It was a big risk for us, it was stressful, it was a lot of hard work. We were riding on a lot of things happening, especially with the site. We stripped back the whole venue and

The beer is kegged and then taken straight to the pub next door, ready to serve to customers.

The fermentation tanks stand proudly in the brewhouse.

re-did it. Brewery-wise, my dad and I dug the drains and concreted it all in. We managed to chip away at it over six months, putting all efforts into the refurbishment. Once the equipment arrived the cranes dropped the tanks into place and everything after that just happened really."

"It was a big risk for us, it was stressful, it was a lot of hard work."

IT'S NOT ALL FUN

Back to the brewery and the mash has finished. Next Renn pulls levers, flicks switches, and connects hoses to move the sweet wort into the kettle, leaving behind the spent grain. While the wort transfers, I follow Renn into a big walk-in fridge that holds all the hops, as well as food for the kitchen. He removes the silver sacks and weighs them out exactly into three different buckets. "I'm adding loads of Amarillo hops for all the fruity, orangey aroma. It should be good!"

The golden, sweet wort is coming up to boiling point while the mash tun next to it is filled with the hot leftover grain. And as I stand with a bucket of hops in one hand and a shovel in the other, I know what comes next. There are two jobs that beer writers get when visiting small breweries: adding the hops and digging out the mash tun. It's a kind of initiation, right-of-passage thing—we're allowed to add the hops because it's fun, we're expected to dig out the mash because it's not fun.

The hops come first. The kettle is boiling and Renn gives me a pair of thick, black rubber gloves before he opens the vessel and tells me to throw in the first hop addition. Steam fills the brewery, sweet smelling at first and then, after I've tossed in the little green pellets, the air becomes fruity and grassy. Renn closes the tank, sets a timer for the second hop addition and rushes off to find some bins for the spent grain. "This is the best part of brewing! A lot of brewers hate it, but it's not that bad." I can't tell if he's serious or not.

Renn positions one bin beneath a door on the front of the tank. He unscrews the door and hot grain tumbles out. He passes me the shovel. "I'm pretty sure you know how to do this."

It was hard work getting the grain in there to begin with and it's even harder getting it out. It's heavy, wet, and hot as I dig the shovel in and drag out the grain into the bin, pulling it out of the tank in heaves, sending steam into the room. I'm just

Renn mans the bar, pouring out a pint of the excellent Reginald IPA.

grateful I don't have to climb inside the actual tank. I've been in many breweries before where that's the only way to do this job. And that really sucks.

I carry on dragging at the grain, trying to remove as much as I can from the bottom of the tank, filling five dustbins. When I can barely scrape any more out, Renn calls me up to the top of the tank and passes me a hosepipe. "Just blast the rest out," he says. This is much more fun, like one of those funfair games where you try and shoot things with a big water gun.

The timer buzzes, the final hops are added, and the beer spins through the whirlpool to separate out the hop trub. Next, the bittersweet liquid cools and transfers into the fermentation tank. This just leaves us with a few more jobs, so while Renn takes some samples of the brew and begins to move hoses back into their proper places, I spray out the green sludge of leftover hops from the whirlpool and then mop and squeegee the floor. The last job is pitching the yeast and the brew is done.

Throughout the whole process Renn is a guy in complete control, and he habitually knows exactly what's happening and what to do next. It's impressive to see a young guy with this much knowledge and skill doing his day job with absolute mastery. He's also the most laid-back guy I've ever met. Even today, when he's brewing a beer he has never made before and with me by his side asking questions, he's still in calm control.

What makes me marvel even more is that this is all Renn and Jess's. This whole space is theirs. They've built it—with help from family and friends—and they are running it themselves. I'm a similar age to these guys and have so much respect for what they're achieving here, because they're making their dream happen.

KNOCKING OFF

By 4pm we're drinking and hanging out in the brewpub that Jess manages (admittedly it's a shortened brewday because I'm visiting). We would've been surfing but the weather was rough. On other days Renn might mash in and run down to the beach for a swim. It sounds perfect but "It's a lot of work, though I always expected that."

Has it been worth it? "It's a pretty great feeling when someone comes up and says they like the beer." His smile grows: "It's amazing." A main highlight was "Definitely pouring the first beers through on tap, that was great. And getting my own beer on tap at different venues, that's a brilliant feeling. There were some very testing times but we're so pleased we opened our own place and are able to share our beers."

This is undoubtedly one of the best-quality ranges of beers I've had.

"Brewpubs have a great feel to them. Food gives a very social aspect. A lot of the places I like drinking at generally have that vibe. Beer and food are important together and we work hard on that."

And the best thing about it? "It's all down to us how we think this brewery should be and we can show that to other people—it's very cool."

Now I finally get to try their beers and I'm left in awe again. I expected them to be good but they are way better than that. This is the final trip I'm taking in 2014. I've been to so many countries, breweries, and bars, but this is undoubtedly one of the best-quality ranges of beers I've had. For my own personal tastes, I can't imagine a better line-up.

Renn and Jess have built something special at Blackman's. They may be grafting non-stop, but they're making delicious beers they love, ones they're proud of, and which go perfectly with great food and great service. And you'll always find Renn in the bar in the evening, either working and talking to customers or seeing friends. As a couple in their late 20s they are making their dream a reality and the fact this can happen in the beer industry is great, because it's creating and shaping the future of what and where we drink.

The shared vision of Renn and Jess has allowed them to create something really special at their brewpub.

CITY GUIDES:

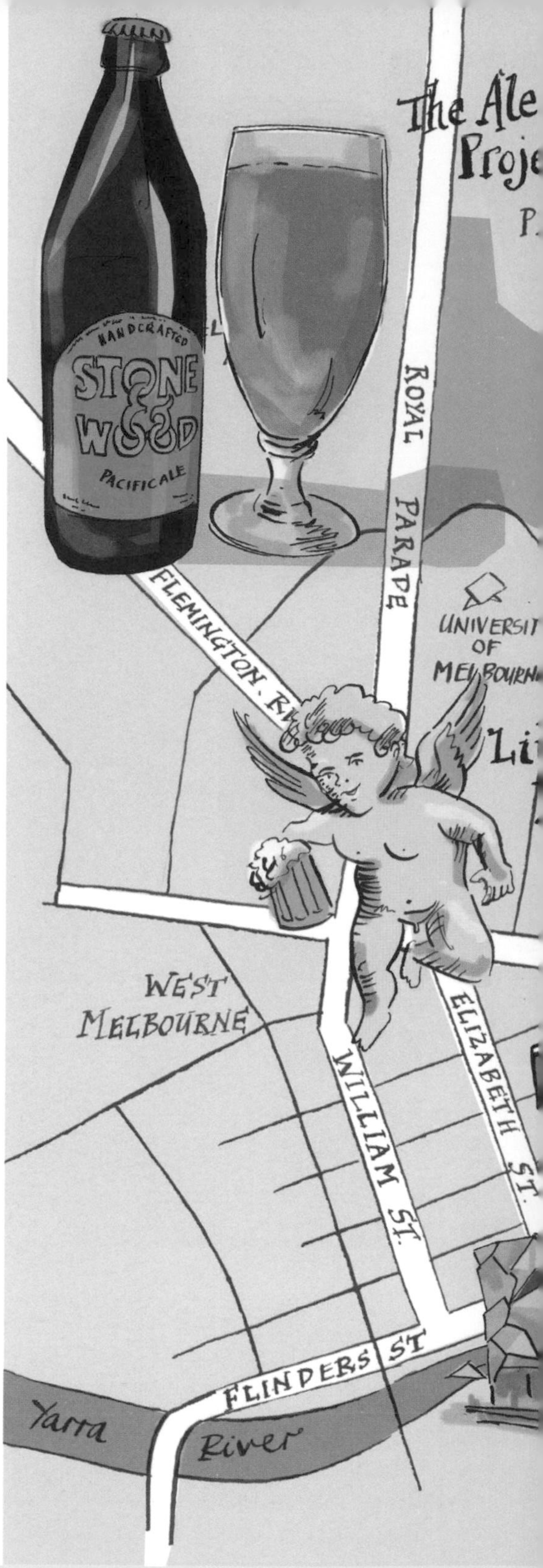

• CITY GUIDE

MELBOURNE

It'd be easy to argue that Melbourne is the best beer destination in the whole of the southern hemisphere. Who could compete? Auckland, perhaps. Maybe Sydney. But for me, Melbourne has it all: first it's simply a cool city, there are small breweries all around making a wide range of beers, there are excellent bars, an unpretentious beer-drinking culture, and a great food scene that benefits from the best-tasting products.

MELBOURNE

Great Northern Hotel

NICHOLSON ST

LYGON

HIGH ST

HEIDELBERG RD.

MOON DOG

QUEENS PARADE

CLIFTON HILL

EASTERN FWY

Yarra Bend Park

PRINCES ST

EASTERN HWY

ELGIN ST

Naked for Satan

Creatures ng Hall

Napier Hotel

COLLINGWOOD

JOHNSTON ST.

HOPPLE ST.

STUDLEY PARK ROA

Moon Dog Craft Brewery

Foresters Hall

VICTORIA PARADE

VICTORIA ST.

Terminus Hotel

kie

EAST MELBOURNE

Royston Hotel

PUNT RD.

Mountain Goat

RICHMOND

MCG

BRUNTON AVE.

The Local Taphouse

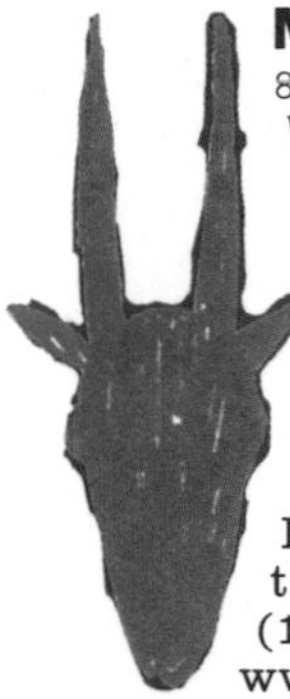

MOUNTAIN GOAT BREWERY

80 NORTH STREET, RICHMOND;
WWW.GOATBEER.COM.AU

I loved it at Mountain Goat. An open space overlooking the brewery and a good range of excellent beers that are all very clean, fresh, and tasty. Steam Ale is gloriously citrusy; Summer Ale is stunning with juicy hops; and don't miss North Street Pale Ale, a beer you can only get at the tap house. The Royston Hotel (12 River Street, Richmond; www.roystonhotel.com.au) is pretty much opposite, so head there for a pint as well.

LITTLE CREATURES DINING HALL

222 BRUNSWICK STREET, FITZROY;
WWW.LITTLECREATURES.COM.AU

Aside from Coopers, Little Creatures is the best-known Aussie craft brewery. And rightly so: the beers epitomize Australian drinking in how they are uncomplicated, refreshing and just really good. Their Pale Ale is one of the best, being balanced and aromatic rather than a wallop of hops. I also really like Roger's Ale which is like an English Bitter. The Dining Room is their Fitzroy spot and it's a bright, breezy place to hang out and have a few pints or pots.

MOON DOG

17 DUKE STREET, ABBOTSFORD;
WWW.MOONDOGBREWING.COM.AU

With comfy couches and homely touches, the tasting room is a welcoming and fun place to hang out. They have six taps of their own beer. A couple will be their core beers, which are very good, plus you'll have some of the most creative small batch beers in the city (I had a Double IPA made with just smoked malt which was insane). Try as many as of their beers as you can. The Terminus Hotel (605 Victoria Street, Abbotsford; www.theterminushotel.com.au) is nearby if you want a beer somewhere else before or after.

COOKIE BEER HALL

252 SWANSTON STREET;
WWW.COOKIE.NET.AU

With over 20 beers on tap and a whole lot more in the fridges, Cookie is a great place to stop for a beer if you're in the CBD where you can taste your way through some of the best Australian brews or pick from others from around the world. The food has an Asian edge reflecting the bar's Chinatown location.

THE ALEHOUSE PROJECT

98-100 LYGON STREET, BRUNSWICK EAST;
WWW.THEALEHOUSEPROJECT.COM.AU

The thing that stood out most about The Alehouse Project was the staff: friendly, knowledgeable, and clearly passionate about the great beers they have on tap. The food menu is all about snacking and sharing, and the whole place has a communal vibe.

FORESTER'S HALL

64 SMITH STREET, COLLINGWOOD;
WWW.FORESTERSHALL.COM.AU

Because my apartment was nearby, I spent a lot of time in this bar when in Melbourne, though saying that, the beer list is so good I likely would've traveled across the city to go here anyway. You'll find a full range of styles, some interesting imports, plus all the best beers brewed nearby.

NAPIER HOTEL

210 NAPIER ST, FITZROY;
WWW.THENAPIERHOTEL.COM

A relaxed old corner pub in Fitzroy, the Napier Hotel has a decent beer list and proper Aussie grub, including peppered kangaroo steaks and huge burgers.

GREAT NORTHERN HOTEL

644 RATHDOWNE STREET, CARLTON NORTH;
WWW.GNH.NET.AU

With 22 taps of tasty beer, the Great Northern is big pub with a suntrap of a garden out the back. Look for beers from the likes of Stone & Wood, Holgate, and 7 Cent.

Standing on the same street corner for a century and a half, the Napier Hotel in Fitzroy is a local institution.

NAKED FOR SATAN

285 BRUNSWICK STREET, FITZROY;
WWW.NAKEDFORSATAN.COM.AU

It might not have the best beer selection but on a warm day head up to the roof and enjoy a drink in the sunshine and some of the best views of the city. Perhaps even push aside your beer glass and have a cocktail instead.

THE LOCAL TAPHOUSE

184 CARLISLE STREET, ST KILDA;
WWW.THELOCAL.COM.AU

Feted as one of the best beer bars in the city, The Local Taphouse in St Kilda certainly has one of the largest beer lists with the best of Australian brews pouring. The food is good pub grub done to a high standard.

TOP 5 BEERS IN TOWN

Stone and Wood Pacific Ale
All-Aussie awesomeness

Mountain Goat Summer Ale
Juicy and delicious Golden Ale

Feral Hop Hog
Australia's best IPA

Blackman's Unfiltered Lager
Brilliantly bangable, hoppy lager

Holgate Temptress
Super sexy chocolate Porter

● CITY GUIDE

SYDNEY

Just being by the harbor and seeing the Opera House is something everyone should experience. Add to this a friendly atmosphere, all kinds of superb cuisine, and easy access to many beaches, and Sydney is rightly rated as one of the world's best cities. Famously thirsty Aussies love a cold one so you're never far from a drink. If you want the best of beer when you're there then here are some suggestions.

Build up your thirst at one of Sydney's stunning beaches.

THE LORD NELSON BREWERY HOTEL

19 KENT STREET, THE ROCKS;
WWW.LORDNELSONBREWERY.COM

Sydney's oldest continually licenced hotel is also Australia's oldest pub brewery. It has a charming British feel which also transfers to the British-inspired beers, like the superb Trafalgar Pale Ale. It's pub fare in the bar or go upstairs for modern Aussie tucker.

THE AUSTRALIAN HERITAGE HOTEL

100 CUMBERLAND STREET, THE ROCKS;
WWW.AUSTRALIANHERITAGEHOTEL.COM

This has a decent tap list without wowing, but come for the busy atmosphere in this V-shaped corner pub near the harbor. They serve the most outrageously Aussie pizza I've ever seen: it's half emu, half kangaroo and called the Coat of Arms.

HARTS PUB

ESSEX STREET, THE ROCKS;
WWW.HARTSPUB.COM

Head to Harts Pub to drink beers from Rocks Brewing Co, who run this place. They also pour plenty of good guest beers. You can visit the Rocks brewery—it's not far from Mascot train station out toward the airport.

REDOAK BOUTIQUE BEER CAFÉ

201 CLARENCE STREET; WWW.REDOAK.COM.AU

With a full range of styles inspired from all over the world, the Redoak beers are all really well made and glittering with awards. The café is great in that it dedicates pairing the beers with the best food, making this the place to come to treat yourself in the center of the city.

BITTER PHEW

1/137 OXFORD STREET, DARLINGHURST; WWW.BITTERPHEW.COM

Bitter Phew is where the beer geeks come to work through the 12 taps of ever-rotating beers. It's a basic space in an attic above Oxford Street with cool music, and they let you to bring in food from Mr Crackles, a brilliant place specializing in hot dogs and meat-filled rolls.

4 PINES BREWING COMPANY

29/43-45 EAST ESPLANADE, MANLY; WWW.4PINESBEER.COM.AU

Get on the ferry to Manly, spend the day on the great beach, and then stop at 4 Pines for some fresh beers. After sitting in the Sydney sun, a glass of their Kolsch or Pale Ale is perfect before catching the ferry back to the city.

YARDARM TAPHOUSE

49-53 N. STEYNE, MANLY; WWW.YARDARM.COM.AU

The Yardarm is opposite the beach so you get a great view of the sea and the surfers while you work through a long list of local brews, including the excellent Riverside Brewing beers.

ROYAL ALBERT HOTEL

140 COMMONWEALTH STREET, SURRY HILLS; WWW.ROYALALBERTHOTEL.COM.AU

This is a small, fun pub that has an English feel in its split spaces. There's a really well selected beer list (look for Feral and Nail) that includes a couple of hand-pulled ales. If you want food then it's burgers and crinkle fries in the bar, or head to the back bar for Chinese dumplings.

LOCAL TAPHOUSE

122 FLINDERS STREET, DARLINGHURST; WWW.THELOCAL.COM.AU

The Local Taphouse—a brother bar of the one in St Kilda, Melbourne—is where you'll find some of the best, most interesting and rare brews, including Australian and imports. While you're drinking, get some food—it's pub grub but you can expect excellent quality. Go up to the quirky rooftop garden on warm nights.

With a view like that and some excellent brews on offer, Sydney is a must-visit destination.

CITY GUIDE

THE CITIES OF NEW ZEALAND

New Zealand is one of the most exciting craft beer countries in the world—but I've never been and it's the one big gap in my beer travels. I want to go for their wonderful local hops, for the best local ingredients in their food, and for the friendly vibe. Because I haven't been, I thank Kiwi brewer Kelly Ryan for these suggestions. He tells me "Wellington is our Portland," so I suggest that as the first stop.

Dominating Auckland's skyline, the Sky Tower is the tallest man-made structure in the Southern Hemisphere.

AUCKLAND

BROTHERS BEER

90 WELLESLEY STREET W; WWW.BROTHERSBEER.CO.NZ

Funky hipster bar and brewpub with an incredible bottled beer selection and usually 10-15 beers on tap from their brewery and others. Cool vibe and in a great food depot, so definitely the place to be seen.

VULTURE'S LANE

10 VULCAN LANE; WWW.VULTURESLANE.CO.NZ

Great beer selection in the heart of Auckland with a focus on finding new brews to put on tap.

GALBRAITH'S ALEHOUSE

2 MOUNT EDEN, GRAFTON; WWW.ALEHOUSE.CO.NZ

One of NZ's institutions as the first cask ale brewpub. Beautiful old building, great cask ales made by their brewer, Sam Williamson, good bottled beer selection, a few tasty guest brews, plus good pub food.

THE LUMSDEN FREEHOUSE

448 KHYBER PASS ROAD, NEWMARKET; WWW.THELUMSDEN.CO.NZ

Great selection of ever-rotating beers (they can pass 200 taps in a year) and great food including excellent hot wings.

BREW ON QUAY

102 QUAY STREET; WWW.BREWONQUAY.CO.NZ

Good bottle range, tasty food, and always a good selection on tap, including Epic Brewing and 8 Wired (because you want to drink Epic and 8 Wired). The building is an old bank and close to the waterfront.

Rotorua is nicknamed Sulphur City thanks to the geothermal activity in the area. The smell is not ideal when you're feeling a little delicate after a night on the beer.

HALLERTAU BREWBAR

1171 COATESVILLE-RIVERHEAD HIGHWAY;
WWW.HALLERTAU.CO.NZ

Based in Riverhead, this is a little out of the city but definitely worth the trip. You sit right in the brewery, you drink very fresh beer brewed on site, and the food platters are great for sharing.

HAMILTON

GOOD GEORGE

32A SOMERSET STREET, FRANKTON;
WWW.GOODGEORGE.CO.NZ

Nice little brewpub now functioning as a full production brewery. Good core range of approachable beers plus great pub food. The pleasant garden bar is a fun place to hang out with friends. It's very close to the cricket and rugby arenas.

ROTORUA

BREW

103 TUTANEKAI STREET;
WWW.BREWPUB.CO.NZ

Great little craft beer bar run by the guys behind Croucher Brewing in Rotorua. Big tourist city that had little good beer before this, making it an oasis in a beer desert.

NEW PLYMOUTH

THE HOUR GLASS

49 LIARDET STREET;
WWW.FB.COM/THEHOURGLASS49

This upstairs bar has been converted into a nice little craft beer space. Excellent ever-changing bottled beer selection, great staff, and the only place where you'll find a bunch of Brew Mountain beers on tap.

Wellington, on the southern tip of North Island, is where some of the country's best beers are produced.

WELLINGTON

THE MALTHOUSE

48 COURTENAY PLACE, TE ARO;
WWW.THEMALTHOUSE.CO.NZ

A New Zealand institution that opened in 1993, it's the original craft beer bar. A massive selection of bottles are all kept at their appropriate serving temperatures across six fridges. Proprietor Colin Mallon and his brilliant staff are super-knowledgeable and can offer a good beer for anyone. This place is highly recommended.

FORK & BREWER

14 BOND STREET;
WWW.FORKANDBREWER.CO.NZ

This is a brewpub with 40 taps of beer and a great food menu. Try the burger or the manuka smoked duck salad. This is where Kelly Ryan brews and keeps 10–15 beers and ciders on tap—try one of the nanobrews that he makes on his 50-liter kit. Good balcony for after-work drinks.

LITTLE BEER QUARTER

6 EDWARD STREET, TE ARO;
WWW.LITTLEBEERQUARTER.CO.NZ

Hidden away in the Edward Street Precinct, this brilliant little bar has an awesome range on tap and in the fridge. It has a great relaxed ambience and top staff who are big supporters of the Kiwi beer scene.

ROGUE & VAGABOND

18 GARRETT STREET, TE ARO;
WWW.ROGUEANDVAGABOND.CO.NZ

Great live music venue with ever-changing and excellent beers on tap. Good food, with pizza a specialty. Situated outside is a fun little common where you can relax on the grass in the sun. Say "hi" to Bruce, the resident bulldog.

THE HOP GARDEN

13 PIRIE STREET, MT VICTORIA;
WWW.THEHOPGARDEN.CO.NZ

This is the place to go if you want a good meal out, a few pints, and maybe a nice bottle of wine as their list is top notch.

GOLDINGS FREE DIVE
14 LEEDS STREET, TE ARO;
WWW.GOLDINGSFREEDIVE.CO.NZ

Eclectic dive bar with a good tap selection, a great atmosphere, and loads of quirky bric-a-brac around the place. Very knowledgeable staff and a great nighttime atmosphere. They've teamed up with a local pizza joint for food.

HASHIGO ZAKE
25 TARANAKI STREET, TE ARO;
WWW.HASHIGOZAKE.CO.NZ

New Zealand's beer nerd bar. It's a basement bar and good to relax with friends at night and have a few imported beers on keg, or a range of local treats.

NELSON

THE FREEHOUSE
95 COLLINGWOOD STREET;
WWW.THEFREEHOUSE.CO.NZ

A converted church with a great beer selection with lots of local breweries represented. Has a Mongolian yurt in its awesome garden bar (and we all love a Mongolian yurt, right?).

SPRIG & FERN
MULTIPLE LOCATIONS;
WWW.SPRIGANDFERN.CO.NZ

There are a bunch of these around Nelson and they all have beer and ciders from the local Sprig & Fern brewery. The Milton Street bar (134 Milton Street, The Wood) has been awarded the best bar in NZ and is a converted house with a cheerful, relaxed atmosphere where you can get fish and chips from the shop next door and bring them in to eat.

THE MUSSEL INN
1259 STATE HIGHWAY 60, ONEKAKA;
WWW.MUSSELINN.CO.NZ

A bit of a drive out of Nelson in Onekaka, Golden Bay, and closed during the winter months, this legendary place is one of the older Kiwi brewpubs. Owner Andrew Dixon built most of it, including his own log cabin house out the back. Classic bohemian styling, mostly local and super-fresh fare on the menu, including amazing seafood. Home to Captain Cooker, a beer brewed with Manuka Tips that are harvested and processed in a machine that Andrew had made especially for the beer. Great live music venue.

CHRISTCHURCH

POMEROY'S
292 KILMORE STREET;
WWW.POMSPUB.CO.NZ

A brilliant family-run pub with an excellent vibe, this is the type of place that you walk into and feel like you're instantly welcome. Warm, cozy, often with some great live music, and a great selection of beers on tap, including some from their attached brewery, Four Avenues. There's a B&B next door.

THE BREWERY–CASSEL'S
3 GARLANDS RD, WOOLSTON;
WWW.CASSELSBREWERY.CO.NZ

There's a wood-fired brewery behind the bar making one of the finest Milk Stouts you'll find—it's great with their homemade pizzas. Head out back and check out The Tannery, a retail area that has been renovated to resemble a Victorian arcade. Incredible detail has gone into its construction.

Hops growing beside a Maori carving in Nelson, the country's main hop-growing region.

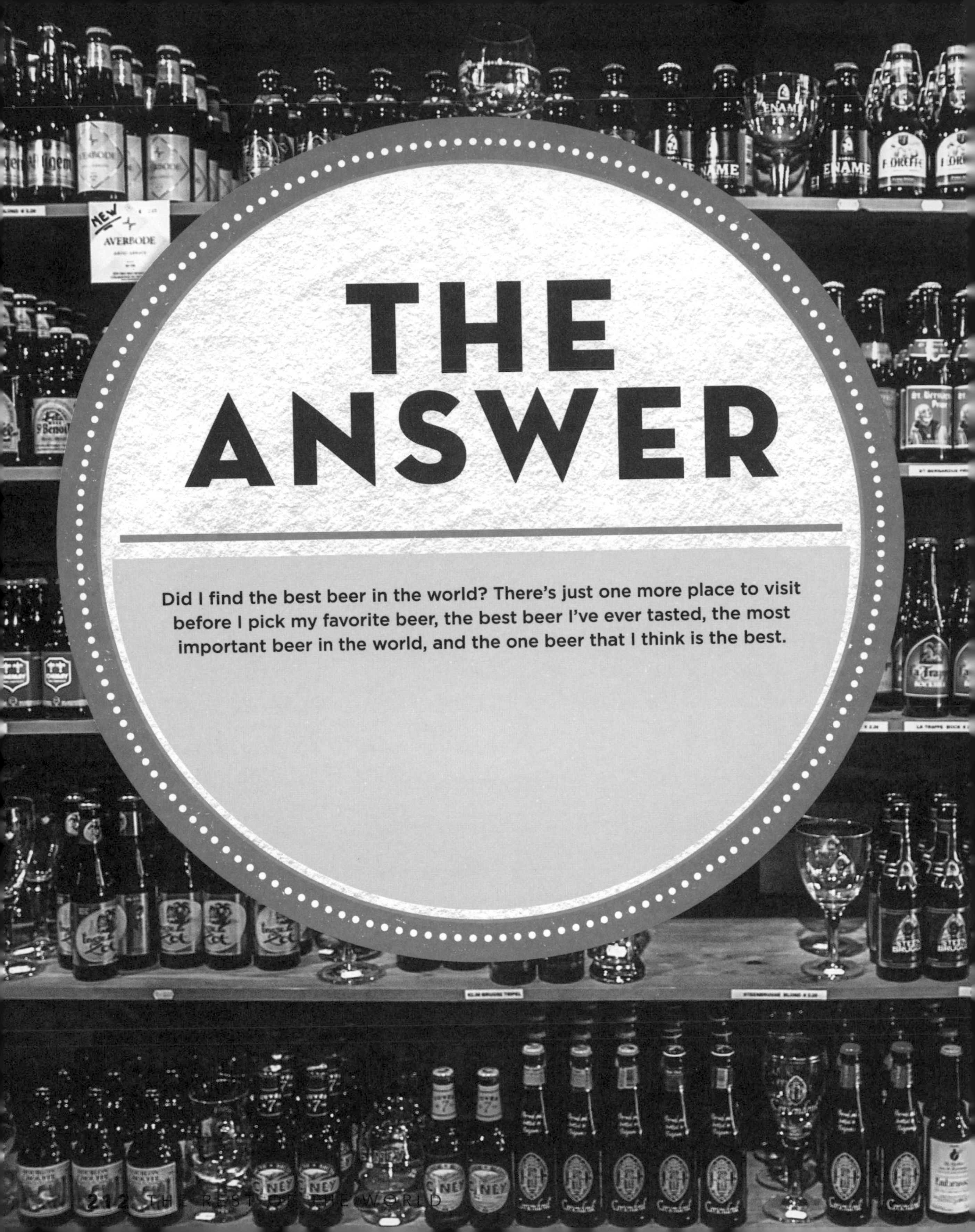

THE ANSWER

Did I find the best beer in the world? There's just one more place to visit before I pick my favorite beer, the best beer I've ever tasted, the most important beer in the world, and the one beer that I think is the best.

A KIND OF PILS PILGRIMAGE

Agostino Arioli has his head inside a hot, steaming tank when I arrive at his brewery with my girlfriend, Emma. He is brewing what I think might be the best beer in the world. But *think* isn't good enough for me; I have to know for definite.

I'm at Birrificio Italiano in Lurago Marinone, a small town about 25 miles (40 km) north of Milan. Since the idea stage of this book I knew that I had to come here and meet Agostino and drink his beer. Specifically I had to drink Tipopils, his Italian Pilsner. If someone had pressed me to give them an answer to the Best Beer question before I started this quest then I probably would've said Tipopils. It's a beer I've had a few times before and it has always seemed to come at important moments in my life (a birth, a book launch, a breakup, a brilliant holiday), so I'm here to drink it fresh from the brewery.

Agostino Arioli with head brewer, Maurizio Folli.

I've also saved this trip until last. In the previous six months I've drunk beer in 18 countries across five continents and visited over 150 different breweries. I had to do all of that travel first, I had to see as much of the beer world as I could, to experience different cultures, to find new beers, taste old favorites, and to try and better understand what I think and what I know about beer. Only after all that could I make this pilgrimage with the proper perspective.

Italy is also a fascinating place to visit for beer. It's a famous wine country, of course, but within just a few years hundreds of breweries have opened with many making seriously great beers.

TALKING TIPOPILS

"The real craft movement, the so-called renaissance, started in 1996," says Agostino. At first glance he's a serious-looking man. Closely cropped hair, a frowning stare—but as soon as he speaks his eyes glow and his smile bursts open with a playful tilt, his hands always moving as if he's sculpting words as he talks.

It was in 1996 that Agostino opened a brewery and started to make different types of German beers—a couple of lagers and a Hefeweizen. That same year Teo Musso started brewing Baladin beers in Piozzo, where he took inspiration from Belgian styles. The year after came more breweries including Lambrate in Milan. And it grew from there. "Now we are something like 800," says Agostino.

The brewing kit at Birrificio Italiano.

"When I started homebrewing [in 1985] there was no chance to find any kind of brewing equipment, so I started in my house, I started to produce my own malt. But I was using the yeast for bread, so I dumped this beer many times because it was really awful," recalls Agostino. Then his father introduced him to Gianni Pasa, a man who worked in the beer industry and gave Agostino raw materials and tips about brewing.

"The reason why I started to brew lager beers and German-style beers is because of that man," Agostino says. "He studied in Germany so he knew how to brew German-style beers but he didn't know anything about English beers."

For 10 years, Agostino essentially brewed just one recipe at home, repeating it again and again to truly understand brewing, ingredients, and processes, and how they interact. That one beer was a German-inspired Pilsner that would become Tipopils.

"What I think is that the American craft beer revolution first came to Europe in Italy," he says. "Because we didn't have our own beer culture we started to brew crazy things and I think still it's a very creative scene. It's different because England has his own beer culture so you always have small breweries but they were brewing real ales. It was the same in Germany—plenty of small breweries but brewing traditional beers. Otherwise we started with crazy stuff, like they did in America."

With influence from England, Belgium, Germany, and America all coming together with local ingredients and local taste, Italy has developed its own beer culture, influencing a generation of young Italians to choose a drink that differentiated them from their wine-drinking parents.

After studying agriculture at university, where Agostino apprenticed in breweries and wrote a thesis about beer, he worked in some small German breweries before returning to Italy. As well as homebrewing throughout this time, he was also working on a business plan to open his own brewpub. Together with 11 business partners, the company officially started up on December 23, 1994. They found a location and started brewing in February 1996, opening the pub and pouring their beers on April 3, 1996.

It was a tough start because Italians were not familiar with the concept of a small brewery at that time. They were sceptical of what they didn't understand, not trusting those small brewing vessels sitting in the front of the pub. But Agostino kept at it and kept on brewing his beer in 200-liter batches.

To help differentiate from the bigger breweries, he used the word Birrificio to describe himself. Looking at Italian craft breweries today, they almost all use Birrificio in their name to the point where I had assumed that it was just the Italian word for brewery. But it's not. Birra means beer; birreria means brewery; birrificio came to mean a small, craft brewery. And it's a word Agostino invented. Not many people can create a word and make it common lexicon in their language; not many people can redefine the image of a wine country.

He moved into the warehouse where we are now in 2012, with the pub still remaining. "Everything was brand new and huge when we moved here three years ago," he says, "but now it's too old and too little." Even though he upped his output considerably, this place keeps getting busier.

Agostino leads us from the warmth of the brewhouse, with its sweet smell of wort, and into the cold cellar with an air that's fruity from fermentation; it's closely packed with big silver tanks all connected by blue hoses the color of the Italian soccer shirt. From here we loop around the packaging area, past pallets of bottles and kegs, then pass through the rest of the brewery, past the cold room, a warm room with maturing bottles, and a barrel store for fun projects.

We complete the walk around by passing through the office and laboratory and into the tasting room overlooking the brewery, with a beautiful, elaborate bar and a long, handsome table.

"How many beers would you like to taste?" he asks.

"All of them!" I say. "But Tipopils first."

Not many people can create a word and make it common lexicon in their language.

HERBAL CHARACTER

Agostino puts a Tipopils on the table in front of us. It's a handsome dark-brown bottle, squat like an old medicine jar with a long neck and a bold hop-green label. "This is my most popular beer," he says. "When people talk about Italian craft beer, they talk about Tipopils. I'm very proud of this." He pops the cap on the bottle and it clinks onto the wooden table. He spreads three glasses in front of him and pours out the pale, ever-so-slightly hazy blonde liquid with a thick white foam. It looks simply incredible.

I was on a beach in Greece, drinking a holiday lager, when I first had the idea for this book. I remember having a cold, refreshing mouthful of beer and thinking that it was the best beer in the world right now. That was five or six years ago and ever since then I've constantly wondered what the best beer could be. Between being on that beach and now being in this brewery, every time I'd tasted Tipopils it struck me as being a serious contender—it just has something special that I've always loved.

I've drunk Tipopils at several key moments in my life, helping to elevate its standing as a great beer in my mind.

I immediately recognize the familiar aroma as the hops bloom from my glass, hugely aromatic, pulling me in. It's even better than I remember—fresher, more enticing. It's elusive yet bold and I chase the aroma in circles around the glass, never quite figuring it out, never managing to eloquently put words to it. Luckily I'm sitting opposite a brewer with a wonderfully poetic way of speaking.

"Herbal character," Agostino says, taking in the aroma. "Like a herbal tea. Resinous, like pine resin. A little fruity. It's difficult to describe the herbal character of the hops. [It's] like when you cut the grass on the mountains... and it dries in the sun. It's a very big mix of different plants and they have a very special aroma, very complex. Herbal. Floral as well."

And somehow that's exactly what it smells like. It's an evocative aroma—of being outside, of being in green fields or up mountains, of freshness.

I take a long, deep mouthful. The carbonation is gentle yet enough to have the beer burst into life as I drink. The body is soft yet dry, the hops give so much flavor and then ease away at the end. It's amazingly balanced and makes me crave another gulp immediately. Tipopils has simple malt depth, hop flavor throughout, that glorious hop aroma, and balance in the bitterness. It's complex, powerful, elegant, all at once.

"The inspiration came from the classic German Pils beers," Agostino says. "Jever Pils, that was my target. My dream. To brew such a good beer like Jever." That's a north German Pilsner, which is famously bitter, dry, and aromatic in its hopping.

"But I was not sure I could succeed," he continues, "So I called this beer "Tipopils" which means 'a kind of a Pils.' It's just to say don't bother me if you don't think this is a real Pils because this is a Tipopils, okay?"

What made, and continues to make, Tipopils different from German Pilsner is that it's dry-hopped, a process which adds more hops after fermentation to give additional aroma.

ON THE TAP

What marks Birrificio Italiano beers out is how they are all different; not just from each other but from equivalent styles made elsewhere in the world. "None of our beers is in style and that's what I like. I call them Agostino-style," he laughs.

There's the Weizen that's spicy and dry and has Agostino suggesting that he might change the name because to him it's somewhere between a German Weizen and a Belgian Saison; Bibock is inspired by amber ales but fermented with a lager yeast that gives plenty of fruity aromas (it's a different yeast to Tipopils), it's also dry-hopped and bitter; Amber Shock is a richly malty strong lager; Vudu is a dark Weizen, spicy and chocolatey; Nigredo is a strong and very hoppy Black Lager; his IPA, which was only introduced in 2015, is full-on fruity with American hops yet has his characteristic dryness of body; Sparrow Pit barley wine is like a bitter, aged dessert wine. Then there are the wooden barrel beers: a Belgian Blonde that's aged in Chardonnay barrels where one variant is herbal, floral, and citrusy thanks to being dry-hopped with Simcoe and another is dry and earthy because it's re-fermented with wild yeast; there's a Merlot barrel-aged version of Nigredo; Scires is a tart red ale aged with cherries; Cassissona is brewed with blackcurrants.

"I knew the English practise in the real ales to add hops into the cask," he says. "In Germany nobody used to do that. And so I was so ignorant about beer—but I'm happy to be ignorant because I'm more free to do whatever I like," he adds with a lowered voice, "So I combined this typical English system with a typical German beer." And by using just German hops, it really showcases their aromas, something few other brewers actually do, preferring the citrusy punch of American hops.

"It was a successful beer from the beginning," he says. So successful that "Many people that started to brew with me, they opened their own breweries and they started to brew their own Pils." As did other brewers and this dry-hopped, pale, aromatic beer became Italy's first indigenous beer style: the Italian Pilsner.

To celebrate this, Agostino started to organize an event called "Pils Pride," which brought together all the Italian Pilsners and poured them in one place. Along with Tipopils, he also makes other Italian Pilsners: Delia is a lighter, more refreshing Pilsner; Extra Hop is brewed using the best German hops Agostino can find, giving as much aroma as possible; Imperial Pils uses freshly picked green hops in a bigger-bodied beer. They are all varied and interesting, yet keep the same characteristics of the Italian-Pilsner style that he invented.

"Is there anything else you'd like to try?" Agostino asks.

"How about some Tipopils from the tank? I want to try it as fresh as possible."

Agostino pauses before replying: "This one is the best. Really," he says, lifting a small bottle of Tipopils. "When I put it into the bottle or kegs, it is perfect." I'm not going to argue with him.

> "I'm happy to be ignorant because I'm more free to do whatever I like."

Agostino is a key figure in the growth of Italian craft beer.

TO THE PUB

From the brewery we go a couple of kilometers away to the pub where Agostino started 20 years ago. A thick golden pipe stretches across the bar with taps poking out the top. Beneath it are glasses of beer sitting mid-pour, waiting for the foam to subside before being topped up. It's busy; people sit with numerous different beers, snacking on bread and meat for aperitivo.

Emma orders a Vudu, which comes in the most unusual beer glass I've seen: it's short and round like a bowl. I have Tipopils that comes in an elegant, thin glass. It's a brilliant gold and the foam is a full crown, pillowing over the top. It smells just as fresh as in the bottle, with that incredibly clean body of malt, a little hint of biscuity sweetness, then that full floral flavor and dry, quenching bitterness. I finish my glass within a couple of gulps and order another.

The pub has always focused on food as well as beer and that's an important link. Italians are famous for the simplicity of many of their dishes. Take tomato, mozzarella, basil, olive oil; it barely gets simpler. But if those four ingredients are each perfect then the dish combines to be even greater than the constituent parts. Beer is similar in Italy, with the best standing out for a complexity of flavor produced from just a few simple ingredients. The bitterness is often dry and high because the collective Italian palate enjoys bitterness more than most nations—think Campari, espresso, salad leaves.

A two-part pour gives Tipopils this great foam.

With Italian dishes, seasoning also can elevate a dish from good to great. In beer, the equivalent of the seasoning is the hops; that's where a beer is transformed. It's where a brew suffers by being boring or over-bitter; it's where it becomes balanced or bold and interesting. And Tipopils is the perfect example of a beer made amazing by the hops.

Drinking this beer now in the pub reminds me of something Agostino said earlier. He knew that Emma had only just started drinking beer with me and he wanted her thoughts.

"Do you think it's bitter or not?" he asked Emma, who shakes her head. "I'm interested in your opinion because you are a beginner," Agostino continues. "You are in this wonderful state of ignorance [and] when we are ignorant we are closer to the truth. Because the truth, when we're drinking a beer, doesn't come from your mind and what you know, it comes from your senses. The more you know, the more you are distracted from your brain and the things you know. So the judgment of simple drinkers is important."

"It smells very strong. But there's no bitter aftertaste," she says. "I really like it."

"I'm happy that you think that," he says with a big animated grin. It made me smile, too.

Unlike Emma, I do need to think about it some more because it's an important beer: Agostino added "Birrificio" to the world beer dictionary; Tipopils became a type of Pilsner that Italy took on as its own style which was emulated by others; and Italiano was the first craft brewery in a wine country with no beer-drinking culture.

Tipopils has all the attributes of something classic: it's definitive, timeless, exemplary of what it is, and something that has influenced many others. It has an important place within the history of Italian beer where it was a modern take on a traditional beer style which combined different elements to create something uniquely Italian. And for a beer that's 20 years old it has remained contemporary in its taste. In fact, it still tastes new and interesting today.

It's a beer that I could give to anyone and think they'd appreciate. It's not like a super-hoppy IPA or boozy barrel-aged Stout; it's familiar yet different, better. This beer is complex yet subtle, one that I could drink all day yet also savor for special moments. A moment like right now in this pub with Emma.

The search for the best beer in the world has been an incredible adventure filled with unforgettable moments but this feels like the perfect end point because it's also the beginning of something new. And I'm very happy that I have a glass of Tipopils in my hand.

THE BEST BEER IN THE WORLD

I've done it. I've traveled the globe looking for the best glass of beer I can find.

The idea was to look at beer's most interesting brews and stories and understand them better. I've tasted the best-selling beer in the world and I've had one which I brewed in my mate's kitchen. I've had the cheapest beer on the planet and I've spent crazy amounts of money on other beers. I've put a beer like Budweiser on a level standing with some of the rarest beers in the world. I've lived like a monk, I've celebrated Oktoberfest with tens of thousands of randy Brazilians, I've watched strippers while I drink IPA, all in the search of great beer and their stories.

The biggest thing I learnt while traveling and drinking is that beer is the most social of drinks. It's best enjoyed with others, ideally in the area it's made, as if the beer is a fabric of its environment. The mood of the place and the beer are inseparable in the same way that the beer is inseparable from the moment you're in. We simply have to travel in order to have the best experiences—you cannot replicate any place or flavor by sitting on the sofa and cracking open a few bottles.

However great the beer you are drinking, it's always made better when drinking in the company of friends.

And that's because beer is about more than the liquid. When I look back on the best beers I've had I don't necessarily remember how they tasted—at least not immediately. Instead I remember where I was, who I was with, how I felt at the time. It's the moments that really matter and I've had some incredible, unforgettable moments. While the search may be over in the sense that I'm writing these pages here now, the reality is that I'll always be looking for that next great beer, for new favorites, for amazing experiences. But we're at the end of the book, so now is the time to come to some conclusions. I hope that in doing so my observations will also encourage you to think about what you might come up with as your own answers.

A FAVORITE BEER?

For me, drinking a favorite beer is like watching a favorite movie or eating some of my favorite foods. It's something that appeals to me uniquely and something I can enjoy often without getting bored. It's not going to be something rare and it's likely something with sentiment attached to it.

I think Duvel is one of the greatest beers in the world. It's complex if you want it to be or it's remarkably simple if you just want a drink. It's equally good on a hot day for refreshment as it is on a cold night for warmth. Bear Republic's Racer 5 isn't the best IPA in the world but it has personal significance to me and I love the way it tastes; just seeing that red and yellow logo gets me excited. As a proud Englishman, I think that a great pint of pale, hoppy cask ale is hard to beat if it's well kept and poured. Something like Moor Beer Co's Revival, with its wonderful mix of traditional ale and modern American hops, is ideal. Then there's the Pils from Berlin brewpub Eschenbrau—I just adore it without being able to explain why.

Then there's Camden Town Brewery. It's a place I worked for a few years and I always have their beers at home. I know each of their beers so well and that brings a certain feeling of comfort each time I drink one. I also now have the sense of following them in the same way that someone follows a sports team—I find myself rooting for them, cheering them on, and always looking out for the next things they do. Camden's IHL, short for India Hells Lager, is a winning mix of clean lager and massive American hops. It's a beer that's exactly to my personal taste, a perfect combo of two of my favorite styles: Pilsner and IPA.

WHAT'S THE BEST BEER YOU'VE TASTED?

Some beers just stick in the memory so clearly because they tasted so good. These beers are often those unforgettable one-off experiences that will likely never be repeated. It might simply be a singular beer that blows your mind or just a fleeting moment when you happened to enjoy a great beer.

One of the first beers Scottish brewery BrewDog made was called Zephyr. It was a Strong Ale aged in whiskey barrels with strawberries and it was just about the most incredible thing I've ever tasted but I'll never get to try it again.

Drinking Orval at the Abbey was surreal and unreal; experiencing the view of the most magnificent monastery with this most magnificent of beers. I have drunk Orval many times before but it was different there, it was special.

And as best man on my mate Matt's stag do in Prague I drank Nomad Karel, a Czech IPA brewed with just Czech hops. I remember being dumbfounded by it when sitting in a dark, smoky bar, surrounded by 15 lads, drinking the most astonishingly vibrant, hoppy beer I'd ever had and just shouting for 20 minutes about how I'm drinking the greatest beer ever brewed. As a beer moment it's a hard one to beat.

WHERE'S THE BEST PLACE TO DRINK BEER?

I think Prague is the world's greatest drinking city. If you like beer then it's the number-one destination on earth, any beer geek will love its great, respectful beer drinking culture. In the city you'll find some of the best pale and dark lagers in the world—all so good when fresh, and especially so when drinking them in classic old pubs. You also have one of the most exciting craft brewing scenes producing some sensational Pale Ales and IPAs. Nowhere else I've been has that combination. Plus there's the added bonus of it being just a brilliant, beautiful city to visit.

WHAT'S THE MOST IMPORTANT BEER EVER BREWED?

There are some beers that have been so significant they've essentially started new phases in the timeline of brewing history. These beers have taken knowledge and inspiration from the past to forge new developments and change the future in significant ways. They are era-defining, classic beers, making them the most important beers ever brewed.

Pilsner Urquell is the original golden lager, taking what brewers knew at the time about pale malts and bottom-fermenting yeasts and combining them to create a new type of beer that went on to become the most dominant beer in the world—it's also still delicious today. The American Budweiser, whatever you think of the taste and the brand, is an incredibly important and pioneering beer, doing so many things before anyone else and growing to become the most recognizable beer brand in the world. Russian River's Blind Pig IPA and Pliny the Elder are craved and loved for their super-dry body and huge hop aroma. They came early on in the ascent of IPAs and Double IPAs to become the most popular style of craft beer, and they have been copied again and again until they have essentially shaped the direction in which IPAs have gone—both created a new template for the style.

Me toasting Tipopils with its creator, Agostino, having just told him it's one of my best beers in the world.

In Britain, the growth of lagers saw Golden Ales arrive, combining pale malt with fragrant hops. These then evolved to become paler and hoppier as New World hop varieties were used to give the biggest citrus and tropical aromas possible. In a way they become like low-strength IPAs and in turn they've influenced Session IPAs, the big style of the mid-2010s.

Finally there's Sierra Nevada Pale Ale. In 1980 this took a classic English style of beer and evolved it into something unrecognizable to an English drinker by throwing new American hops at it. This Pale Ale gave a completely new flavor profile to American drinkers and it was a brave beer to brew when the market was so dominated by light lagers. Since then it has been ever-present through the rise of craft beer, where the allure of the aroma and flavor of American hops is possibly the reason you like beer as much as you do, and maybe even the reason you're reading this book right now. It's hard to say what the world of beer would look like today without these key beers and they remain important by the fact that we can still drink them today.

WHAT'S THE BEST BEER IN THE WORLD?

The best beer could be any of those already mentioned, but subjectively for me it needs to be a combination of them all: a favorite beer that was a great experience to drink and is a significant timeline-shifting brew.

Pilsner Urquell is a special beer, one that is both historically relevant and tastes great. It's the perfect drink to discuss beer's past but also a hoppy session beer in the modern sense. And any visitor to the brewery cellars will know it's an unrivaled beer experience.

Another contender is Tipopils, the beer that was in the back of my mind when I started this book. It remakes pale lager by giving it this huge, delicious hop profile and aroma from being dry-hopped, where using all German hops gives us a different kind of aroma than we're used to, making it complex and interesting. It has an American sensibility, a German accent, and Italian style. It's already a classic that created a new national style; it's celebrated by beer geeks but at the same time is approachable for beer novices. It's simply just amazing to drink and also one of my favorite beers.

The idea of classic, era-defining beers and their place on the timeline of brewing leaves me wondering what's next? Pilsner Urquell ultimately shifted the look and taste of beer. Budweiser created the modern mass-market brand and made the world know it's name. Sierra Nevada kick-started craft brewing and gave us hops, forever shifting the flavor profile of beer. IPA and Double IPA took those American hops and threw them right in our faces. British cask Session Ales also used those US hops to create a new, vibrant beer, which could be drunk all day—the pale and hoppy—and that in turn brought us the Session IPA. Tipopils, and others like it, remade lager into something exciting and more in line with the flavor profiles of craft while keeping the classic qualities we expect in the best lagers, again shifting our drinking.

Something else will have the same impact on the world of beer—perhaps it already has—and I'm excited to taste it, excited to always be drinking the best beers I can find.

INDEX